A

SOLOVYOV
ANTHOLOGY

A
SOLOVYOV
ANTHOLOGY

Edited by S. L. Frank

With a new preface by Cardinal Giacomo Biffi
and an introduction
by Cardinal Hans Urs von Balthasar

The Saint Austin Press
London
MMI

THE SAINT AUSTIN PRESS
296 Brockley Road
London   SE4 2RA
Tel   +44 (0) 20 892 6009
Fax +44 (0) 20 8469 3609

Email: books@saintaustin.org
http://www.saintaustin.org

First published 1950, SCM Press Ltd.
This edition published under by arrangement
with the original publisher.

Pages vii ff. © 2001 SCM Press Ltd
Preface © The Saint Austin Press, 2001.
Introduction © T & T Clark, Edinburgh.

A catalogue record for this book is available from the British Library.

ISBN 1 901157 19 9

Printed by Newton Design & Print Ltd, London, UK.   www.newtondp.co.uk

CONTENTS

Note

For anyone who studies the writings of men with names
properly spelt in the Cyrillic alphabet there will always be
problems of transliteration. Hence we read *Solovyov* and *Soloviev*.
S. L. Frank favours the latter, von Balthasar
(and most modern scholars) the former.

FOREWORD TO THIS EDITION

Vladimir Sergeivich Solovyov: an unheeded prophet[1]

H.E. Giacomo Cardinal Biffi, Archbishop of Bologna

Vladimir Sergeivich Solovyov died one hundred years ago, on 31st July (August 13th, by our Gregorian calendar) of the year 1900.

He died on the threshold of the twentieth century: a century whose troubles and vicissitudes he had foretold with an uncanny degree of accuracy; a century which would, however, in its deeds and prevailing ideologies, tragically contradict his most important and original teachings. His teaching role was therefore a prophetic one, and one which at the same time went largely unheeded.

Prophetic teachings

In the lifetime of this great Russian philosopher, the most common view – amid the carefree optimism of the *Belle Époque* – was that mankind would have a peaceful future in the century which was about to begin. Under the guidance and inspiration of the new religion of progress, and a solidarity freed from transcendent motivations, the nations would know an age of prosperity, peace, justice and security. In the *Excelsior* dance – which enjoyed a great popularity in the final years of the nineteenth century (and which gave its name to an endless procession of theatres, hotels and cinemas) – this new religion had almost found its own liturgy. Victor Hugo prophesied: 'This century has been a great one, and the next will be a happy one'.

Solovyov however did not allow himself to be enchanted by such secular ingenuousness, and indeed predicted with lucid foresight all the calamities that would come to pass.

---

[1] Address given on Saturday March 4th, 2000 on the occasion of the centenary of the death of Vladimir Solovyov, at the opening of a conference entitled 'A Passion for Unity': Vladimir Solovyov (1853–1900), organised by the Enrico Manfredini Cultural Centre, and by the Russian Christian Foundation. It is here published in translation with the approval of the author.

Already in 1882 – in his *Second Discourse on Dostoevsky* – he seems to have predicted and condemned in advance the folly and atrocity of that tyrannical collectivism which a few decades later would afflict Russia and mankind:

> 'The world must not be saved through recourse to force... It can be imagined that men might work together towards some great task, and that all of their individual activities might be related and subjected to that task; but if this task is imposed upon them, if it comes to have a fateful and threatening meaning for them, ... then, even if such unity were to embrace all mankind, a universal humanity would not have been achieved, but we would merely end up with an enormous "ant's nest" '
>
> ('La Casa di Matriona' Italian Edition, pp 65-66)

It is this 'ant's nest' which was in fact later realised in the blunt and merciless ideology of Lenin and Stalin.

In his last published work – *Three dialogues and the Story of the Anti-Christ*,[2] which he completed on Easter Sunday, 1900 – it is impressive to note the clarity with which Solovyov foresaw that the twentieth century would be the 'age of the last great wars, of civil strife and revolutions'. After which, he said, everything would be in place for an end to the importance of the 'old structure of separate nations, and almost everywhere the last traces of the ancient established monarchies would disappear'. Thus would be established the 'Union of the United States of Europe'.

What is most striking is the clear-sightedness with which he describes the great crisis which would strike the Christian faith in the final decades of the twentieth century.

He depicts this using the iconography of the Anti-Christ, an entrancing character who would succeed to some extent in influencing and conditioning everybody. In him, as he is represented here, it is not difficult to recognise the symbol, almost the hypostatisation, of the confused and ambiguous religious tendencies of our own times: he would, says Solovyov, be a 'convinced spiritualist', an admirable philanthropist, a

---

[2] The concluding part of this work is reproduced on p. 229 of this anthology.

committed and zealous pacifist, a dedicated vegetarian, a resolute and active proponent of animal rights.

He would also be, amongst other things, an expert exegete: his biblical studies would even merit him a degree *honoris causa* from the faculty of Tübingen. Above all else, he would show himself to be an excellent ecumenist, capable of creating dialogues 'with words full of sweetness, wisdom and eloquence'.

He would bear 'no hostility in principle' towards Christ; indeed he would esteem his most elevated teachings. But he will not be able to go along with his absolute 'unicity', and for that reason he would criticise it; and therefore he would not allow himself to admit nor declare that Christ rose again and is alive today.

As we can see, what is being outlined – and criticised – here is a Christianity of 'values', of 'open-mindedness' and 'dialogue', where it would seem that little room remains for the person of the Son of God crucified for us and risen again, and for the salvific event.

All of this gives us food for thought. Zeal for the Faith is reduced to a humanitarian and vaguely cultural form of action; the message of the Gospels is equated with an irenic meeting with all philosophies and religions; the Church of God is exchanged for an organisation for social progress: are we sure that Solovyov did not truly foresee that which has in fact come to pass, and that this is not today the most dangerous snare for the 'holy nation' redeemed by the blood of Christ? It is a disturbing question, and not one to be avoided.

Teachings left unheeded

Solovyov understood the twentieth century like no one else, but the twentieth century did not understand him.

Not that he suffered from any lack of recognition. His position as the greatest Russian philosopher is not usually disputed. Von Balthasar considered his thought 'the most universal speculative creation of the modern era'[3] and he went so far as to place him on a par with Thomas Aquinas.

---

[3] See p. xi of the introduction to this edition.

Yet it is undeniable that the twentieth century, taken as a whole, paid him no attention whatsoever, and indeed set off deliberately in the opposite direction to the one he had indicated.

The attitudes which prevail today are far removed from the Solovyovian vision of reality, even among Christians who are committed to the Church and *in tune with her culture*. For example, amongst other things:

– A selfish individualism, which is increasingly affecting the evolution of our behaviour and our laws;

– A moral relativism, which tends to make people believe that it is legitimate and even praiseworthy to adopt positions in the legislative and political spheres which are at variance with the norms of behaviour to which one personally adheres;

– Pacifism and non-violence – in the mould of Tolstoy – confused with the Gospel ideals of peace and brotherhood, to the extent that we end up surrendering to bullies and leaving the weak and the upright with no defence;

– A theological extrinsicism which, for fear of being accused of extremism, forgets the unity of God's plan, renounces the task of shining the light of divine truth into all areas, and resigns from every obligation to Christian coherence.

The twentieth century has, in a special way – in the way in which it has unfolded and in its social, political and cultural consequences – loudly contradicted the great moral edifice of Solovyov.

He had characterised the fundamental ethical postulates as a threefold primordial experience – innately present in every man – as decency, mercy towards others, and the religious sense.

The twentieth century, then – following a sexual revolution which was selfish and devoid of wisdom – has arrived at a state of permissiveness, of showy vulgarity and public shamelessness, whose scale seems to have no equal in human experience.

Furthermore, it has been the most oppressive and bloody century in history, devoid of respect for human life and devoid of mercy. We cannot of course forget the horror of the extermination of the Jews, which can never be sufficiently abhorred. But it is worth remembering that that was not the only atrocity: no one remembers the Armenian genocide which straddled the first World War; no one commemorates the tens upon tens of millions killed under the Soviet regime; no one ventures to count the victims sacrificed pointlessly in the various parts of the world on the altar of the Communist utopia.

As for religious sense, the twentieth century in the East has seen, for the first time, a state atheism proposed and imposed upon an enormous body of men, while in the worldly West an atheism of a hedonistic and libertarian kind has become widespread, to the extent that we have even arrived at the grotesque notion of the 'death of God'.

To conclude: Solovyov was undoubtedly a prophet and a teacher; but a teacher who was, so to speak, out of tune with his times. And this, paradoxically, is the reason for his greatness and his value for our own era.

A passionate defender of man and yet allergic to every sort of philanthropy; a tireless apostle of peace and yet an opponent of pacifism; a champion of Christian unity and yet a critic of all irenicism; a nature lover and yet far removed from modern infatuations with ecology: in a single word, a friend of truth and an enemy of ideology. It is precisely this sort of guide that we so desperately need today.

INTRODUCTION
To this edition

SOLOVIEV: HIS VISION AND FORM OF WORK[4]
Cardinal Hans Urs von Balthasar

Soloviev,[5] writing a century after Hamann, was heir to all that had occurred during the intervening period; the French

---

[4] Reproduced from Vol. III of Hans Urs von Balthasar's *The Glory of the Lord.* (T&T Clark)

[5] Unfortunately, I am obliged to quote Soloviev's works in translation, so far as they are available (there is a complete Russian edition in 9 volumes, 1901-1907, and another in ten volumes, 1911-1914, plus four volumes of letters, Petersburg, 1908-1911, 1923). There is one work in French, *La Russie et l'Eglise universelle* (Paris, 1889).
A German "collected edition", which brings together the major works, has been appearing under the imprint of Verlag Erick Wewel since 1957 (four volumes have appeared so far, *II, III, VI, VII*; these are quoted as W). The deficiencies in this edition can be supplied from other translations, above all from that of Harry Kohler, which appeared as *Wladimir Solovjeff: Ausgewählte Werke* (two volumes, Diederichs, 1914, 1916). The projected third volume never appeared. This edition (=D) becomes the fourth volume in the *Philosophical and Anthroposophical Library* published by Verlag Der Kommende Tag (Stuttgart, 1918-1922; = A). What is not available in D, we shall quote from A.
Other translations referred to include: the French version of Soloviev's doctoral thesis, *Crise de la philosopie occidentale* (translated by Maxime Herman, Aubier, 1947); *Drei Reden über Dostojevsky* [*Three Addresses on Dostoyevsky*], translated by Th. Gräfin von Pestalozza, Grünewald, 1921: *Die historischen Taten der Philosophie* [*The Historical Achievements of Philosophy*], an inaugural lecture, translated by E. Keuchel, Sarja, Berlin, 1925. There are some shorter pieces, particularly letters, translated for the first time in *Wladimir Solovjew: Übermensch und Antichrist* (selected and translated by L. Müller, Herder, 1958). Parts of the work on *Judaism and the Christian Question* are translated in Bubnoff-Ehrenberg, *Östliches Christentum, Vol II,* 299-332 (Beck, Munich, 1925). A short passage from the *Critique of Abstract Principles* is reproduced in Kobilinski-Ellis, *Monarchia Sancti Petri* (Grünewald, 1929), an extensive anthology of texts on the ecumenical question from Soloviev's writings.
What is not translated of the major works had to be taken on the basis of the painstaking and brilliant analyses of Soloviev's work by D. Stremoukhov in *Vladimir Soloviev et son oeuvre messianique* (Strasbourg, 1935; quoted as Str.) and other studies (such as that of Szylkarski, in *Solovjews Philosophie der All-Einheit,* Kannas, 1932).
To provide some general perspective, we here list Soloviev's major works:
The Crisis of Western Philosophy The Crisis of Western Philosophy (1873); quoted as *Crisis,* following the French translation.
The Philosophical Principles of Integral Knowledge (1877); quoted as *Princ.,* following Stremoukhov.
The Critique of Abstract Principles (1877-1880); quoted as *Crit.,* following Str., one chapter in Kobilinski-Ellis.
Twelve Lectures on Godmanhood (1877-1881); quoted as GM, from A III (ET, *Lectures on Godmanhood,* trans. by P. Zouboff, Poughkeepsie, 1944).
Three Addresses on Dostoyevsky (1881-1883); following the translation already mentioned.
The Spiritual Foundations of Life (1882-1884); quoted as GG [*Die geistliche Grundlagen*], from W II (ET, *God, Man and the Church,* trans. by D. Attwater, London, 1938).

Revolution, German idealism, the Hegelianism of the Left together with Feuerbach and Marx, Comte's positivism, Darwin's evolutionism, Nietzsche's doctrine of the superman; and the fashionable pessimism of Schopenhauer in the form finally given it by E. von Hartmann. The controversy between the religious confessions had acquired a broader, worldwide perspective, turning into a dialogue between East and West, the Byzantine-Muscovite world and Rome. The Great Schism had once again become an issue of present relevance and its theological meaning was being reexamined. Soloviev's thinking has an urgency attained by no one since Hegel, and it operates on the same level as Hegel's, dealing once more in purely and consistently universal, "catholic" terms. It has an almost hallucinatory spiritual clarity, like the northern Alpine valleys when the dry warm wind of that region is blowing: all objects seem to be brought very near to the eye; they can be grasped in sharp outline and arranged in ordered relations one with another. The reason why this, the "most universal intellectual

---

The Great Schism and Christian Politics (1883); quoted as GS, from W II.

The History and Future of Theocracy (1885-1887); quoted asTh., from WII.

La Russie et l'Eglise universelle (1889); like the smaller French works, this will for the sake of simplicity be referred to in the German version in W III, and quoted as R.

The National Question in Russia (collected essays from the period between 1883 and 1891); quoted as Nat., following A IV.

The Justification of the Good (1897); quoted as RG [*Die Rechtfertigung des Guten*], following D II (ET, by N. A. Duddington, London, 1918).

Theoretical Philosophy (1897-1899); quoted as Th. Phil., following W VII.

Essays on aesthetics, sexual love, *The Drama of Plato's Life* (1889-1899); from W VII.

Numerous articles on philosophical matters in Brockhaus-Ephron's dictionary; quoted from W VI.

Sunday and Easter Letters; quoted as SO [*Sonntags-und Osterbriefe*], from D II.

Three Conversations (1899-1900); quoted as Gespr. [*Drei Gespräche*], from D II (ET in *A Solovyov Anthology*, ed. by S. L. Frank, London, 1950).

Soloviev's poems (about 150) are in part available in German translation. The following editions are noted:

Gedichte von Wladimir Solovjew, trans. by L. Kobilinski-Ellis and R. Knies (Grünewald, 1925).

Gedichte von Wladimir Solovjew, trans. by Marie Steiner (Dornach, 1949).

Wladimir Solovjews religiöse und philosophische Lyrik, trans. by Hunnuis and Engert at the end of the above-mentioned work by Szylkarski (Kaunas, 1932); relatively speaking, the most complete collection, but poetically unsatisfactory.

Russische Lyrik, selected and trans. by W. von Mattey (Schwabe, 1943).

Neue russische Lyrik, ed. and trans. by J. von Guenther (Fischerbücherei, 1960).

Bibliography in Stremoukhov; on Soloviev's aesthetics in particular, Leonida Gancikoff, *L'estetica di Wladimir Solowiow*, in *Sophia* (Naples, 1935), 420ff.

construction of modern times",[6] has its place in the context of this present work is not only that it is "a work of art on a massive scale", a drama and epic, a hymn of the universe; nor is it just because it is "beyond question the most profound vindication and the most comprehensive philosophical statement of the Christian totality in modern times". It is, rather, that this system aims at bringing a whole ethical and theoretical scheme to perfection in a universal theological aesthetic – a vision of God's coming to be in the world. By this means, Soloviev both delivers his final verdict on Kantian and Hegelian formalism, and at the same time secures a place for the theological aesthetic already in existence but not hitherto recognized as a proper discipline of thought, by giving it at least the outline of a formal structure. He is also "the only Russian writer to have left us an aesthetic system".[7] This is no accident: he alone among the Russians had had some feeling for the specifically Roman form of the Church, not, as one might suppose from an exclusively aesthetic standpoint, in the manner of the Romantics or of the *Action Française* (with whose precursors he did indeed come into contact),[8] but from an ethical and social perspective.

Soloviev arrived at the Catholic conclusion[9] because, for him, it provided a link between two formal concepts. The first originates with Hegel and corresponds to his distaste for any kind of subjectivism, any clinging to particularity and differentiation. The subject is a person only because it becomes objective spirit: this spirit mediates between the subject and that which lies outside it, and as such it has structure and form. But so long as this form remains limited by the particular – especially the national – the spirit has not yet acquired the universality that properly belongs to it. Confronted by this Hegelian law, the scales fell from the eyes of the young slavophile Soloviev: even the greatest spokesmen of this school – Khomiakov, Kireevsky, Aksakov – stay within their national

---

[6] Keuchel, in the introduction to the inaugural lecture, ed. cit.

[7] Herman in the introduction to *Crisis* (ed. cit.), 137.

[8] GM, lectures 11-12 A III 219, n.

[9] The proof that Soloviev actually converted in earnest to Catholicism – a fact ever more strongly contested time and again from the Orthodox side – is to be found in Heinrich Falk, *Wladimir Solowiews Stellung zur katholischen Kirche*, in *Stimmen der Zeit*, 1949, 421-435.

frontiers and inevitably, for good or ill, are bound to impose this limitation on Orthodox Christendom as such. Hegel's all-embracing intellectual structure in its systematic as well as its historical aspects has been of invaluable service to Eastern Christianity, a means for it to transcend its national limitations, leading it back to its true identity.[10] Even the cyclical view of culture defended by Danilevsky (the Russian Spengler) is entirely superseded by it.[11] And the catholic spirit can be attained only through the mediation of an objective form that is itself international and catholic; so adherence to the form of Roman Christianity is a means, not an end in itself.

But there is a complementary Hegelian principle, the law of process, understood as the progressive determination of the undetermined, so that by this means determinacy and universality or plenitude develop simultaneously. This principle provides the transition to the second ultimate formal concept. *Process, or evolution*, is the great word of the century, a concept in which temporal and historical consciousness encounters the metaphysical question of meaning and is brought within the latter's sphere. And for Soloviev this concept stands at the centre of his system. It is securely grounded upon the abiding intuition that was the basis of German idealism, and it is confirmed by the cosmology that was established empirically only subsequently (cosmology seen in terms of a process of hominization) and by the study of cultural history (seen as a preparation for the incarnation of God); confirmed, finally, by the evolution of christological truth in the dogmatic development of the Church – sketched by Soloviev almost more painstakingly than by Newman and deployed against the rigidly retrogressive Eastern Church.[12] By this means, the total meaning of the world's evolution is clearly established for the future: the development of humanity and the totality of the world into the cosmic body of Christ, the realisation of the eschatological relation of mutuality between the incarnate Word and Sophia, who receives through the Word her final embodiment as his Body and his Bride. The theme and content

---

[10] Th., foreword W II 374-375.
[11] Reply to N.J. Danilevsky, W II, 347-360; art. on Danilevsky in Brockhaus-Ephron, W VI.
[12] Th. XXIII W II 476ff.

of Soloviev's aesthetic is nothing less than this: the progressive eschatological embodiment of the Divine Idea in worldly reality; or (since the Divine Spirit is indeed in and for itself the highest reality, while the material being of the world is in itself no more than indeterminacy, an eternal pressure toward and yearning after form) the impress of the limitless fulness and determinacy of God upon the abyss of cosmic potentiality. This also means the bringing into submission, the conquest, of the nondivine on the basis (in Baader's terms) of the image of God already printed upon it. This is the complete triumph of God's omnipotence, which can manifest his plenitude and totality and cause it to prevail even in what is opposed to it – in what is finite, separated, egotistically divided, evil.

Here, then, is the same universal trend of thought as in Hegel; but in place of the Protestant "dialectic", which relentlessly transcends all things to find its term in the absolute Spirit, the basic conceptual model in Soloviev's thought is the catholic "*integration*" of all partial points of view and forms of actualization into an organic totality that annuls and uplifts (*aufhebt*) all things in a manner that preserves that which is transcended far more successfully than in Hegel. It establishes God's becoming man as the abiding pivot and organizing focus of worldly reality and its relation to God. What is preserved is the eternal, ideal kernel of every person in so far as it has been integrated into the entirety of the cosmic body of God; which means that its real bodily form is preserved in the same way. There is no ultimate absorption of all things into an absolute spiritual subject; instead there is the resurrection of the dead. So for Soloviev aesthetics and eschatology coincide, in practical terms; and in connection with this we must note simply that if God has become man in Christ, the Kingdom of God does not break in "unilaterally" from above and from outside; it must necessarily grow to maturity just as much from within. Soloviev's skill in the technique of integrating all partial truths in one vision makes him perhaps second only to Thomas Aquinas as the greatest artist of order and organization in the history of thought. There is no system that fails to furnish him with substantial building material, once he has stripped and emptied it of the poison of its negative aspects. This process succeeds smoothly and painlessly even with wholly anti-Christian ways of thinking like ancient Gnosticism and contemporary materialism; and the integration is so powerful that no trace is left in the completed structure of eclecticism or of a process of compilation; just as, through the skill of composer and conductor, all the instruments of an orchestra articulate precisely that symphonic consonance (for the production of which their parts were differentiated in the first place) as a consequence of the ideal pattern worked out beforehand. It is not so much that integration is made possible by the capacity to distinguish necessary and unnecessary aspects in a system – though such a capacity is eminently present and available and is indeed brought into play.   Far more importantly, such integration is achieved by a technique of allocating to each element in turn a place in the system in accordance with its value and specific gravity. And by this means, the limitation of the particular original world view appears of its own accord in the perspective of an inclusive totality of vision. This style of thinking is made possible primarily by means of a concept of God that is alike beyond personalism (God as the free *hen*) and beyond vulgar pantheism (God as *pan*). The Greeks emphasized the *pan,* the Jews the *hen;* but the Christian God is in the truest sense both *hen* and *pan.* God is not exhaustively defined in terms of personality. He is not only an independent entity, He is everything, not only a distinct individual but the all-embracing substantial being of things, not only an existent but Being itself[13] – and precisely in that respect freely exalted and all-powerful over every individual existent, so that his being as totality is in no way simply the sum of all finite substances.[14] Thus the Christian reality of participation by grace in this *hen-kai-pan* in Jesus Christ must mean the opening up, in full consciousness, of the limited, finite spirit to this total plenitude; it must mean the breaking apart of every variety of egotistic will-for-self, allowing it to emerge as a love free from jealousy, which lets all things be (and so is a self-negation).[15] The divine and eternal integral wholeness is answered from the side of

---

13 GM, lecture 5 A III 91.
14 *Ibid.*, lecture 6 A III 105.
15 *Ibid.*, lecture 1 A III 15.

created reality by a progressive integration into that integral wholeness.[16]

If Soloviev is set against the background of the Christian *past,* one can say that it is idealism (especially in the form given it by Schelling) that has provided for him the impulse to free himself from the limited forms of mediaeval and Eastern Christianity as it provided the same impulse for Karl Barth (in the form of Schleiermacher and Hegel), who used it in overcoming the limited vision of Luther and of Calvin (in their doctrine of predestination). Schelling confronts Soloviev with ancient gnosticism as an attempt to reduce Christianity to its own terms in a systematic way. Valentinus is hailed by Soloviev as "one of the greatest intellectual geniuses of all time";[17] all the main motifs of his cosmic poem are taken over, but their direction is reversed. As Valentinus builds the Christian doctrines of incarnation and salvation into a surrounding system alien to them, so Soloviev integrates gnosis into Christianity. This implies also that the two streams that here flow together – the Oriental (including the Indian doctrines of freedom and of *nirvana* and their resurrected modern forms in Schopenhauer and Hartmann) and the Greek (most centrally in the shape of Plato and all his imitators, Eastern and Western) –are employed in the most positive and deliberate fashion and with distinct tasks to perform. India provides the first form of the doctrine of pan-unity, and so also of the doctrine of freedom; but this alone remains negative and exclusive. It presents a theory of the world as infinite potentiality ("thirst", or "urge", or Schopenhauer's "blind will"), but redemption from this world remains again something negative.[18] Greece, in the person of Plato, discovers the divine in the shape of the Idea that fully answers the "urge" or "longing" (*Drang*). The latter can be understood as Eros directed toward the good and the beautiful; but the divine world of ideas does not embody itself, and the Idea is manifested only in a contemplative sense, its embodiment in ethics and politics comes radically to grief. There is no thinker whom Soloviev, the ostensible Platonist,

---

[16] *Ibid.*, lecture 7 A III 138.
[17] Art. on Valentinus, W VI.
[18] GM, lecture 3; A III 51f.

takes to task so severely as Plato. Soloviev saw the greatest tragedy of human history in the fact that Plato, who owed the whole of his philosophical impulse to the liberating influence of Socrates, had finally and shamefully (in the *Laws*) betrayed his master and his master's ideas – in that, in this late work, he judges anyone who subjects the authority of the state's laws to any kind of critique to be worthy of death.[19] But even without this catastrophe, the Platonic Eros remains only a beginning, incapable of following itself out to a proper conclusion, or indeed of understanding itself to the limit. Plato had not unravelled the mystery of what the process of "generation in the Beautiful" means.[20] He could not, for he had no knowledge of it from within; for that, some sort of radical conversion was necessary, like that provided by biblical religion in its transferring of the initiative from God-seeking Eros to the gratuitous descent of Agape, and in its making humanity the object of God's quest. To understand what is central in Soloviev's turning away from Plato and the whole of Platonism, one has to let the following statement sink in.

> Before Christianity, the natural principle in human nature was the given object (the fact); divinity was something that was sought for (the ideal), and it worked on man in an "ideal" way, simply as the object of seeking. But in Christ what was sought was given to us, the ideal became fact: "Here the inaccessible (that is, the unattainable) happens, the indescribable is here enacted." The Word became flesh, and it is this new spiritualized and divinized flesh that remains the divine substance of the Church. Before Christianity, the firm foundation of life was human nature (the old Adam); the divine was the principle of change, motion, progress. After the appearance of Christianity, the Divine itself, incarnate now for evermore, stands over against man as a firm foundation, as the element in which our life exists; what is sought is a humanity to answer to this Divinity; that is, a humanity capable of uniting itself with it by independent

---

[19] *The Drama of Plato's Life* (*Lebensdrama Platons*) XXX W VII 333. Similarly, in the very detailed article on Plato for Brockhaus-Ephron, W VI, and further, in GG W II 53ff. 66-67.
[20] *The Drama* ... XXII W VII 318-319.

action, appropriating it for itself. As the object of seeking, this ideal humanity here becomes the active principle of history, the principle of motion and of progress.... The outcome must be man divinized, that is the humanity which has taken the Divine into itself.[21]

Or, briefly put: "In Christianity, Plato's ideal world is transformed into the living, active Kingdom of God, which does not operate 'over against' the material being of the factual reality of this world with indifference, but rather endeavours to make this world the vessel and the vehicle of absolute being. . . . The harmony of the ideal world, the inner unity of all things, reveals itself in Christianity through the power of the divine-human personhood of Christ as its living reality."[22]

Logically, then, Soloviev's true starting point in the Christian past is Greek patristic thought before the Schism, especially in its definitive form in the work of Maximus the Confessor, who systematically makes the Chalcedonian dogma (that is, the synthesis between God and man in Christ) the foundation upon which the entire structure of natural and supernatural reality in the world is erected. To the static element provided by this world picture, Soloviev added nothing of substance except the dynamic element of German idealism – the evolution of nature towards man, of history toward Christ, and of the Church toward the Kingdom of God in its completeness. The christological development of patristic thought in the great councils constitutes for him an adequate basis for discussion between Eastern and Western churches. Maximus in particular – "the most significant philosophical spirit in the Christian East after Origen, the only significant philosopher of that era in the whole Christian world, the link between Hellenic Christian theosophy and the mediaeval philosophy of the West"[23] – is repeatedly cited as chief witness for the fundamental idea of Soloviev's evolutionism: that, since Christ God has been given to men: that now it is man who is sought; everything from now on depends on the free acceptance of the grace of this gift – the

---

[21] GG II W II 134-135.
[22] Inaug. lecture 10-11.
[23] Art. on Maximus in Brockhaus-Ephron; W VI.

"art" of the Kingdom at work, and the redemption of the cosmos. Maximus's defence of the free human will of Christ against all the encroachments of platonizing monophysitism provided a decisive vindication of the Christian cause.[24] If Maximus, with his christological philosophy of Godmanhood,[25] represents the truth at the heart of Hegel's thought; so it is Hegel who gives Maximus his topical relevance at the end of the nineteenth century; in the pattern thus arrived at, all the theoretical and practical strivings of the age find their magnetic centre.

This is so much so that Soloviev also anticipates in prophetic fashion the great developments of the twentieth century. As compared with the methods of eidetic classification used by Dilthey (forms of Spirit), Spranger (forms of life), Leisegang and Rothacker (forms of thought) and Spengler (forms of culture), Soloviev is indeed well in advance with his method of integration. He analyses independent forms only within the context of the whole and in order that they may fructify the whole. In the approach of his theoretical philosophy (1897f.), he comes very close to Husserl's earliest approach to philosophy. He surmounts the monadic idealism of this system simply by implanting the whole of theoretical philosophy in the context of an ethical reference, the sphere of act and freedom (like Blondel and his disciples). In his presentation of themes, his kinship with Scheler is astonishing: there is the same religious approach as in *The Eternal in Man*, the same struggle against Kantian formalism in ethics (for both of them the decisive impulse and point of departure for their own particular concerns), the same phenomenology of the ethical – the sense of shame, the sharing of suffering (*Sympathie*) and the sense of

---

[24] GS 3 WII 231,242. Clarificatory comments in W II 328-329, 332; Th. 17, W II 449. *On St Vladimir*, W III 123; R introd., W III 163, 170-171; ch. 9 W III 239, etc. On the meaning of Chalcedon: GS 3, W II 24ff.; Th. 16, W II 444ff.; ch. 23, W II 475 (Chalcedon as a criterion); R ch. 14, W III 319-324 (Chalcedon and Rome).

[25] The extent to which we have to speak of a christological philosophy in Soloviev is illuminated by this principle: "A free and interior union between the absolute divine principle and human personality is possible only on the basis of allowing human personality itself an absolute significance. Human personality therefore can unite itself with the divine principle only in freedom, out of its own interiority, since it is itself, in a certain sense, divine, or, more accurately, participates in the divine" (GM, lecture 2; A III 22). This "divinity" of man, however, has its preeminent and supreme instance in Christ and thus has its foundation in Christ.

honour and reverence (*Pietät*). There is the same broadening
out into sociology (society and the forms of knowledge),[26] the
same basic tension in man between the materially real and the
divinely ideal. But where the later Scheler is broken by this
tension, Soloviev holds out as a Christian and avoids that fatal
philosophical notion of the twentieth century that sees driving
instinct as power and spirit as impotence. Nonetheless, he
comes close to Freud in freely accepting the theory of
sublimation as something pervasive within this tension: the
forces of egotism are given to man not to be destroyed but to
be transformed, just as God himself creates good out of evil.
The dark "ground" is constantly in need of being brought to
illumination.[27] Most astonishing of all, though, is the
relationship of the whole vision to that of Teilhard de Chardin.
One might well say out that none of the latter's intuitions is
alien to Soloviev. He accepts the process of the hominisation
of nature as established fact, as much on the idealistic and
speculative level as on the empirical scientific level of
palaeontology; it is so self-evident as not to need recapitulation.
Likewise, he accepts the progress of cultural and religious
history toward the God-Man, Christ. And on the basis of both
these assumptions, the collective evolution of humanity and the
cosmos toward the complete coming into being of God in the
world, in the mystical Body of Christ, appears no less self-
evident to him. If Christians eighty years ago had taken
Soloviev's world picture seriously, there would be no cause
today for all the anxious efforts to refute Teilhard. But, quite
apart from Soloviev's incomparably greater speculative power,
his picture has this in its favour: at the end of his career,
Soloviev was confronted by the apocalypse, by Antichrist; and
this serves as a salutary counterpoise to his evolutionism, a
counterpoise lacking in Teilhard right up to the end.

---

[26] All this appears most clearly in *The Justification of the Good* but is also to be found in the
earlier *Spiritual Foundations* and *Lectures on Godmanhood.*
[27] GG II 4: "The essence of the Good is made present through the activity of God; but
nothing other than the transformation of the self-assertive power of personal will, when
overpowered and converted into a condition of potentiality, can provide the energy to
produce the manifestation of the Good in man. So in the holy man, potential evil is the
precondition of actual salvation: the saint is great in his holiness because he might also be
great in evil." W II 85-86. Likewise GM, lecture 10, A III 201; RG I 2,4, D II 55ff.; *ibid.,* 62,
RG II 8, 7, D II 192f.

Soloviev's achievement for his own age was to have affirmed so far as possible all the distinct paths and streams in the construction of world views. If he went along with German idealism in its basic concerns, the idealism to which all the varieties of rationalism since Descartes had been leading, so also he agreed with the check to idealism offered by Feuerbach's humanism. After all, if it is true that the human spirit has developed out of nature, why then refuse any justification to the material aspect of man?

> The material principle in man that links him with the rest of nature, which Buddhism attempted to deny, from which Platonism sought escape and liberation – this principle, according to Christian belief, has an established role in the life of man and of the universe. Christianity sees material life as the necessary foundation for the realisation of divine truth, the embodiment of divine spirit.... It asserts the resurrection and eternal life of the body.... The reinstatement of the rights of matter was a necessary operation in the process of liberation wrought by philosophy, for it is only the acknowledgment of matter in its true significance that sets us free from actual slavish dependence upon it, from an involuntary materialism. So long as man does not feel material nature in himself and outside himself as something that is his own, something akin to him, he does not love it, and he is not yet free from it.[28]

But in the same connection Soloviev exposes crude materialism as philosophical naiveté and the concept of pure matter as a contradiction in itself, a contradiction that Leibniz and, more particularly, Schopenhauer and Hartmann, show him how to resolve. With materialistic socialism, the same contradiction breaks through in the ethical sphere,[29] and its concerns must find a haven at a higher spiritual level, in a christological socialism, in what Soloviev dreamt of and sketched out as "universal theocracy". This integration will be bound to take its

---

[28] Inaug. lecture, 13-14.
[29] GM, lecture 1: the opposition between a renunciation of egoism and individual separateness in the interests of a collective egotism of material welfare.

aspect of formal absoluteness from rational idealism, but the real fulness of substantive historical content from empirical "materialism". In Christ, the real and the ideal have become archetypally one, and so Soloviev now seeks ideological schemata that can chart the process of the world's divinization that begins at this point.

These schemata must in each case be developed with an encounter in mind: the encounter between a divine reality, understood in its maximal, most concrete fulness, and a human and worldly reality, taken equally in its maximal concrete fulness. In this way they must indicate the basic form of the *hieros gamos*, the sacred marriage, of Heaven and earth. Thus Soloviev harks back to the gnostic idea of *syzygia* (the primordial couple, *Ur-Paar*), a syzygy between the fully incarnate deity (as Logos and Christ) and the fully divinized reality of the world (as the *Sophia* that is led upward to God, back to its source in God). Intently and enthusiastically, he follows through the history of Western Sophiology in its various changing guises, from Valentinus by way of the Kabbala to its baroque representatives – Böhme, Gichtel, Pordage, Rosenroth, Arnold – to Swedenborg and to Franz von Baader. But because in reading all these and many others he fully appropriates them for himself, the muddy stream runs through him as if through a purifying agent and is distilled in crystal-clear, disinfected waters, answering the needs of his own philosophical spirit, which (in contrast to that of so many of his speculative compatriots) can live and breathe only in an atmosphere of unqualified transparency and intelligibility.

Sophia is the eternal feminine in the world, the eternal object of God's love; it is the essence of the world, gradually moulded, elevated, purified, emerging in its proper selfhood in the primordial image of the Church, the *Panagia*, the spotless virgin and mother of Christ, but then broadening out to become the real principle of the whole of redeemed humanity and creation. This Sophia is Soloviev's "immortal beloved". To her he dedicates most of his poems, though there too, as normally elsewhere, she is still not named directly. She appeared to him in visionary form three times during his life,[30] and it is worth at least airing the question of whether these are not in fact apparitions of Our Lady. Soloviev always saw and acknowledged that Mariology and Sophiology pervaded one another from within and so welcomed the application of Sophiological texts in Scripture to Mary and the promulgation of the dogma of the Immaculate Conception by Pius IX. Despite occasional and impassioned relationships with earthly women, which remained, however, unrequited or unconsummated, signifying for him no more than transitory embodiments of his "secret mistress", Soloviev lived in an habitual state of "baptized Eros" directed toward Sophia. His only desire was to see all things in her light; not only relations with the individual human "Thou", but also relations with human society and the cosmos in general must be "a living relationship of Syzygy."[31]

It is out of Sophiology that there issues the outline of that system that might be called "theosophy" (in Baader's sense), that is, a science conceived as the integration of philosophy and theology. It is not, however, an integration in the way in which it was conceived in German idealism, which simply assimilated both into the ideal of absolute knowledge; it is based rather on the foundation of the Christian assumption that the free acts of a free God are a revelation of the highest kind of rationality surpassed by nothing else and so are *necessitates* in the Anselmian sense. Once we know that God has redeemed and divinized the world in Christ, the immediate issue of that knowledge for human understanding is the recognition that everything in history and nature, as far back as the act of creation itself, must be intelligible in this perspective, which excludes all others, and that it could not be otherwise. Within the total overall scheme, then, the logical connection of the several elements can manifest itself in the form of a "postulate",[32] as "logical

---

[30] These visions are described in the great poem frequently translated, "Three Meetings: Moscow, London and Egypt". Soloviev said of this that it contained the most important thing that had ever happened to him so far. Kobilinski-Ellis (see n. 1) provides, together with his translation, a commentary on the whole of Soloviev's Sophiology, in which more extensive confirmation of and testimony to its mariological significance is adduced.

[31] *The Meaning of Sexual Love* 4 W VII 269.

[32] GG I 4 W II 87.

inference",[33] as something "entirely natural, necessary and rational" (this expression is used in connection with the resurrection of the body).[34] "By virtue of their deepest meaning, and because they are absolutely congruent with reason, [Christian dogmatic statements] can be developed into the most perfect of philosophical systems."[35] This holds true even for the doctrine of the Trinity, so far as its "formal aspect" is concerned.[36] What this means is clarified by the statement that

the eternal and divine world ... as the ideal plenitude of all things and the actualization of the good, the true and the beautiful, presents itself to the understanding as something that must stand as a norm, in itself and for itself. As the absolute norm, it is logically necessary to the understanding; and if understanding as such cannot assure us of the presence and accessibility of that world, that is because the understanding alone is in no way the organ by means of which we can know any *actual* reality. Such reality can be known only through genuine experience. The ideal necessity of a divine world and of Christ as the centre and pivot of this world, absolutely universal, and at the same time, for that very reason, absolutely, uniquely individual, a central point in whose complete fulness the world participates – all this is plain to speculative thought.[37]

Accordingly, Soloviev (contradicting the traditional affirmations) says that God's *essence* is accessible to reason while his *existence* must be the object of faith.[38] Soloviev's ecumenical purpose is "to vindicate the faith of our fathers and to raise it to a new level of rational consciousness: to show how this ancient faith, when freed from the fetters of local isolation and national egotism, coincides with eternal and ecumenical truth".[39] The role of philosophy in all this is that of "defactualising" the

---

[33] GG I 5 W II 91.

[34] SO 12 D II 176.

[35] GG II 2 W II 129-130.

[36] GM, lecture 6 A III 127-128.

[37] GM, lecture 8 A III 150.

[38] *Ibid.*, lectures 2and 3 A III 28f., 40f., 43: "That God is, we believe; who he is we experience and know."

[39] Th., foreword W II 363.

Christian and churchly reality that had by its superficiality obstructed the understanding of faith, both in the mediaeval Western world and in the East.[40] What is achieved is an enrichment of the patristic and of the mediaeval Christian world view with all the contributions made by modern speculation and the results of modern science. In this way, all partial aspects are integrated into the central theosophic and "logosophic" system as *logoi spermatikoi*. And among these also there actually appears the Roman Catholic ethic of ecclesiastical obedience and practical discipline; for Soloviev this seems to be demanded unconditionally by the idea of a social world-organism, just as it saves to complement the strongly individualist-ascetical component in his spirituality.[41]

In Russia and in the West as well, Soloviev was a completely solitary figure. However, various bonds linked him with his most important contemporaries: between him and Dostoyevsky there was the closest friendship and the most intimate commerce of soul and mind, so that (for instance) we do not know which of them first conceived the figure of the Grand Inquisitor or the notion of applying the three temptations of Jesus to the Church and to Catholicism in particular. It is in fact more likely to have been Soloviev.[42] The two of them went on pilgrimage together to Optina Pustyn (in June 1878) to visit its renowned Starets Amvrosy. Both were equally impressed: the Starets was to become the prototype of Zosima, and Soloviev, the "secular monk", the model for Alyosha Karamazov. Soloviev lived out his ideal of practical Christianity to the point of folly: "He was almost always without money, he let all and sundry take advantage of him, he would give the contents of his wallet to anyone who asked anything from him, and, if his wallet were empty, he would take off his coat and give that, so that in winter he regularly had to borrow clothes from his friends. He would even give his shoes to beggars in

---

[40] Inaug. lecture, 11-12, 15.

[41] Particularly clear in GG.

[42] W. Szylkarski, *Soloview und Dostojewskii* (Schwippert, Bonn, 1948). By the same author: *Messianismus und Apokalyptik bei Dostojewskii und Solowjew,* which appears as an epilogue to Antanas Maceina's *Der Grossinquisitor, Geschichtsphilosophische Deutung der Legende Dostojewskijs* (Kerle, 1952).

the street."[43] Animals loved him, and flocks of birds besieged his hotel room. He died far too young, worn out by a quixotic life of constant wandering and by overwork. A lasting affection drew him to Tolstoy, so different a character from himself. Soloviev always believed that he could win Tolstoy back to a genuine Christian belief, although Tolstoy dismissed the *Lectures on Godmanhood* as "rubbish" and "childish nonsense". Common social concerns brought them together again; it was only reluctantly that Soloviev, obedient to his convictions, attacked Tolstoy's pacifism and moralism in the *Three Conversations*. His encounter with Leontiev, however, was crucial. At first, Leontiev beset him with an impassioned adoration, an almost unhealthy love; but he became less and less willing to forgive him his religious belief in progress. Leontiev, torn between an aesthetic and an ascetic and religious existence, a Russian Kierkegaard, could not cope with Soloviev, the supreme Hegelian. If Soloviev's ideological constructs seemed to him far too deceptively lucid, his very style of life seemed opaque and ambiguous; so the ardent love turned to a hatred that embittered his last years. He demanded Soloviev's exile from Russia and elaborated a complete campaign of persecution. In an article written after Leontiev's death, [44] Soloviev had no difficulty in showing him to be a contradictory thinker, never able to unite his Byzantine hostility to progress, his asceticism and his cult of beauty.[45] But the encounter with Leontiev was unexpectedly portentous for Soloviev; it was on this rock of opposition that his firm and rounded faith in progress splintered (though indeed it had already been undermined by his disappointments in ecumenical negotiations). There now rose up on the horizons of his spirit the dimensions of the scriptural apocalypse: it might be that the line of development from the head of the Church on his cross to the Kingdom in its fulness and the deified cosmos would run only through the eschatological battles between the opposing forces in the world, finally revealed in all their contradictoriness. So Leontiev's objections to Soloviev (as Ludolf Müller impressively

---

[43] Herman, introd. to *Crisis*, 149f.
[44] For Brockhaus-Ephron; W VI.
[45] On the relations between the two men, see N. Berdyaev, *Constantin Leontjeff* (Paris, n.d.) 201-229.

demonstrates) in fact led him to a conclusion in the theology of history that – as the theologian of the three temptations of Christ – he could have drawn for himself and would have been obliged eventually to draw for himself: the conclusion "that the ways of history do not lead directly upwards to the Kingdom of God"; they pass by way of the final unveiling of the Antichrist, who conceals himself under the last mask to be stripped away, the mask of what is good and what is Christian.[46] We shall see how this tension between progress and apocalypse (which is missing in Teilhard) moulds the shape of Soloviev's aesthetic. Here the total opposition between Hegel and Soloviev comes out into the open, between Hegel's dialectic of absolute knowledge (which again first takes flight – as the "owl of Minerva" – in the twilight of the end of history) and Soloviev's Christian programme of integration. For the former, evil can be no more than Socratic ignorance; for the latter, it is a clearly acknowledged act of saying No to love. And this contradiction shatters any systematic clarity in the cosmic "process"; it explodes into a battle to the death, a battle of mounting intensity, that, in Soloviev's eschatological consciousness, could not be other than directly imminent. And so it is into this fiery inferno that his entire system flows.

Soloviev's work divides into three clearly delimited parts. The first period is dominated by the construction of the theosophical system (1873-1883); the second is taken up with the ecumenical project for reconciliation between the churches of East and West and with paving the way for the advent of "universal theocracy" or "free catholicity" (1883-1890); the third period, after the failure of his union schemes, returns again to philosophy, outlining the system in its final form, with the accent this time on "theurgy" and apocalypse (1890-1900).

After a preliminary enquiry into *The Mythological Process in Paganism* (1873), which takes its bearings from Schelling, the first period opens with a critical survey of modern Western thought from the Middle Ages to the present. *The Crisis of*

---

[46] Ludolf Müller, *Wladimir Solowjew: Übermensch und Antichrist: Über das Ende der Weltgeschichte*. Selections from the complete works. Herder-Bücherei 26 (1958), 148-149.

Western Philosophy (1874) was already internally adumbrating the method of integration and indeed was already making use of it to a limited extent in pointing beyond rationalism (idealism) and empiricism (positivism) to the true point of departure for philosophy. The first positive outline of a system, in fact, was to be entitled *The Principles of Universal Religion*; never in fact carried through to completion, it nonetheless led in to the later structure. The earliest extant outline seems to be the foreword to the next work, which remained no more than a fragment, *The Principles of Integral Knowledge* (1877).[47] According to this, philosophy should be made up of three parts: first, the logical part, which has for its object the Absolute in its necessary a priori determinations; then the metaphysical, which investigates the Absolute in its relations with the created world; then the ethical part, which deals with the integration of the world into God and God into the world. While the book aforementioned treated of logic, it is the work that follows it, the *Critique of Abstract Principles* (1877-1880) that undertook to set out an ethical system (or a religious doctrine of self-realisation). In this work, which deals in an epilogue with Kant's formal moral principle, the parallels with Scheler are particularly striking; not only do we find a substantial ethic of value, but a new ethic of being (developed from idealism) in process of construction. In this latter, human self-realisation is seen within the framework of the total self-realisation of God in the cosmos, so that the close connection, close to the point of full identity, between ethics and aesthetics is evident.[48] The appropriate metaphysics, though partly overlapping with ethics, is represented by the *Twelve Lectures on Godmanhood* (1877-1881), while the aesthetics remained unwritten. Instead there appeared an outline treatment of spirituality, *The Spiritual Foundations of Life* (1882-1884).

After the assassination of Alexander II, Soloviev, who had pleaded for Christian compassion to be shown to the murderers, resigned his chair at Moscow. Dostoyevsky urged him to be more active; so, even more strongly, did Fyodorov (for whom, in his *Philosophy of the Common Task*, the only

---

[47] Stremoukhov, 52f., 69-78.
[48] *Ibid.*, 60-62.

legitimate account of the world was to be found in the resurrection of the dead, the fathers being raised to life by their children). But Soloviev's concern about the state of the Russian Church led to his rather abrupt turning toward the Roman communion (1882); [49]and the works of his second period stem mostly from his residence abroad. First there came *The Great Schism [sc. between East and West] and Christian Politics* (1883); and after that a *magnum opus* in three volumes was planned, *History and the Future of Theocracy: An Examination of the Path Towards True Life in World History.* Of this, only a foreword and a first book, *An Introduction to the Whole Work*, appeared (1885-1887). The second part was to have included a "philosophy of biblical history", and the third a "philosophy of church history".[50] The essence of this work was preserved in his French essay, *La Russie et l'église universelle* (1889). Side by side with this went studies on Israel and its relation to Christianity and theocracy, as well as prolonged polemical debates with representatives of Eastern Orthodox nationalism and slavophilism.

The failure of his schemes for reunion led him, now a much fatigued man, back to theosophy and the final stage of construction of his system. From the second period there still remained a belief in the primacy of ethics, so much so that the theoretical element, much restricted as to its sphere of competence, was only just squeezed in between ethics and aesthetics. The new ethics was first to have been a revision of the earlier version (in the *Critique of Abstract Principles*), but it grew into a major independent work. *The Justification of the Good* (1897) emerges as the most luminously serene work of this wise man. The *Theoretical Philosophy* (1897-1899) remains fragmentary; the radicalism of its approach makes it extremely difficult to see how it might have been developed. Cartesian methodological doubt is pursued to its conclusion; as regards the object as well as the subject, the essay suggests no way out of a phenomenalist position; that is, it denies to pure thought any capacity for breaking through into being. Whatever was to have followed, we may be sure that the further step upward would have derived from consideration of the ethical claim.

---

[49] Details in Wladimir Szylkarski, *Solowjews Weg zur Una Sancta*, in W II 153-205.
[50] W II 363.

Everything flows into Soloviev's aesthetics, and for this only sketches and drafts survive: *Beauty in Nature* (1889), *The Universal Meaning of Art* (1880) and the essay on Eros, *The Meaning of Sexual Love* (1892-1894). The early material shows how much his controlling interest drew him toward this conclusion to his work. "The task of humanisation now emerges as the solution of an aesthetic question, a solution for which the Beautiful in nature prepares the way and which art continues. Contemporary art, then, is obviously inadequate to the embodiment of Wisdom: what is needed to fulfil such a task is a genuinely theurgic art."[51] The essay on Eros witnesses to something of this: it achieves meaningfulness only in connection with Christ's "humanisation", his becoming Man. "Aesthetics thus becomes the science of the progressive embodiment of the idea.... The new position of the philosopher is that he now treats the world process from the aesthetic viewpoint, instead of confining himself to the theocratic dimension."[52]

---

[51] Str. 225.
[52] *Ibid.*, 267; *cf.* Herman, 132f.

2. LOGIC AND METAPHYSICS

Soloviev paves the way toward his system of pan-unity by a preliminary delimitation of the field of philosophical thought. Only the independent subject is capable of self-reflexive philosophising, and this activity contains as much reality as the independent being as such. The subject, however, finds itself belonging to a common, suprapersonal, generic nature, finds itself caught up in a social and. political life; and the realities of language and religious expression itself belong of necessity to this social and political life – an individual can as little "invent" them as the individual bee can invent the honeycomb. But the subject also acts beyond and outside himself in aesthetic work, which expresses a more than individual inspiration.[53] In the *Crisis of Western Philosophy*, Soloviev shows the consequences of philosophy's identification of these suprapersonal relations with the subject itself. Such a move inevitably condemns philosophy to formalism; that is, to confusing the demonstration of the conditions of the possibility of suprasubjective knowledge within the subject with the reduction of what is known to the subject itself. In the late and fragmentary *Theoretical Philosophy*, the same point of departure appears in radicalised form. Here what is given in the finite subject is strictly reduced to a *noesis* and a *noema* conceived, respectively, simply as "appearance" and that which appears; while the positing of the *noema* as real transcends the whole sphere of what is merely *theoretically* given and derives in fact from that sphere of act or will, which is also the only thing capable of giving the subject itself its ontic dignity. The separation of the subject from the total cosmic subject and the divine subject is, as it stands, as much a fiction as the act of isolating the phenomenal object from the total interconnectedness of existing reality.

The major currents of Western philosophy – rationalism, from Descartes, by way of Spinoza, Leibniz and Wolff, to Kant, Fichte, Schelling and Hegel; and empiricism, from Bacon by way of Locke, Berkeley and Hume to Mill and Spencer – have absolutised either one aspect or the other of the structure of cognition, either the concept or the experience, and turned a

---

[53] *Crisis*, 162-163.

merely formal element into the whole of the reality. This ultimately issues in the identifying of an abstract function with the concrete reality that performs that function; in Hegel everything is reduced to "*the* Reason", in Schopenhauer everything is reduced to "*the* Will", in Hartmann to "*the* Unconscious". But who is it who *is* rational, who wills, who is unconscious or superconscious? The twofold historical development can be expressed in two syllogisms. For rationalism, the major premise is this: "what is truly knowable is known by a priori thinking" (Descartes to Wolff). The minor premise runs thus: "but a priori thinking can know only the forms of our own thought" (Kant). And so the conclusion is: "therefore what truly exists is the forms of our thought; being and concept are the same" (Hegel). Likewise for the empiricist tradition. The first premise is: "what truly exists is known experientially" (Bacon); the second: "but only discrete empirical states of consciousness can be experientially perceived" (Locke, Hume and Berkely); and the conclusion: "therefore what truly exists is discrete states of consciousness" (Mill).[54] These statements are mutually exclusive, but they are at one in the one respect of elevating a single element in actual knowing into the whole act. Soloviev dubs this "abstract formalism", "because where there exists neither knowing subject nor known object, only the form of knowledge remains".[55]

In the *Crisis*, Soloviev generally finds his stimulus in those philosophies that carry on the train of reflection beyond the primitive Cartesian allocation of "spirit" exclusively to the subject (*noesis*) and "matter" to the object (*noetna*). Matter (the concept of the atom in particular) conceived as pure extension and pure passivity is a contradiction in itself Leibniz rightly sees the need for some active principle in matter, a power working against infinite divisibility, analogous to the spiritual principle, and so also a kind of unity in plurality – whether it is that a temporary state of affairs unites plural elements in a unity (*Perceptio*, cognition), or that the power working within effects an unbroken transition from one cognition to another (*appetitio*,

[54] *Ibid.*, 318-320.
[55] *Ibid.*, 320-321.

will).[56] In Schelling, this analogy of subjectivity (the idea of a principle existing in the object as "nature" and in the subject as "spirit") is acknowledged as a starting point; but it loses its primacy in the process of advance toward final identity. This identity (of subject and object), however, remains a questionable conclusion, since the "absolute subject" is conceived on the pattern of the finite subject, which achieves its selfhood from what is *not* identical with it; and thus formalism is still present in the system.[57] Schopenhauer emerges as the first to break through that formalism that culminates in Hegel; he clarifies the whole sphere of cognition from the perspective of the will that surrounds it on all sides. But if will, understood as a blind urge – that is, as something preceding all cognitive activity – is postulated as absolute, then once again it remains vacuous and meaningless; the world is as little illuminated as God, and its real existence as little vindicated. An absolute "will for life", an infinite, unsatisfied striving, a hunger for being and so also for suffering, is a contradiction in terms; and the ethic of "sympathy with the finite creature" erected on this basis, the ethic in which every sufferer transcends the egoism of his own particular existence to identify with the Other, is no less contradictory.[58] But if the obscure drive within all finite reality is not itself the Absolute, then equally it is not to be identified with the finite knowing ego; it is rather that reality that alone can illuminate the objective world in its existence as matter and as phenomenal life and that comes into its own in the knowing subject as knowledge and will. On the other hand, these elements that come into their own in the reflective activity of the human subject – will and perception, reality and ideality – must always have been part of each other if the formal and elemental realities are to be rendered intelligible. In other words, the world process *exists* as truly as does the Absolute that must be posited before and beyond any world process – as truly, that is, as God, understood as that which is not in process of becoming but which exists eternally in the perfect identity of spirit and nature, ideality and reality.

---

[56] *Ibid.*, 180-181.
[57] *Ibid.*, 198-201.
[58] *Ibid.*, 256-260.

The "crisis" in the attempt to explode the formalism of Western philosophy comes, therefore, in allowing the self-reflexive finite subject to make a twofold claim as the condition of its own possibility. On the side of the "object", the demand is for a total reality that is always volitional but not identical with the particular subject (this will be christened the "world-soul" in subsequent books), although it is at the same time the "real" condition presupposed for the subject's own existence. On the side of the "subject", what is required is a subjective reality in which the two moments of finite cognition, each of which presupposes but never becomes identical with the others – that is, general concepts (form) and particular perceptions (content) – have a prior identity.   In other words, what is required is God.[59] Soloviev grounds this second demand for the time being by means of inner experience (Jacobi), which he describes as "faith" (as opposed to finite objective knowledge) or direct intuitive penetration (*Mystik*); but it would be unfair to accuse him at this point of a flight into the irrational. His path toward God is (as with Baader) philosophically precise, well thought out and logical. Later, at the beginning of his *Theoretical Philosophy*, he shows that he is also able to dispense with appeal to supposedly "direct" mystical experience.   It is only a terminological question whether or not one wants to call the (finite) personal subject's reflection on his act of knowing "philosophy"; if one does so, no problem remains about calling the actual step beyond the boundaries brought to light by this reflection (boundaries that themselves demand this step beyond), "ethics" on the one side – the step toward the world – and "theosophy" on the other – the step toward God – leaving the name of "metaphysics" for the relation between God and the cosmos (the world-soul).

So at the end of the *Crisis*, we are confronted with three postulates (though they are not as yet clearly articulated) for a comprehensive ontology, coming clearly to light in the subsequent works of the first period correspondingly as they are worked out in detail.

1. We must be committed without qualification to the achievements of modernphilosophy as regards the world

---

[59] *Ibid.*, 329-331.

process in its twofold cosmological and historical shape (hominisation and divinisation), but without identifying the subject of this process with God. It can only be a comprehensive subjective reality over against God, in process of self-integration; it may be designated as world-soul, cosmic will, humanity or, finally, "Sophia". If this assumption is not made, even the most limited of material objects will remain inexplicable.

2. God's existence over against the cosmic process makes it impossible directly to identify the finite with the infinite subject; and above all it makes possible the relation of love that had always been impossible in idealism. The merely formal (ideal) sign of the divine in man cannot be given content except through God's free opening of himself (grace, revelation). God, as the identity of real and ideal, being and spirit, identity and nonidentity, is also the totality of what is outside himself, since he is wholeness *in* himself. He exists "for himself" only in so far as he exists as "not for himself" (as love), as totality both within and without himself.

3. Thus there falls a shadow over any being that exists "for itself", in a state of separation that is not wholly and purely a condition of and an opening to wholeness in the world. The individual ego (as philosophising subject) is bound on its own level to degenerate into formalism, since pure separation is ontically abstract and unreal, a state of fallenness from the concrete fulness of God; it is exiled from fulness, so that it has to recapture this fulness in the process of integration, starting from the opposite pole, from sheer nullity, so as to be "God outside God," the representation of God in the twofold freedom of creator and creature and therefore the absolute form of artistic activity.

We shall now proceed to deal with these three metaphysical perspectives in turn, though in different order.

1. Since the doctrine of the world-soul and the world process presupposes the doctrine of God, we shall first present this latter in the form in which it appears in subsequent works, above all in *the Principles of Integral Knowledge* and the *Lectures on Godmanhood*. God is the Absolute in the twofold sense of being both a reality detached from (unconditioned by) all that he is not, and a reality subsisting entirely independently in isolation

(and perfectly); which is possible only if, while being limited by no other reality, he also possesses the power and freedom to be himself in any other reality.[60] He is in fact not a part of all things; if he were only that, he would be the actual being of what is other to him. But if in fact he has free sovereignty over what is other to him, if he is its principle, then he is himself both in himself and in what is other to him, which therefore cannot be the negation of God in its otherness from him. And it is as the one who in his freedom and power possesses what is other to him as both subordinate to himself and behind himself, that he is Trinity: this important and suggestive conclusion Soloviev shares with Schelling, though he does not understand it in quite the same way, since he fills up the idealistic form with what he considers to be (and wants to be grasped as) Christian content. As the ground of all that is (*quod est*, the subject), God is Father; as paradigm of existing reality (*essential* the object), he is Son; and as that which unites both (*esse*, identity),[61] he is Spirit or being. This explains why it is that the finite subject cannot in itself attain by philosophical reflection to the ground of being (and of spiritual being); it can do this only by self-transcendence – by its subjectivity (*noesis*) transcending itself in movement toward the absolute subject, the Father, and its object-reference (*noema*) transcending itself in movement toward the absolute object, the Son. Soloviev can dispense with the Cartesian self-affirmation of the finite subject in its intuition of itself as "thinking substance" only because he has in the background this conception of the *imago Trinitatis*.

Because God the Father has by his side a Son identical in substance with himself,[62] he has within himself the perfect reproduction and self-presentation of his own totality, independently of whether this is manifest in himself or in the other that is also himself. In his Logos, he contemplates his own absolute divine power and freedom – freedom to do all things, and so power over all things.[63] The infinity of this free power becomes truly present for God in the Son; he possesses this in himself both as his potentiality and as his own actuality.

---

[60] Str. 70.
[61] *Ibid.*, 72, 74; *cf.* R III 1 W III 327.
[62] Th. 13 W II 435.
[63] GM, lecture 6 A III 110.

But he does not wish to possess it only in and for himself, as he is unenvying Goodness; he wishes to give this freedom and power to his potentialities by giving them self-subsistent actuality. By this means, in the first place, he demonstrates fully that "he is an absolutely unified reality in his innermost essence, which cannot be superseded or negated by any plurality within his unity".[64] He rules from all eternity over all the plurality that stands against him as power and as ideal reality; but he also wills to rule over it as Good, and to do this he must let it attain real plurality.

> God cannot be content with being stronger than chaos only *de facto*; he must also be so *de jure*.... Thus he must separate off his perfect wholeness from the chaos of plurality and respond in his Word to every possible expression of plurality by an ideal expression of true unity, a rational ground that demonstrates the intellectual, or logical, impotence of chaos when it seeks to maintain itself *as* chaos.... God's absolute superiority must emerge not only as *against* chaos but also as *for* it, in that it gives to chaos more than it merits, allows it to share in the fulness of absolute life, allows it to perceive the truth that divine plenitude is superior to the empty multiplicity of an unredeemed and corrupt infinity by living inner experience, not only on the grounds of objective rationality.[65]

This rather later formulation softens the abruptness of certain expressions in the earlier writings, in which the distinction between the necessary begetting of the Son and the free creation of the world seems to have been obliterated; in these texts God appears to be obliged by his own eternal character to create the world, to let his free power triumph over chaos and to let the glory of his love illuminate the self-orientated life of his creatures.[66] The immanent Trinity would then have to be seen as in its very expression already orientated toward the world itself. "The Logos is God revealing himself; but that

[64] *Ibid.*, 110-111.
[65] R III 3 W III 341-342.
[66] 62 *Cf.* for example, GM, lecture 5 A III 75, and *ibid.,* 88; also lecture 6, *ibid.,* 105; lecture 7, *ibid.,* 142, and lecture 8, *ibid., 152.*

presupposes an Other for whom or with reference to whom God reveals himself; that is, it presupposes man."[67] Accordingly, in *The Principles of Integral Knowledge* the relation between the Logos and the material principle, *Hyle*, seen as the external presupposition of the intradivine being-other of the Second Person, becomes very close.[68] Finally, Soloviev makes the link between God and the three transcendentals: in that he comes forth from himself, God is Goodness; in that he knows himself, he is Truth, in that he experiences himself, he is Beauty. But these determinations are in each case made in relation to God's revealed existence in the "otherness" of the world; so that Truth is at the same time God's self-manifestation as the Kingdom of God, brought to perfection in Christ, and Beauty is God's full actualisation of his selfhood in the other, his highest degree of materialisation. "Good is the prescribed goal, Truth the necessary means for determining it, and Beauty the actual realisation of it. In other words; because Being itself affirms the ideal as Good, it bestows upon it, through the mediation of Truth, a realisation in the Beautiful."[69]

But what precisely is this ideal reality or totality of ideas? What (to introduce the term that now becomes necessary) is God's *Sophia?* Is it the plenitude of the modes in which his essence can be imitated (which exist already as absolute reality in his essence), coming to light through his power and freedom? or is it the plenitude of possibilities realised through his free power and grace, possibilities that are (eschatologically) linked with the form of preexisting ideas? The question is of some importance for aesthetics; from the viewpoint of the aspirations of reality, does the Beautiful lie in the sphere of ideal being only? or does ideality eternally include reality in itself? For Soloviev, however, the question can be left as insoluble, since for him the opposition of real and ideal no longer had ultimate significance as in the idealist system of God's coming to be; in God, the idea is always his own reality, and it is this reality that draws the still imperfect creation, existing for itself alone, home to himself.

---

[67] *Ibid.*, and lecture 8, 153.
[68] Str. 73.
[69] *Ibid.*, 75.

This also becomes clear from the fact that the process of the subjectivising of the idea, its fulfilment in being properly and independently itself, is curiously underemphasised in all this. In the Logos there exists, first of all, "'the sphere of pure intelligences, objective ideas, hypostatic thoughts of God ... and these constitute the world of ideas; they are entirely contemplative, passionless and immutable essences, fixed stars in the firmament of the invisible world, and so they stand above any desire, any will and thus also any kind of freedom". Over against this world stands the sphere of the "responsive activities of the Holy Spirit, which are more concrete, subjective and lively and which constitute the spiritual world, the sphere of pure spirits or angels.... They experience not only intellectual contemplation but states of emotion and will, they possess motion and freedom" (the significance of the fall of Lucifer is illuminated by this).[70] In the former sphere, the intelligences are so much "in" God that they exist only beyond themselves; in the latter, the spirits also exist in themselves. The former have "only an ideal individualisation", while for the latter "the divine will seals their independent unique subsistence".[71] We may properly observe here that for Soloviev, individuation is in no way accomplished *rations materiae*; for him it is precisely the personal that is truly and properly "ideal", while, conversely, that which is purely generic and anonymous is assigned to matter. The tendency to "neutralize" (so to speak) the act of creation, and in certain respects to negativise it is of importance here. This is the old neo-Platonic-Gnostic-Kabbalistic tradition, about which more will be said later on.

Sophia, then, is the divine substance *qua* "pan-unity", "the plenitude or absolute wholeness of being", in which "indeterminate plurality has never existed as such but has from all eternity submitted itself and reduced itself to the absolute unity of being in its three inseparable hypostases".[72] In a figurative sense, it can be described as "the body of the divine, the material being of the Godhead, penetrated by the divine principle of unity". Or else it may be described as his "nature";

---

[70] R III 5 W III 354-355.
[71] GM, lecture 9 A III 171.
[72] R III 3 W III 339-341.

since it is precisely in this way that God distinguishes himself absolutely from the nature of the world, it is necessary that "an eternal nature of his own, a special eternal world of his own, be accorded him'.[73] As such, though, it also includes in itself "the power that unites the fragmented and disrupted being of the world". It includes this not in its form as active divine Logos, but rather as "the feminine origin or the feminine consummation of every entity". "If it *exists* substantially in God from all eternity, then it comes into actuality in the world, embodying itself progressively in the world. In the beginning, it is *reshith* – the fertile idea of absolute unity, the only power whose calling is the unification of all things. At the end, it is *malkuth*, the kingly rule of God, the perfect, wholly realised union of creator and creature. It is not the world-soul – this is only the vehicle, the means and the basis for its realisation.[74] On this basis, then, Sophia is defined in terms of the tension between, on the one hand, God himself in his perfect presence and perfect representation in the totality of being (thus over against the Logos, understood as the locus of divine generation and the active moulder of that totality), and on the other, the Kingdom of God as the perfected issue of the world process, together with the humanity that is brought to completion through that process. But if humanity is necessarily threefold – Man, Woman and Society – "then its union with God is also necessarily threefold, though forming only one unique divine-human essence – Sophia incarnate, whose central and perfect personal expression is Jesus Christ; whose feminine complement is the Holy Virgin; and whose universal extension is the Church", this last-named being officially held together by the person of Peter. Nevertheless, Christ remains in himself the incarnation of the Logos as the divinely personal power that actively shapes the world. Over against him, as both fertile feminine womb and his created, formed issue, stands Mary, who is also the Church, *Maria-Ecclesia*, eschatologically the "Bride and Consort of the Lamb", the personal and social form taken in the world by Sophia in the stricter sense of the term.[75]

---

[73] GM, lecture 7 A III 145-146.
[74] R III 5 W III 352-353.
[75] *Ibid.*, III 7 W III 366-367.

The bodily element in this process of incarnation is essentially that of the one eucharistic body of Jesus, made ready beforehand in the animation of all bodily existence in the world, but finally given concrete structure by God. This living form of the body of the world, which finally finds its own plastic expression, is the form of God's Sophia, of his divine mode of articulation itself.[76] This is not contradicted by the *Lectures on Godmanhood*, where he sees Sophia as "the ideal, complete humanity, determined for eternity in Christ",[77] not only collectively but thoroughly individually, since it is a reality in which "each single individual is eternal as a part of total humanity" and has "an eternal and unique substantiality".[78] The world-soul was previously distinguished from Sophia as being only an "outer husk" for the perfection of humanity; but in so far as it is structured in all respects by Sophia and so enters into it as its goal, it also can now be called Sophia in its own right; it is "the complete organism, simultaneously universal and individual, total humanity as the eternal body of the Godhead and the eternal soul of the world".[79]

2. Both the remaining aspects of Soloviev's metaphysics – the complex of ideas centring on creation, separation from God, and the Fall, on the one hand, and the question of the world-soul and the world process on the other – are in fact inseparable, and this inseparability is precisely what characterises the contribution of Eastern Christian theology to the *Una Sancta*, the theme that it brings to be incorporated in it. The actual coincidence of Creation (the creature's emergence from God and from ideal form) and Fall (the creature's falling away from God) is expressly taught by Maximus the Confessor,[80] epitomising a long tradition that is by no means exclusively Gnostic. The "subject" of the world process as a whole, normally called the "world-soul", begins its development in a position of extreme inferiority, a state of absolute fragmentation and separation. In accordance with gnosticising Christian tradition, Soloviev believes that this state cannot be

---

[76] *Ibid.*, 368.
[77] GM, lecture 8 A III 152.
[78] *Ibid.*, 158.
[79] *Ibid.*, 157.
[80] *Cf.*, my *Kosmische Liturgie: Maximus der Bekenner*, 1961, 184-185.

comprehended without supposing a dimension of turning away from God, a dimension of guilt, embracing the whole process.

Before we introduce the question of "process", – that is, of the essence of Creation, Fall and development, a word about the essence of the world-soul is in order. According to the article in Brockhaus-Ephron, "The world-soul is the uniform inner nature of the world", in so far as this unity is conceived not only as "the highest ideal unity, which reposes in the absolute principle", but also as a real "subordinate principle", as in Plato's *Timaeus* and in Plotinus. "The idea of a world-soul, which disappeared in the Scholastic period, becomes a matter of pressing concern once again in the Renaissance Platonists and at the beginnings of the modern era," in Goethe and Schelling, for instance; while Schopenhauer and Hartmann go further back still, beyond the Greeks, to the monism of Indian thought. Soloviev himself dismisses this monistic conception of the world process: "If we presuppose a world-soul as the unique fundamental principle, such a world process would have to be a constant generation of something absolutely new, an uninterrupted creation *ex nihilo*; that is, pure miracle." However, natural philosophy makes it perfectly plain that there is a uniform centre of nature (as, indeed, the Soloviev of the *Crisis* had demonstrated): "If the component elements of the cosmic whole, the atoms, are to be traced back to a dynamic source of determination (centres of active powers), a determination that in turn finds its exhaustive definition in the psychic characteristics of aspiring and imagining, then we are necessarily bound to grant that the natural ground of unity in these powers also possesses the same psychic nature."[81]

If "atoms" are active centres of energy in reaction against a principle of passive dissolution proceeding *ad infinitum*, then "pure matter" is a limit concept, a "postulate", that is entirely imaginary; it cannot even be followed through to a logical conclusion.[82] "In order to act upon another reality outside itself, any power or energy must strive to go out of itself. In order to receive the influence of another energy, it must, so to speak, make room for the other, draw it to itself or set it before itself.

[81] Art. "Weltseele" in Brockhaus-Ephron W VI.
[82] GM, lecture 2 A III 30.

It follows from this that any fundamental or primordial energy necessarily finds expression in this way, in aspiration and representation."[83] In action, it becomes real for others; in experiencing outside influence, other things become real for it. So the purely quantitative dimension is already superseded: the centres of atomic entities are acting and aspiring monads, living elemental substances (if they were not so, they would have no rationale for their aspirations). "In nature there is no such thing as pure mechanism or absolute soullessness."[84] If we start our investigations at the lowest levels of the process, it is still the forward-striving energy of nature that appears as "elemental basis of the cosmic whole, as blind natural will". In this, two tendencies are simultaneously recognisable: there is the capacity for a deeper submission to the ideal principle of the cosmos, and thus the readiness to receive forms; and at the same time, because of the blindness of the act of aspiration, there is the opposite capacity for resistance to the ideal principle, the tendency toward chaos.[85] Pure "striving", "blind yearning" (*désir aveugle*) *is* what characterises this stage, precisely because the energy has not yet achieved any kind of interiority, and cannot transcend the separation of the particular individuated centres of energy that "exist side by side with one another in the formal unity of infinite space – a completely external and empty image of the objective substantial wholeness of God".[86] This "pure striving" is "pure indeterminate potentiality",[87] and as such, it is "the first of all creatures, the *materia prima*, the true substratum of our created world".[88] Soloviev does not want to abandon to their own inner and autonomous fertility and creative fantasy the products of the world-soul as they follow one upon the other, the gradations of astral, geological and biological processes leading up to humanity; rather, in reaction against a monistic idealism, he puts them all under the irradiating activity of the divine creative Logos, but in such a way that in the inmost depths the mother and matrix of all

---

[83] *Ibid.*, lecture 4 66.
[84] RG, introd. 4 D II, 20, n.
[85] "Beauty in Nature" ["Die Schönheit in der Natur"] 8 W VII 152-153.
[86] R III 4 W III 349.
[87] *Ibid.*, 348.
[88] GM, lecture 10 A III 180.

forms shares in the successive acts of their information, since this matrix itself attains a deeper interiority in every one of its products and so acquires greater generative power. On its own, it is a "barren womb";[89] but when it is fertilized by the Logos, it is no longer possible to say whether the forms generated are more the product of the Logos or more the product of the world-soul. What at first is imposed upon the world-soul as an external "law", (what, therefore, it experiences as pure limitation) it now takes into itself and, as it ascends towards consciousness, experiences as inner life and light and so as liberation. Whereas the world-soul "originally, as simply aspiration, does not know what it should aspire to and does not possess the idea of pan-unity", the Logos for its part cannot realise "its ideal purpose directly in the divided elements of material existence". So the world-soul is the necessary principle of mediation, just as much for the Divine Logos (whose desired goal is the coming to be of God in the world) as for the world itself, which can only attain to freedom through a process of prolonged assimilation of the ideal "law" into its own distinct life. So if the question is asked as to why the goal is not reached "by one single act of creation", "why such pain and fatigue is necessary in the life of the cosmic whole", "the answer [lies] in a single word that expresses something without which neither God nor nature is conceivable: freedom".[90]

Now the world-soul becomes "free" and "self-aware" for the first time in man: "In man nature transcends herself and, in attaining her conscious being, passes over into the sphere of absolute being."[91] In man the world-soul "comes to itself": all that has gone before is only a process of "hominisation"; and so the world-soul can be identified in its meaning and its goal with humanity.[92] "As the living core of all creatures and at the same time as the real form of the divine, the unified wholeness of humanity, or 'world-soul', is both the true subject of creaturely

---

[89] R III 6 W III 357.
[90] GM, lecture 10 A III 181-183.
[91] *Ibid.*, 186.
[92] *Ibid.*, 187. *Cf.* 174: "The world-soul, or ideal humanity", "the prototype of humanity or the world-soul"; 188: "The world-soul in man, or man himself"; 190: "Human consciousness, i.e., the world-soul."

existence and the true object of divine action."[93] Man is the one truly free being who stands between God and the world; his freedom may, of course, be no more than a natural exercise and thus be limited and conditioned, but it has only itself to blame for this. So if we say that "by a free act of the world-soul, the world that it held together as a unity has fallen away from God and fragmented into a multitude of warring elements",[94] then this cosmogonic "falling away" (at least in so far as it includes an element of guilt) has to be seen as one and the same event as the fall of man. "Eternal humanity" (the "Adam Kadmon" of the Kabbala) is, in the ideal purpose of God, the world-soul that has "come to itself": only in man does it attain to that state of suspense between God and the world that can result in a falling away from God. Man "possesses first the elements of physical existence that link him with the natural world; second, an ideal consciousness of total unity linking him with God; and, third, because he unites himself exclusively neither with one nor the other, he emerges as a free ego.... He is free to will the total unity that God possesses; and by willing it as God wills it, he can will to exist beyond himself, as does God."[95]

It would be nonsense to think in terms of two "falls", especially as Soloviev consistently impresses on us the identity of world-soul and humanity (*qua* content of the cosmos of which it is the consciousness). But Adam Kadmon is man in a general no less than an individual sense; Soloviev recognizes no such thing as an hypostatized universal, only "ideas" concretely filled out with their individual content.[96] He speaks of "the sinfulness of universal man", as a consequence of which humanity, "which ought to constitute the unifying rationality of the universe, found itself fragmented and scattered over the globe".[97] Like Maximus the Confessor, he speaks of the "splitting of a single human nature into many individual

---

[93] *Ibid.*, lecture 9, 174. *Cf. The Meaning of Sexual Love* I, W VII 215:"[Man] is aware of himself as the centre of the general consciousness of nature, as the soul of the world, as the self-realising potentiality of absolute total unity."

[94] GM, lecture 10 A III 183.

[95] *Ibid.*, 187.

[96] GG II 1, 5 W VII 89: "By the figure of the natural Adam we should understand not merely an individual person over against other persons, but a wholly united personal being, including in itself the entirety of natural humanity."

[97] R, Introd. W III 151.

natures".[98] He sees the totally unified essence of man and the world as having emerged from God's eternity into a sphere that is not historical ("fallen") time, in which preexistence (the preexistence in unity of all things) and immortality (after time) are absolutely one and the same and support each other. "That which comes into being only in time must also disappear with time; the notion of an entity eternally perduring after death cannot be logically harmonized with belief in its antenatal nonexistence."[99] The paradox is inescapable that for Soloviev the temporal world process (the world-soul's coming to consciousness in man) depends upon a supratemporal decision of the same reality in its freedom – depends, that is, upon its "eternal humanity". This indeed is the only possible resolution of the apparently contradictory assertion that death came into the world through one man's sin (Rom 5. 12) and yet must have existed, in terms of evolutionary history, long before the first man. It is possible that Soloviev also has in mind here Schopenhauer's doctrine of the unconditioned will and its subjugation at the level of phenomena to the principle of sufficient reason. He offers a painstaking exposition of this: "Every willing individual is, from one point of view, entirely conditioned in its manifestations; but, from the other side, it is entirely free in its inmost essence. Although all its acts are determined by its innate character, this innate character of the person is at the same time conditioned in its metaphysical essence by its own free Will."[100] Quite apart from the fact that, in Soloviev's work, the whole process is set out in dualistic rather than monistic terms (in terms of the distinction of cosmic will from God), the resolution of the world-soul problem must be sought in this direction. The world-soul itself is aspiration and will, but in an indeterminate condition (it is *aoristos dyas*),[101] "an unconditioned and unconfined principle" (*apeiron kai*

---

[98] RG II 7, 10 D II 164.
[99] GM, lecture 8 A III 159-160. *Cf.* 167-168: "The efficient cause of evil cannot be in the individual as an earthly phenomenon, conditioned in advance; *rather it must be sought in an absolute, eternal essence, in which the direct pristine will of this individual is contained*"
[100] *Crisis*, 249.
[101] R III 4 W III 348.

aoriston);[102] in order to define itself as will, it requires the consciousness that it attains only in man.

Once again, it is clear from all this that the world-soul is in no sense to be equated with Sophia,[103] although as the wisdom and the total unity of God progressively embody themselves in it, the more the activities of the creative Logos are taken up by it, at an ever more interior level, and marked as its own. In this sense, at any rate, Sophia and the world-soul can be equated,[104] or rather the world process can be described as Sophia coming to be.[105] Thus it could be envisaged as in one way comparable to the Augustinian City of God (*Peregrinans*), or else as the universal Church.

The world-soul is that which carries forward the cosmic process that begins with Creation. At the point of Creation, the only thing established as the ground of created being is pure potency (the world-soul as *materia prima*, as mother or matrix of all things); and there then follows the bestowing of form on this by the irradiation of the creative Logos (which represents the ideal world, *divine* Sophia, over against this primal matter). So Soloviev, following Augustine on the one side and Schelling on the other, can describe the act of creation almost in negative terms as the "removal" of God's triumphant power, that power for which the chaos of pure potentiality is always a possibility that is already in the past, already transcended. God "wills chaos to exist since he is able to lead back into unity the rebellious life of creatures and fill the infinite void with his overflowing life. Thus God gives freedom to chaos, he denies himself.... the power of reacting against it in his omnipotence."[106] This negative guarantee of security for the order of potentiality by means of the already victorious power of God holding itself back is at the same time a positive act of will, "since this other reality only attains its existence by a free act of the divine will".[107] God

---

[102] *Ibid.*, III 5 W III 356.

[103] As Stremoukhov rightly stresses (82, n. 65).

[104] GM, lecture 9 A III 174.

[105] *Ibid.*, lecture 10 A III 182.

[106] R III 4 W III 345; *cf.* 354.

[107] R III 4 W III 346.

desires that finite essences should possess a real life of their own. It is to this end that he brings his divine will out from its absolute substantial unity and directs it toward the multiplicity of the ideal objects and thereby confirms their independent and individual existence.... God confirms and establishes the "other" – that is, being (*to apeiron*) – by not retaining this will in himself as the One, but objectivising and actualising it for himself as total unity.   However, because of the natural unique particularity that belongs to the life of this "other" – that is, to every divine idea, every objectivised form, and in virtue of which it is simply "*this*" reality – these forms with which the divine will has linked itself do not behave at all indifferently with regard to the divine will; they remould the activity of this will to conform to their own particularity, pouring it, so to speak, into their own particular form.... In this way, the will ceases to be exclusively divine.... It now both belongs to the objectified form in its particularity as well as being an expression of the activity of the divine essence.   The infinite energy of existence (to *apeiron*) which in the Godhead always remains hidden behind and within its realisation . . . , ceases to conceal itself in an individual essence behind its realisations, since these actions are not the whole but only a distinct part of the whole.   So every individual essence loses its direct unity with the Godhead, . . . it separates the divine *act* of will from the absolute and immediate unity of the divine will as such, taking it *for itself*, and through it acquiring the living power of reality.[108]

Here one need only replace the word "will" with the word "being" (*actus essendi*) – as indeed Soloviev himself does – to see appear the classical Thomist doctrine of the *limitatio actus essendi per essentiam ut potentiam*, with the whole profoundly problematic element that this contains (since the inner potentiality, or "openness", of this divine act of being, as it externalises itself in the cosmic act, the *apeiron*, is already articulated in and with the process of *limitatio*).   The consequence also follows that the world-soul (*qua* humanity), which has already been designated as

---

apeiron, is nothing other than this divine act of being itself, transcending itself in the Other and pouring itself out into the Other.

The world then becomes "the God who is coming to be" vis-à-vis the God who exists as eternally contemporary to all things. It becomes, as Soloviev constantly reiterates, a mirror image of God's reality,[109] which constructs itself a second time beyond itself, constructs itself out of a pure potentiality for being. Why so? So as to point to the ultimate proof of its Divine Being, to the fact that he is both *hen* and *pan*; that, in its total being, it is contained by no "other" reality and limited by no "other". It is wholeness both in himself and outside himself.

This is where the difficulties start, at the point where the limitation of the act of being is described as a separation and a "taking for self" of the divine will. To avoid identifying the coming into reality of nature with the Fall, identifying separateness with egotism, we must stick to those texts that are quite clear in tracing the Fall back to a (transcendental) free decision, which establishes the form of fragmentation in cosmic life. It is through this decision that evil enters in at the root of the sensible world as the contradiction between the infinity of the basic blind urge or "thirst" and the finitude of the forms in which it is realised and which it wills to make absolute. The central phenomenon in which this destructive contradiction becomes manifest is the life of the various species; though when thus manifest, the contradiction is ipso facto denied and resolved at a higher level. Such a life is based on sexual desire and necessarily ends in death. It nourishes itself from an alien life (killing so that it itself may live) and yet can live only in order to die.[110] Again this is a decidedly Eastern way of thinking. The positive concept of form means the removal and elevation of this endless and unsatisfied craving in finite being to another level: "The boundary of matter is to be found in God."[111] Thus the world's condition is evil, since all beings burn with the hellfire of insatiable craving, they burn with "false and evil life". Only from God can it receive definition and limit –

---

[109] R III 4 W III 346. "A negative counterpart to the divine"; RG III.8, 3 D II 184.
[110] GG I, Introd. W II 13-15.
[111] GG I 1 W II 33.

initially, by means of an external and harsh law that, as it is gradually interiorised, brings this dark blaze of desire into the light; and by doing so it shows itself to be truly grace, something the creature can never bestow upon itself, something, therefore, that requires faith in a higher gift, given from outside,[112] something that thus requires prayer.[113] The finite in itself is parasitic and insatiable; the infinite, on the other hand, is always a matter of a definite task, a definite responsibility, and so constitutes the form that determines the "matter" provided by the basic urge or drive.[114]

Adam exists in three conditions. He is, first, wholly real in God and potential in himself. He then becomes real in his own right, and *as such* has only potential (ideal) reality in God. Finally, in Christ, he becomes real both in himself and in God *en duo physesin*.[115] "The animal shape in which humanity appears to us at the dawn of history is only a distortion of the image of God in man."[116] So far as it includes the process of hominisation, the establishment of the world's reality is indeed the result of alienation. The latter is "a displacement of certain essential elements"[117] and thus "a false relation" of individual entities to one another,[118] whereby "the root of the perversity of our existence is constituted by impenetrability; that is, by mutually exclusive essences standing in opposition to each other".[119] The centring of the self *in* the ego and the stubborn clinging *to* the ego, clinging to the differentiated existence of separation and division, this above all puts individual existence "outside the truth" and condemns it to death and decay.[120] "The oppressive, tormenting dream of our egotistic separateness",[121] the contradiction of wanting to be at one and the same time the whole of reality *and* one's own self, this "root of all

---

[112] GG I, Introd. W II 19-25.
[113] *Ibid.*, 25f.
[114] GS I W II 211-212. Also R III 6 W III 357.
[115] GG II 1, 5 W II 92-93.
[116] GG I 2 W II 51, n.
[117] GM, lecture 9 A III 165.
[118] GG II 1, 2 W II 74.
[119] *The Meaning Of Sexual Love* 4 W VII 268.
[120] *Ibid.*, 2 VII 215.
[121] GM, lecture 9; A III 162.

suffering",[122] existing in opposition to the corporate fulfilment of nature, is transcended first and foremost in Christ and in the Mystical Body. In ordinary sexual relationship, the contradiction is at best only masked – that is why sexual Eros is so close to cruelty and to rending hostility;[123] and thus too, marriage is not a real means of salvation – sexual continence is far better. Again, childbearing can only be the transmission of the same finite, egotistical and therefore mortal life, despite the hope that the temporal world will get "better" with the children; the sacrament of marriage does not alter any of this.[124] For that one would have to be able to elevate the meaning of Eros, purified and clarified by sexual continence, into true love. And then to pass beyond both marriage (which will always remain the only possibility for the common run of men) and negative asceticism (beyond which the Christian monastic tradition has rarely penetrated), into that rare and supreme possibility of authentic love, in which the eternal, androgynous syzygy which is the heart of Eros, now redeemed from its fallenness to sexuality, is taken up into God, into the relation of Logos and Sophia.[125]

But it is worth remembering at this point that matter – that is, a state of absolutized separation and fragmentation – is no more than a limit concept (a "postulate") that is in reality impossible, and that the "will", energy or impulse, that constitutes the kernel of all life is already in reaction against this tendency toward a flight into chaos. However, the power to penetrate and overcome this chaotic tendency toward absolute separation varies: the cosmic process is the gradual illumination and redemption of the will (of the world-soul), its deliverance from this perverse potentiality that it possesses. Here we should note merely that it is only when it becomes conscious in the free human subject that the blind "impulse to separation" opens up to the diabolism of freely willed evil; and so the world process can be perfected only in a process of historical and apocalyptic decision for or against the true Good.

---

[122] *Ibid.*, 164.
[123] GG II 1, 3 W II 77.
[124] RG II 7, 4 D II 15 154f.
[125] This is the theme of the essays on sexual love; VII 201-272.

We shall not attempt here to trace out the stages of the cosmic process in detail, though the description given of them (modelled on the accounts of Schelling and Hegel) is of the highest visionary power. God does not create directly, but only through the medium of the world-soul: this is an indispensable notion of which we must never lose sight.[126] Through "blind groping", "through unfulfilled projects for never-realized creatures", the world-soul ascends with difficulty, from chaos to cosmos. So the stages of the world's coming to be are to be interpreted as the steps leading up to the coming to be of man and of Christ. The "universal force of gravity" binds disparate things to one another in a mechanical and external fashion; it is "a primordial expression of cosmic altruism". Subsequently, a new, refined and dynamic form of matter, the "ether", embraces the elements and binds them together as light, electricity and so forth; "this active energy is characterised by pure altruism, an unlimited extension and a continuous act of self-giving". "The world-soul, the earth, beholds in the radiance of the ether the ideal image of its heavenly beloved, but it does not in reality unite with it"; it strives toward it by absorbing the light into itself, by "transforming [it] in the fire of life", and now begins to develop organic forms. These represent the Logos in so far as it has come into being as immanent in the world, the Logos that finally, after endless efforts, struggles through to come to consciousness in man, and so too to come to the form of total being, that form in which the God, who is all in One, can be present as ideal structure. At this point, the historical process begins, the process that so deepens and alters the ideal forms of thinking about God that the dwelling of God in a real man, as the constitutive reality of a real man, becomes possible in consequence. By these stages the world ascends toward its peak in the God-Man. Soloviev constantly goes over them again: from the abstract Indian idea of God (corresponding to the abstractness of the principle of gravity) we move to the luminous, contemplative ideal world of the Greeks (corresponding to the stage of the irradiation of matter, but still lacking active interiority of life) and thence to Israel's real and active relation to God (corresponding to the organic process of

---

[126] R III 6 W III 157-159.

nature) – a relation, though, in which God still remains "Other".

"That which is fresh and original in Christianity does not lie in general conceptions but in positive facts, not in the speculative content of its ideal structure, but in this idea's embodiment in a personality. This fresh and original character can never be taken from Christianity; it is not at all necessary in establishing this to demonstrate, in the face of all historical fact and all sound human understanding, that the ideas of Christian dogma come on to the scene as something entirely novel, fallen from Heaven, so to speak, in their perfected shape. Nor would this be a view shared by the great fathers of the Church."[127] Soloviev does not mean to say that Christ is only a particular case of the genus "Godmanhood": he is much more its unique and all-transcending peak, God's becoming real in man – previously no more than an unrealisable ideal for humanity. He is "the absolute synthesis of the infinite with the finite",[128] "manifestation of the new man ... [as] the focal point of world history".[129] However, this is not "a miracle in the crude sense of the word, not something alien to the general order of existence; this new and unprecedented phenomenon was being made ready in all that had gone before; it represented what all the earlier phases of life had yearned for and striven for and hastened toward: the whole of nature had aspired and gravitated toward man, and the whole history of humanity had been directed toward the God-Man".[130]

Soloviev's Christology reaches its climax in the affirmation that the realisation of the God-Man Christ is to be seen as grounded upon a reciprocal sacrifice – God's sacrifice in entering into humanity no less than man's in entering into God. In this lies the perfection of human love, and thus too the perfection of human freedom. In the state of total "innocence", Adam Kadmon existed really in God while existing only potentially in himself; then, when he came to be

---

[127] GM, lecture 6 A III 102-103. *Cf.* lecture 7, 141: "Christianity has its own proper content ..., and this is uniquely and solely Christ"; and 142: "The only novelty, the only specifically distinguishing feature, [is] Christ's teaching about himself, this pointing to his own person."
[128] R III 11 W III 408.
[129] GG II 3 W II 136.
[130] GG II 1, 5 W II 91-92.

real in (and for) himself, his being in God was only potential. The pristine unity cannot be simply reproduced, it must be "achieved; it can be only the issue of free action, of a free deed, in fact, of a twofold deed: a self-abandonment on the part of the divine just as on the part of the human". Now the whole cosmic and historical process rests upon "a kind of self-sacrifice" by the Logos, "since on the one side, the Logos here renounces, by a free action of his divine will or love, the manifestation of his divine glory. He forsakes the repose of eternity and engages in the struggle against the principle of evil, subjecting himself to the whole consequence of the rebellion of the cosmic process by appearing within the imprisoning constraints of an existence external to himself, within the limits of space and time ... hidden rather than manifest. On the other side, however, is cosmic and human nature, in the form of its actualisation at any particular point, unceasingly divesting itself of itself as it experiences an unremitting yearning and strives after ever new modes of appropriating the divine prototypes." Nevertheless, for the time being this twofold *kenosis* remains incomplete; "it first comes to perfection when the divine Logos truly empties himself and takes the form of a servant (Phil 2.7)", since at this point he

> determines [the human principle] no longer by means of external action, by setting limits to it without himself changing at all but rather by an interior self-limitation making space in himself for the Other and taking up into himself what is human. So on the one hand, the divine Logos takes human limitation upon himself; not indeed in such a way as wholly to enter into the limits of human consciousness, which would be impossible, but by experiencing these limits in any actual given moment as his own. And this self-limitation of the Godhead *in Christo* sets free his humanity, since it allows his natural will freely to renounce itself in favour of the divine principle – regarded not as an external force (which would mean that the self-renunciation was   unfree) but as an interior good through which man can then come to share this good in full reality.[131]

---

[131] GG II 1, 5 W II 94-96 (collated with Kohler's translation in D I 78-80).

This is a crucial text for the whole of Soloviev's theology and theological aesthetic: in God's *kenosis* (which perfects the whole process of creation by transcending it from within), human *kenosis* is freely given space in God so that the human consciousness may give itself over absolutely to the divine. In this act, man is freed from all sinful isolation for him who is total unity; and this indwells in him, no longer simply as a pure abstract form of thought (Western rationalism from Descartes to Hegel remained fixed at this level), but rather as real plenitude. And this is possible, not through some Promethean will to understanding on the part of "absolute Spirit", but through dedication in response to the eternal Father. This twofold *kenosis* is the essence of the person of the God-Man no less than of his work, his death on the cross, and it is at the same time absolute glory in twofold form – the self-glorification of God in his creation as much as the glorification in God of the whole man, the man who, in the voluntary death of love, is victorious over all the disastrous contingencies of the material world and so has achieved for himself and for all humanity and the cosmos the resurrection of the body.[132] In this connection, Soloviev insistently stresses the necessity of the christological doctrine of Christ's twofold will, which alone guarantees the *kenosis* and the glorification of the God-Man himself as well as of the whole creation through him. This doctrine alone makes possible the threefold temptation of Christ, which becomes intelligible precisely in virtue of this developed Christology (the idea that Christ's human nature exists in and because of a surrender to the person of the Logos who makes space for it in himself). It is a temptation to bring more and more of the divine power into play for the work of salvation – which would, however, mean the loss of life lived in self-surrender and so the loss of the only possible salvation. The renunciation of a glory that can be deployed at will is the attainment of an authentic "glory in the act of all-conquering love: 'We beheld his glory, glory as of the only Son from the Father, full of grace and truth'."[133]

---

[132] GG II 1, 5 W II 99-101.
[133] GG II 1, 5 W II 96-99.

With Christ, the spiritual man comes on to the scene; the law of his being lies in the saying that only he who loses his soul (in so far as it is separate, limited and worldly) will save it.[134] And he wins in exchange for it not only his own self in Christ and so in God, but also, as a necessary consequence, the divine and worldly total unity itself. He has consecrated himself to the work of atonement, to the coming to be of God's Kingdom; and that Kingdom in its coming to be is the Church.

3. ETHICS AND ECCLESIOLOGY

Soloviev's basic idea is the notion of "realisation", realisation as the becoming real of the ideal, as the descent of Heaven to earth, as the setting free of man for God and for himself by the process of God's becoming man. To this end it is of first importance that the level of *theoria* (as pure knowledge and perception of the idea) be transcended; and it is transcended by God as he makes himself known in the Judaeo-Christian tradition as the *realissimum* (beyond the Greek ideal of contemplation and the formalism of Kant), which in its work of grace sets limits on human freedom for the actual task of collaborating in the building of God's Kingdom in the cosmos. Thus the "will" of God, that which he has invested in the world as his own reality in the Other, returns again to him in a threefold manner.

So clearly does Soloviev see in the process of the absolute ideal – God becoming real – the abiding and obvious achievement of Christianity for the human race, that he does not consider it as a philosopher might, going back behind the process, abandoning what has actually been attained in the interests of some kind of pure philosophical method. Still less is he minded to offer a rationalistic unravelling of the Christian phenomenon in order to surpass it. For if God's coming to be real has not been consummated on the soil of historical and empirical fact in the uniqueness of the God-Man, then everything remains still in the partial and prejudiced state of *theoria*, "absolute knowledge". However, the projected system

---

[134] GM, lecture 5 A III 59.

of the late "theoretical philosophy" shows a concern to build into itself this realm of absolute knowledge as pure phenomenalism and formalism. The later ethics, the *Justification of the Good*, accomplishes both steps at once: worldly reality (of the so-called "external world" as well as of the ego) is unfolded and secured primarily in ethical fashion – and the reality of God unfolds itself in the same act as the inner reality that makes possible every ethical action and is presupposed by it. For in order to exist, man must act; and in order to act he must presuppose that existence has some meaning; but this presupposition implies the existence of a *giver* of meaning.

> Any creature striving toward the goal of its existence necessarily becomes convinced of the fact that the attainment of its goal or the final satisfaction of human desire does not lie in human power; that is, any creature endowed with reason comes to recognise its dependence on an invisible and unknown reality. Such dependence is impossible to deny. The only question is whether that on which man depends has a meaning or not. If it has no meaning, then a life conditioned by this meaninglessness is itself meaningless.... We are able consciously and rationally to do good only if we believe in the Good itself, in its objective, independent significance in the world – only if (in other words) we believe in a moral order, in a purpose, in God.... We must believe that the good that reason demands of us is no subjective illusion but has a real ground, and that it brings truth to expression.[135]

Soloviev has no trouble in showing that all the great ethical systems (all those, that is, with religious content) of the various races are constructed on this assumption, and that the ethical systems of eudaemonism on the one hand[136] and Kantian rigorism on the other[137] extract only one aspect from the total

---

[135] RG I 4, 4-5 D II 98-100.
[136] RG I 6 D II 128-148.
[137] RG II, 713-714 D II 170-177. "Morality is in reality autonomous; Kant was not deceived in this respect. And this massive issue from the sphere of human consciousness, which is implied in its very name, will not forsake man. Morality is autonomous precisely for this reason, because its essential core is no abstract formula, hanging in the air; rather it is

phenomenon. He himself constructs his system (as always) with an eye to the final integration of the "total unity"; the norm is the wholeness of man,[138] and a broad inductive survey of ethical phenomena, conducted with magisterial sureness of touch, demonstrates "from below", from the concrete facts of history, what Kant proves a priori (and thus no more than formally).[139] The three basic phenomena of shame (the elevation of spirit over the world of instinct), sympathy (communication with one's fellow man, with everyone who is a neighbour) and *pietás* (in the sense of reverence for the higher reality upon which one depends – parents, clan, country, ancestors, gods, the living God) support the cosmos of virtues and duties, the universal human integration as personality, society and Church, or Kingdom of God.[140] Here again the concept of process, this time at the historical level, is for Soloviev "an historical fact that cannot be contested with any well-founded degree of certainty".[141] Each man on his own level can of course, in some way do what is right, strengthened by providential grace. "But just as neither a formless organic piece of matter nor an inadequately evolved living body such as a sponge, polyp or cuttlefish can produce a human being, even if it possesses it potentially within itself, so also the Kingdom of God (in the sense of the perfection of human and cosmic social life) cannot take shape directly out of a horde of savages or an inadequately evolved and barbarous political organism."[142] Just as the first Adam's arrival on the scene was a seed sown in the world requiring infinite time to evolve, so too the seed of the second Adam will require a long passage of time before the whole "dough" of world history and the cosmos is leavened. However, the eschatological Kingdom of God does not fall from Heaven any more than Christ's own advent occurs

---

autonomous because it carries in itself all the conditions of its own reality. And those realities presupposed by a moral life, the existence of God and an immortal soul, do not represent the demand for something other, added on to the sphere of morality; they are its own inner basis. God and the human soul are not postulates of the moral law, but the very formative powers of moral reality." *Ibid.*, p. 175.

[138] RG II 7, 10 D II 162f.
[139] RG, foreword *ad fin.*; D II xxii-xxiii.
[140] *Ibid.*, I, ch. ii-iv.
[141] *Ibid.*, II 7, 14 D II 176.
[142] *Ibid.*, II 8, 5 D II 188.

without mediation; it comes in the fulness of time, when the womb of the virgin – and the womb of earth itself as well – is perfectly ripe for the reception of the divine seed. While the Church fathers had to answer the question of why Christ came so late, at the end of the ages,[143] Soloviev has to deal with the opposite question, why he came so early and delays his return so long. If "the Kingdom of God could be revealed as little among cannibals as among wild animals, if it is necessary for humanity to make its way from an animal, formless and chaotic condition to intelligible organization and unity, then it is as clear as day that this process is not yet concluded, that the idea of Christ has not yet leavened all the dough".[144] Soloviev is no Pelagian,[145] so little does he recognise any independent achievement by men and by humanity without the prevenient assistance of the "nourishing" work of grace,[146] that we must fear almost the exact contrary – a dissolution of the natural order (where, at the end of the day, nature would still exist really only as pure potentiality, while an ideality stems from the Logos) in the order of grace. But the expressions he uses here should not be pressed too far: Soloviev thinks as a Christian who can never posit a pantheistic dissolution of creation and creaturely freedom in God; his teaching on the Kingdom of God seeks indeed to integrate all particular individual freedoms in the one mystical Body, in the communion of saints, but seeks precisely in this integration to preserve and eternalise the authentic freedom of authentic personalities.

Since the event of Christ, this process of the integration of humanity into the Kingdom of God is necessarily bound to the reality of the *Church*. The Church is, on the one hand, the God-Man really living on in a community of love, realised ethically as well as sacramentally; but, on the other hand, it is also, necessarily, the pattern of the ideal universal form of the Kingdom of God. It is ideal in so far as it has not yet really been integrated and realised in the historical process; but in Christ it is already real, and, in inchoate form, it is realised in the Church and in humanity. The Church as founded by Christ is the place

---

[143] Henri de Lubac, *Katholizismus als Gemeinschaft* (1943), 145f., 216f.

[144] RG II 8, 5 D II 189.

[145] *Cf.* the detailed article on Pelagius in Brockhaus-Ephron; W VI.

[146] RG II 7, 14 D II 176.

where the ultimate is made present; in it the false and contradictory species life that exists in the flux of temporality is done away with: in the Church is abiding fatherhood and abiding filial *pietas*; it is "natural humanity transsubstantiated".[147] And it is so from a starting point in the real and particular that the ideal sought for is no longer simply God but the perfected body of humanity.

> The God-man is individual, the true Man-God is universal as the radius is the same for the whole circle and determines equally the distance from the centre to any given point on the circumference, it is thus in itself the formative principle of the circle, while the points on the circumference can make up the circle only in the sum of their totality. Outside this totality – that is, outside the circle – they have taken individually no definition; and the circle also is unreal without them. In the human world, the Church represents this circle. When human personality is united with the Church, man comes to be *integrated*. He receives true and healthful life, and the Church itself is fertilised and can now act effectively.[148]

Everything then depends on the integration of humanity into the Church, so that it can receive there a share in the form of divine-human universality, and on the other hand, on the Church's integration into humanity, so that it can shed the abstractness that is foreign to it because of its essential centre, but which it still retains because of the refusal of men to accept it. It is of course equipped by its founder, for the sake of its task of integration, with a *form* of universality, that removes it from the limits of any finite worldly form (nationalism in particular); but this form, which culminates in the finality of papal authority and in the doctrine of infallibility, is not *in itself* abstract. For in the first place there is absolutely no such thing as abstract truth in the Church; further, the form of being in truth corresponds to a real existence; in truth, an existence

---

[147] R III 10 W III 396-397.
[148] GG II 2 W II 135.

which has its ground in the immaculate virgin Mary,[149] and finally, the form of infallibility is always embodied in a concrete Church order, "grounded in the real and living unity of the prince of the apostles," the one who, in the place of all and in the name of all, was the first to make a free confession of the divinity of Christ, to "the messianic idea in its absolute and universal form," and thus the one to whom the keys of the Kingdom have been entrusted.[150] So the concept of form that is practically applied in the polity of the Catholic Church is, as was noted at the onset, the concept of a means, a way of mediation; but it is only possible and meaningful if it arises out of a form that has its end in itself (the Godmanhood of Christ as the expression of God in the world) and advances toward a form that equally has its end in itself (the complete embodiment of Christ in humanity, the Kingdom of God). Only when considered in the light of this purposive dynamism is the form of the Church not vacuous or abstract, but a plenitude in the process of coming to be, supernatural ethic in practice and so itself an expression of Christian love. For it is love alone, and can only be love alone, that transcends all forms of egotism, whether of individuals, or of groups, so that it may liberate them in "a real act of submission or love toward the Church"[151] for Christ who is total truth and total unity. It is in virtue of this love, which is at work beyond all limited personal or racial loves, that "the Church as a whole is more real and more alive than all persons and races, just as the whole body surpasses the individual organs and cells in its vital power".[152]

In the *Spiritual Foundations of Life,* Soloviev had already, in a superb survey, outlined the forms of ecclesial catholicity; it is a survey oriented to the practical "catholic" task of the permeation of all humanity but does not yet enter into the debate between the Western and Eastern Churches. Although, as Soloviev says in this work, the Church stands above all natural organisms, it possesses in common with them those qualities that belong to any kind of life in the world. "Any real determinate life also requires a corresponding determinate

---

[149] R II 1 W III 249.
[150] *Ibid.,* 250-253.
[151] *Ibid.,* II 4 W III 267.
[152] Th. 23 W II 476.

form", a body. This is more than a mere aggregate of parts; it involves (1) the entirety of its component elements, (2) the organic form that produces the real body out of these elements, (3) the actual vital energy itself, which expresses itself in all the operations and movements of the separate parts in subordination to the whole. In the Body of Christ, the elements are human beings, the form is the Church and the vital energy is the Divine Spirit. By virtue of the ecclesial form, the Divine Spirit elevates particular individuals above their limited existence, so that they come together formally in the total unity of Christ; and it further happens, again because of the ecclesial form, that the enduring limitations of sinners do not damage the dignity of the Church as a whole. A natural body too can be diseased in particular members, but it will die only if the central organs are affected. But in the Church these organs are invulnerable: the head is the God-Man, the heart is the immaculate Virgin and, with her, the whole invisible Church of the saints. So the ethical task proper to all who belong to the Church becomes the conforming of its life to the divine life, whose seed and whose structure are preserved in the sacred form of the visible Church. Any form originating with man is innerworldly; by contrast, everything "provided by the Church universal, has the form of unconditionality (absoluteness)." This comprises (1) the true faith as the Church understands and proclaims it in her role as representing the powers of human knowledge penetrated by Christ's spirit, to which the individual has to surrender his isolated, "fleshly" understanding; (2) the right relationship to all men, which the Church in her hierarchical form is able to uphold, the hierarchial form "in which every member occupies his place and fulfils his destiny not in his own name, but in the name of him who has commissioned that member for his work, in which this whole ordered existence leads directly up to the source of all truth, to Christ, the one true High Priest and King"; (3) the human destiny to rule over the cosmos and mould it into the body of God. But for this last the Church carries in itself only the seed, the germ of the new and higher nature (in the.Eucharist), "the absolute form of transfigured matter," with which we communicate in the organic existence of the Church, so that, starting from there, freed in principle from the servitude of the material order, we can actively help the world to be transfigured.[153] The universal form of faith, universal hierarchical obedience, and the receiving in the sacraments of a universal eschatological quality of life, these three things together elevate man in his fragmented and limited existence to a state of participation in the fulness of divine catholicity. And the ecclesiastical form directed toward that goal cannot be invalidated by the "matter" that is unified by it: "The Church is not only the assembly of believers; it is, before all else, that which assembles them – that is, a substantive form of unity given to men from above, by means of which they can come to share in the Godhead."[154]

Soloviev emphasises very strongly the mediatorial nature of ecclesiastical form. We are not to "confuse the bed with the stream"; the Church is the Kingdom, not in the state of fulfilment but only in becoming, and there can be no doubt that the grace of God has always been at work in the world. But since Christ's incarnation, this grace has taken on a visible and tangible form: "In the Christian Church, the divine is not only an interior and intangible working of the Spirit, it appears also in determinate shape, already realised, in bodily manifestation. The Old Testament Church too had its forms, but there they were only allegorical foretypes and signs. On the other hand, the sacred forms of the New Testament Church are true and authentic images of the presence and work of God in humanity." Because of the imperfection of the human beings who enter the Church, "these forms appear only as the inception, the pledge, of divine life in humanity ... but even at the present time the New Jerusalem, the city of the living God, does not consist purely in the thoughts, wishes and inner feelings of Christians: the divine forms represent the real foundations, here and now, of that city of God, on which the divine building will be erected – which, indeed, is already in process of construction in a mystical sense. So, of course, not everything in the visible Church is divine, but the divine is already something visible within it. And these visible foundation stones are unshakeable and unchangeable; without

---

[153] GG II 2 W II 108-111.
[154] *Ibid.*, 112.

them there is no Church."[155] The Church is, it could be said, the process of gestation, the perfected Kingdom is the event of birth.

Soloviev's doctrine of the necessary interpenetration of an immutable structure with the living evolution of the same structure arises out of this conception: if an entelechy is vital and active, then precisely for that reason it must change as to the forms of its manifestation if it is to remain itself. "Thus the visible forms of the divine, though always present in the Church, were at first very rudimentary and imperfect, just as the visible form of a seed is rudimentary and imperfect and shows very little correspondence as yet to the full form of the plant, although it contains this form potentially in itself." So it would be foolish for someone to reject the full-grown tree so as to preserve the seed, to "reject the more fully revealed forms of God's grace in the Church, preferring absolutely a return to the structure of the primitive Christian community".[156] And yet the whole plant is present in the seed; and thus the choice of a new apostle to complete the original number is made at Peter's suggestion. It is not done "aristocratically", with the Apostles exercising their own plenitude of power, nor "democratically", by ballot, but "theocratically", through prayer and the drawing of lots. In this way, the divine influence on the community is the outcome of the free concord of the disciples under Peter's leadership; so that "already the polity of the Church emerges with complete clarity as a free theocracy".[157] The Church that is sent out into the arena of world history will always have to express its life in the fact that, through the indwelling Spirit of God, it is equal to ever-new historical situations and tasks. It will, in consequence, have to elucidate its faith in the rich Graeco-Roman systems of learning and conceptuality and to develop the expression of it accordingly, precisely if it wishes to remain true to its own primitive tradition;[158] and the definitions promulgated in its ecumenical councils as the expression of the self-understanding of its faith will be binding on all believers.[159]

---

[155] *Ibid.*, 114-115.
[156] *Ibid.*, 118-119.
[157] *Ibid.*, 120.
[158] *Ibid.*, 121.
[159] Th. 7 W II 414f.

At this point, the Great Schism intervened, the schism between East and West, between the Byzantine-Muscovite world and Rome, and between the slavophiles and Soloviev, with Soloviev pleading the cause of Rome – but also the cause of the ecumenical councils-with such superiority in his grasp of the issues involved. We need not and cannot summarize here this brilliant apologia, although in its clarity, verve and subtlety it belongs among the masterpieces of ecclesiology. One or two observations must suffice. Both the great schisms, Eastern and Protestant, are pure scandal; they cannot be justified from a Christian point of view in any way at all. The East, which adhered to the legitimacy of the great ecumenical councils, had in fact acknowledged the authority of Rome in these very councils (especially at Chalcedon); no council ever condemned Rome, and, since the time of Photius, the East has recognized its inability to convene an ecumenical council on its own behalf. It has ossified in the position it held at that time, whereas Rome has never ceased to renew itself in vital fashion, facing up to the contemporary historical situation. Before the separation of the churches, the Byzantine Church, out of loveless political envy and the lust for honour, had surrendered itself to the service of the emperor and so deprived itself of its catholic, supranational liberty. This bondage to the state was its legacy to Russia, which totally dispensed with the Church's liberty by finally establishing the tsar as head of the Church in 1885. By rejecting the living, contemporary Polity of the Roman Church, Byzantium had no alternative but to elevate the stagnated tradition and, in consequence, formalism into a principle; thus it became the Church of the past.[160] It was a profound historicophilosophical logic that the heir of Byzantium was Islam.[161] Whoever, as a Christian, only preserves without creating has indeed suffered the interior loss of his treasure: "When cut off from its living form of *coming to be*, existing only in the forms of expression that *have* already *come* to be, the Church's holiness necessarily loses its infinite quality. It becomes hidden and bound by limited, dead, ... already-

---

[160] GS 3 W II 240. *Ibid.*, 4, 258f., 5, 268f., 272f.; and SO 12 D I 183f.
[161] GS 3 W II 243-248; R, Introd. W III 174-177.

exhausted forms that weigh upon the living consciousness as purely external things."

"In such a situation, what is essential and eternal in ecclesiastical structure is confused with the contingent and the past; the stream of Church tradition itself, forced into narrow channels by the dead hand of fundamentalist literalism, no longer has its proper unbounded ecumenical breadth."[162] Thus the flight into contemplative monachism was likewise logical, a flight by which the profane world and the Christian nation were abandoned to a purely secular political order and left without Christian nurture.[163] Byzantium is now no more than "a deserting Church".[164] Indigenous Russian Orthodoxy, with its healthy and vigorous beginnings under St Vladimir, was too heavily weighed down by its fateful heritage to be able to escape the disease of sterile conservatism.   The indigenous Russian schism, the controversy between Avvakkum, the leader of the *raskol*, and the patriarch Nikon, revealed the hopelessness of the inner situation and the cruel lack of any decisive ecclesiastical court of appeal.   Peter the Great did the only possible right thing when he abolished the patriarchate and established the Synod: "Russia, thank God, was rescued both from the Oriental stasis of the Old Believers as well as from a superfluous and belated parody of the mediaeval papacy!"[165] On both sides we see the lack of interior catholicity; but the saviour figure, Peter, who "legitimately and lawfully abolished"[166] the ecclesiastical power that had been so abused, was also the one who opened a door to the West – and thus to the universalist thinking of German idealism. Compared with this, Peter's own rationalism and that of the slavophiles who followed was something already surpassed from within.   If Khomyakov understood the notion of an ecumenical Church "as a living organism of truth and love", and still at the same time wished to cling to Russian national messianism, then logically he ought to have accused the whole of the West of a falling away from love.   For Soloviev, this is a "monstrous assertion" from the Christian point of view

---

[162] GS 5 W II 272.
[163] R I 1 W III 192-193.
[164] *St Vladimir* W III 105.
[165] Th., foreword W II 367, 370.
[166] *Ibid.*, 371.

as much as the historical (when considered in the light of the actual events leading to the Great Schism).[167]

Soloviev himself is unsparing in criticism of the Roman Church, but only so as to separate wheat from chaff, to set out the Petrine principle in its purity and indispensability. Rome is the form of the sacred, the living counterpart of the frozen Byzantine Icon,[168] grounded upon the resurrection of Christ, which demonstrates "that bodily existence is not excluded from the covenant between God and man, and that external, palpable objectivity can and must become a real instrument and a visible likeness of divine power".[169] But this sacral form is holy only as a means to the realisation of God's Kingdom;[170] the more it appears as a humble servant and the less attention it draws to itself, the more Christlike it is.[171] "The authority of the Roman See was never more generally acknowledged or more powerful than under the least assuming popes."[172] The besetting temptation for Christian Rome, as the heir of the pagan caesars, was, again and again, the exploiting of power to achieve spiritual goals. An "authority possessed of a mystical religious foundation had no need of reinforcement from without or of formal juridical documents"; but an "all-too-active concern with their own power" led the popes to strive for such secular guarantees, and in this way they inevitably became entangled in politics and even in waging war. "The Church militant became the Church in arms", and the spiritual theocracy to some extent assumed "the character of a coercive regime".[173] So little does Soloviev extenuate these abuses and what he calls the "abstract clericalism" of Rome,[174] that he can portray Protestantism's reaction in the direction of Christian liberty as in fact inevitable,[175] although he denies that Protestantism has the

---

[167] *Ibid.*, 375-377.
[168] "The apostolic chair in Rome: this wonderworking icon [sic!] of universal Christianity": R, Introd. W III 161.
[169] *Ibid.*, 160. On the theology of the icon, *cf.* Th. 17 W II 450-455.
[170] R II 2 W III 259.
[171] R II 8 W III 284. "So it is clear that the central authority of the papacy has a purely conditional and functional meaning": GS 6 W II 288.
[172] GS 6 W II 289.
[173] *Ibid.*, 288-291.
[174] W II 161.
[175] GS 4 W II 257. *Ibid.*, 6 W II 304f.; GM, lecture 2 A III 22.

character of a Christian Church because of its refusal of an objective and universal ecclesial form.[176]

The great lesson to be learned from the twofold schism is that the Roman form is still necessary for the Church's survival, but that the Church cannot be united by force, any more than it can rule the world by force or man be saved by force.[177] There is nothing more needful for the stability of Christianity on earth and its effectiveness among men than the reunification of its three branches. Each of them preserves one distinctive element of Christian life: the Graeco-Russian East preserves tradition (the past); Rome preserves the means of spiritual power (the present, as the constant renewal of the presence of Christ); Protestantism preserves freedom and prophecy (the future), though this can in no way present itself as authentically Christian without both the other principles.[178] Soloviev is not arguing for the "branch theory" of the Oxford Tractarians; but he does see the values that have been stolen from the Church's centre in Rome and are still withheld from it because Orthodox and Protestants stand aloof. Only a pure act of love can help the Church over these difficulties, a love, though, that renounces any kind of egotistical clinging to the national or to a freedom of conscience conceived in purely individualistic terms, a love that acknowledges the form of universality. What is required is an "ethical act of self-denial on the part of persons and nations"; this alone can open the way for the total unity of the Church of Christ;[179] for it is only when animated by the Spirit of the Church that the individual can be free: "Such men as surrender religiously to the Church in its holiness and obey it humbly in its authority share in the Church's freedom in full measure; for in their life the Divine Spirit lives and works, and where the Spirit of the Lord is, there is freedom. Any other kind of freedom, which is not purchased at the high price of self-denial in faith and obedience, is counterfeit coin in the ethical world."[180]

---

[176] GS 6 W II 306. *Ibid.*, 7, 323.

[177] *Ibid.*, 6 W II 307-308.

[178] *Ibid.*, 4 W II 263f. *Cf.* the rather different division in Th., foreword W II 382-385, and R, Introd. W III 152-153.

[179] GS 4 W II 253.

[180] *Ibid.*, 255.

For Soloviev, with his lucid spirit and its search for order, one thing self-evidently, necessarily and immediately needed resolution: the ecumenical problem of the mutual estrangement and hostility of the churches. He made a representative confession of faith to the Roman Church in the name of all Russians:

> As a member of the true and venerable and rightly believing Eastern or Graeco-Russian Church ... I acknowledge ... as supreme judge in matters of religion him whom St Irenaeus, St Dionysius the Great, St Antony the Great, St John Chrysostom,
> St Cyril, St Maximus the Confessor, St Theodore the Studite, St Ignatius, et cetera also acknowledged: namely, the apostle Peter, who lives on in his successors and did not receive that Word of the Lord in vain: "Thou are Peter – ..." et cetera. You know, O immortal spirit of the blessed Peter, invisible servant of the Lord in the government of His holy Church, that there is need of an earthly body for its revelation. Twice, indeed, you have granted it to be embodied in a society, first in the Graeco-Roman, then in the Romano-German world ... and after those two preliminary incarnations it awaits the third and final one. A complete world, full of forces and longings but lacking a clear consciousness of its destiny, is knocking on the door of world history; what word is to be spoken to it, O peoples of the Word? ... Your Word speaks of a free universal theocracy, the true solidarity of all nations and classes, the realisation of Christianity in social life, a christianised politics, freedom for all the oppressed, protection for all the weak, social justice and true Christian peace.... I have come to utter this Amen in the name of one hundred million Russian Christians in the firm and full conviction that they will not dissociate themselves from me .... [181]

---

[181] R. Introd. W III 188.

4. AESTHETICS AND APOCALYPTIC

The protests against Rome failed;[182] Rome possessed that form of catholicity that alone can unite the world and lead it toward the Kingdom of God. Soloviev wished to see this formal principle applied entirely realistically in the free subordination of the state – that is, of particular states – to the spiritual authority of the representative of Peter. Only so can national egotism be overcome, and "the universal brotherhood of races" be realised.[183] "The free ethical sacrifice of the national spirit" could make real the "supremely free unity of the Church", whose ecumenical reality would appear to us "no longer as a lifeless idol, nor as a body possessed of soul but bereft of consciousness, but as self-conscious, ethically free, a nature itself working for its own actualisation, as Sophia, the true Beloved of God . . ."[184] Soloviev's dream was to open up the sphere of realised secular achievements, of state and culture, to the influence of a Church that is unified and thus fully aware of its task, in the kind of free reciprocity that the Middle Ages had indeed sought, but never wholly realised. Only through the Church can the concerns of the state achieve a supratemporal significance for the Kingdom of God, only through the Church can the indubitable fruits of cultural and technical progress be given meaning in the light of eternity. "If social progress aims to be authentic progress, it must have an absolutely worthy, an ideal and perfect purpose."[185] Like Dante, Soloviev dreamt of the unification of the world, not in a totalitarian monarchy, but in a total free theocracy, into which all things, secular and spiritual, must be integrated. Did he seriously hope to see this distant goal of his ecumenical efforts attained? In any event, after his failure to achieve the proximate goal of ecclesiastical unity, his hopes vanished into thin air, leaving him a disappointed man.

And so the last years of his life – the years that take up again the speculative work of the first period and attempt to bring it to a conclusion – move into a curious twilight. The direct

---

[182] GS 6 W II 308-310.
[183] Th., Introd. W II 384.
[184] *Ibid.*, 385.
[185] GG II 3 W II 149.

activism in ecclesiastical politics which marks his ecumenical period recedes, to give place to his own theoretical work, which (as was demonstrated at the beginning) seeks to open the whole of philosophy to aesthetics, starting with ethics and working through to theory. The aesthetics which has to perfect the whole scheme was never written; we have only fragments of this. It was to have been an aesthetic that was the issue both of the "realisation of the good" (the idea taking form) and of perfected truth (the idea, that which is worthy of being, becoming real), and so a "science of the apocalypse", of the revelation of God's Kingdom, God's ultimate coming-to-be in man and the world. In the light of Rom 8. 19f., both basic words, *apocalypse* and *glory* move closer together: "This revelation, and the glory of God's children that all creation awaits in hope consists in the fact that the free union of God and man is to be fully realised in the whole of humanity, in every sphere of its life and activity . . . , all these spheres must be led into the condition of divine-human, harmonious unity, must enter the state of free theocracy in which the Church Universal will attain to the full measure of Christ's maturity."[186]

But if the meaning of *apocalypse* is here reduced entirely to "aesthetics as ultimate harmony", the other meaning of apocalypse in the Bible makes its impact felt ever more strongly as the years pass. Indeed, it swells to thunderous volume until at last it produces a quite opposite result and completely swallows up the first meaning, "aesthetics as harmony". Free obedience, free sacrifice, free theocracy, all will flow into the divine freedom in an apotheosis of creaturely freedom. But what if the creature uses its freedom to say no? Had not Soloviev's earlier philosophy already established that all true freedom rests upon the overcoming of the power to say no, and that the depth of denial that is possible increases in proportion to the increase of consciousness and spirituality? The unconscious world-soul is chaotic, but only the free spirit is demonic. Thus there irrupts into Soloviev's world picture a force that had always been latent there but had never been given its true weight. At the beginning Soloviev had attacked Western abstract thought; but was not the construction of the

---

historical process, as a continuation and a reflection of natural process, still itself abstract? Did it take seriously enough the freedom of the creature? Even if we want to assume that the historical process is entirely in the hands of the Logos, who is becoming and finally has become man – this "real suprahuman field of activity, giving nourishment to the whole life of humanity and conditioning its ethical progress by the fulness of this nourishment"[187] – even so, we still have to ask

whether what we know of the incarnate Logos gives adequate grounds for expecting this kind of progress within history. As the powers of good advance through history, so too do the powers of evil, since progress can in no case outplay the free decisions of humanity, least of all if we conceive the world-soul as "coming to itself" in man, and if man is not cast down from his throne to be a mere function of a monistic *Weltgeist*.

But what then is the content of the total aesthetic scheme? it is a revelation (an apocalypse) of the truth of God and of man – of God as God-Man and man as man-God – each opened to the other in their apocalyptic depth; and above all it is the unimaginable and incomprehensible justification of the good in and through this death-dealing reciprocity. But this means that the law of death and resurrection remains the ultimate law for world history, no less than for the individual. Certainly we would be less than just to Soloviev if we did not acknowledge that even in the period of his undisturbed faith in progress, he always had the resurrection of the dead before his eyes as the horizon of his eschatological aesthetics, and that the whole of the aesthetic element in nature and art appeared to him purely as an adumbration of the resurrected cosmos. But this view so dominated his thinking that he was in consequence inclined to overlook the realism of death or to cloak it in the enveloping terms of the "process". For him, "the Kingdom of Death" was subspiritual nature, which included the sexual sphere; all truly spiritual entities in which the eternal, ideal world is already to be seen appeared to him to constitute the unique path to immortality and resurrection. The heavenly crucifixion of the Logos was for him (as it was in Valentinus' myth) a painless, dialectical matter, and the earthly crucifixion was something

---

[187] RG II 7, 14 D II 176.

viewed exclusively from that standpoint. In the very few places in his work where the cross appears, it is only as "the sign of spiritual power that can overcome all suffering".[188] In this area there was a great deal still to be done. Soloviev wrote his *Three Conversations*, including the *Tale of Antichrist*, with his last failing energy, and he did indeed say a decisive word with these. But death itself left him no time to deal more thoroughly with the mystery of death.

It remains for us to deal in order with the first fragmentary outlines of an aesthetic, then with the subsequent, apocalyptic aesthetics that extend so far beyond the first.

From the very beginning, Soloviev wanted to complete his theosophy with a universal aesthetics.[189] He prefaced his essay on natural aesthetics with Dostoyevsky's dictum that "beauty will save the world."[190] The *Critique of Abstract Principles* had proclaimed that "the realization of pan-unity in its external actuality is absolute beauty", so it is as little something "given" as is "pan unity" itself; it is a task assigned to humanity, and human art is a vehicle of its realisation. Soloviev promises to develop, at the end of his work, "the common axioms and rules of this great and mysterious art that brings all beings into the form of beauty".[191] According to another declaration, the sphere of aesthetic realisation should be divided into three areas: the material (technology), the formal (the "fine arts") and the absolute (mysticism).[192] For Soloviev, however, mysticism is not only passive devotion to the divine or direct contact with it; it also is the active art of bringing the divine from Heaven to earth, and, in this sense, "theurgy"[193] – it is concerned, that is, with the realisation of the ideal: this is why Soloviev becomes a bitter opponent of classical idealist aesthetics, according to which beauty is allowed to be "only" appearance, not reality, only an illusory reflection, not even a true promise or foretaste. "An infinity that existed solely for an instant would be an

---

[188] GG II 1, 6 W II 105.

[189] As in the outline of the *Philosophical Principles of Integral Knowledge, Str.*,75.
He refers back to this in his later philosophy of art: W VII 174, n.

[190] *Beauty in Nature*, W VII 119.

[191] *Cf.* the introd. to *Shorter Writings on Aesthetics* W VII 337.

[192] *Principles of Integral Knowledge,* Str. 114, 273.

[193] Article on "Mystik" in Brockhaus-Ephron; W VI.

unbearable contradiction for the spirit; a bliss existing only in the past would be a torture for the will."[194] Thus too Goethe's Faust cannot embody any authentic idea: "The heavenly powers and the 'eternal feminine' appear from above, and so from outside; they do not reveal themselves from within, in the very content of reality itself." [195] Even Dante's Paradise is "not sufficiently living and concrete – an essential deficiency that not even the most euphonious verse can make good".[196] "According to Hegelian aesthetics, beauty is the embodiment of a universal and eternal idea in individual and transitory phenomena; in this embodiment, moreover, these phenomena remain transitory, disappearing like individual waves in the stream of the material process. Only for a moment do they reflect the light of an eternal idea. This is possible only if the relation between spiritual principle and material phenomenon is accidental. True and perfect beauty, on the other hand, since it expresses the full solidarity and mutual penetration of these two levels, must necessarily allow one of them (the material) to come really to share in the immortality of the other."[197] If true embodiment is lacking, "the powerlessness of the Idea to give its inner content a direct external expression" becomes manifest. Thus Soloviev welcomed the shift toward literary realism, even in the materialistic form that it assumed in Chernyshevsky:[198] he was a declared enemy of all "art for art's sake".[199] In ancient culture, "poets were at once prophets and priests", and it is only in the subsequent division of labour that poets elevated an isolated art to the status of an idol: "For such priests of pure art, perfection of external form comes to be the main consideration." Realism quite rightly reacted against this; but "in the ineffectual hunt for pseudo-real detail, the actual reality of the whole is once more lost". Dostoyevsky had an eye for true inner reality, and he is the pledge of the poetics of the future. In this way he unmasks in prophetic fashion the anti-Christian side of modem utopian social progress – movements

---

[194] *Sexual Love* 5 W VII 257.
[195] *The Meaning of Art* 3 W VII 188.
[196] *Ibid.*, n.
[197] *Ibid.*, 2 W VII 179-190.
[198] *First Steps Towards* a *Positive Aesthetic* W VII 351.
[199] *Ibid.*, 346f., and the essay on Lermontov W VII 405f.

orientated to the future; his vision grows in the true "houses of the dead", of the "insulted and injured", as he recognises the solidarity of saints and sinners. His ideal is the Church, the Kingdom of God, and not a particular nation. "The Church as positive ideal was intended to become the central idea ... of *The Brothers Karamazov.*"[200] The more truth, the more beauty, always: "The full truth of the world consists in its living unity as one spiritualised and God-bearing body; in that lies the world's truth and the world's beauty."[201] Following on from that, the task in hand is "to embody the content of salvation and truth in the sphere of things perceptible to the senses by giving it the form of beauty" – and that immediately means ascesis for the soul that lives through its senses, a submission of blind, inordinate impulse that has no interior goal to the chains of the spiritual idea that captures it and gives it form.[202] But what exactly is the idea that seeks thus to incarnate itself?

Soloviev defined it quite strictly in relation to his aesthetic. Ideal being is being such as merits to be and therefore *shall* be. It is existence in complete unity such that in it (1) "the elements do not exclude one another but stand in complementary relationship and exist in solidarity"; (2) these elements "do not exclude the whole, but maintain their individual existence on the one common ground"; (3) "the ground in its totally unified character does not suppress or absorb the individual elements, but gives them full play within itself by developing itself in them". Being of this kind is at once true, good and beautiful. If one of the three elements is lacking, falsehood, evil and ugliness arise. "Anything is ugly where a part grows disproportionately and unchecked, dominating other parts, where unity and wholeness are absent, where, most particularly, there is no free diversity."[203] In short: "The plenitude of the Idea requires that the greatest unity in the whole be realised in the greatest independence and freedom in the partial and particular elements *in* them themselves and *through* and *for* them."[204] This idea of beauty is indeed eternally real in God himself, in so far as he

[200] First address on Dostoyevsky, in *Drei Reden* (1921), 9-26.
[201] GG, foreword W II 10.
[202] GG I 3 W II 64.
[203] *The Meaning of Art* 2 W VII 176-178.
[204] *Sexual Love* 3 W VII 266.

exists as the eternal actuality of all his potential in the fullest degree of freedom. It is, at the same time, the reality of the Kingdom of God in its coming to be in the world as it realises itself eschatologically through the ascent of natural and historical forms. Christ and Mary, the Logos incarnate and Sophia incarnate, represent in this process the ever-perfect primordial form of beauty, the norm by which reality as it takes on form can measure and align itself.[205] The threefold characterisation of the Idea (as the mutuality of parts, their free submission to the whole and the whole's allowing the parts to be themselves) can be summed up in one word: love. "Love in the extended sense in which this concept coincides with that of unanimity, harmony and peace, the concept of the totality of the world, the concept of *kosmos*. In this sense, the Good, the True and Beautiful are only the various images of love.... The will of the Good, however, is in its essence genuine love, or love's source, the Idea of the Idea."[206] And as the good that is longed for, this love is Eros, and, as that which is realised out of God's plenitude, it is Agape. It is plain that, for Soloviev, to distinguish between Eros and Agape in their essences is completely unthinkable: Christian love is the level where natural Eros is fulfilled, where what it vainly longed for and sought to embody is granted to it – the true presence of God in man, immortality, resurrection.

The essays *Beauty in Nature* and *The Universal Meaning of Art* belong among the best of Soloviev's work, but this is not the place to rehearse their argument in their particular details. For our purposes it is important that in the essay on nature the idea of progress, which allows the beautiful to be perfected as a free and living organism, only gradually and with dramatic setbacks (monstrosities in nature, the disproportionate growth of individual functions, excesses, et cetera), provides the basis of the eschatological hope of glory for the entire cosmos in its interior development. The Kingdom of God is coming into being from the beginning of the world process onward. Beauty in nature is neither pure illusion nor can it be simply explained in terms of psychological stimuli; it is just as objective in its

---

[205] W VII 199.
[206] GM, lecture 7 A III 138-139.

forms as it is subjective for the one who beholds or experiences it. It may be encountered anywhere where the more spiritual reality overcomes the material and makes it transparent: in the diamond, for instance, where the light so shines through and plays with the material reality that both seem to have become one, "what results is translucent matter and embodied light."[207] In living beings, the penetration becomes more and more an interior thing; the lower level of being can be changed, illuminated, sublimated in different degrees by the Idea. "Thus the material instinct of sexuality can, in the nightingale's song, clothe itself in the form of harmonious notes", "the instinct comes to embody the idea of love".[208] Of course the beautiful is not to be found simply in the adequate embodiment of any kind of content (otherwise an animal such as a pig, embodying pure voracity, would be beautiful, as would a Worm, embodying formless and blind instinct), but only in the embodiment of a content worthy of existence, which alone merits the name "Idea". In order to embody the latter, the art of the creative Logos struggles with the chaotic element in the world-soul;[209] and so long as the supreme equilibrium is not reached, any harmony is menaced from within, because it is only provisional: "Every fresh victory opens the possibility of a fresh defeat", since the primaeval chaos, which is pure hunger for existence, the "necessary background of any earthly beauty", is not yet finally informed and transfigured.[210] "Even the most beautiful of butterflies is no more than a winged worm";[211] in the higher animals, the "worm-like" element is forced inward and made unnoticeable by a beautiful outer covering. But such a covering is not yet a complete transfiguration: only in the resurrection of the body is the inwardly necessary goal of the world process achieved, the resurrection as the complete illumination of chaotic matter by the loving spirit; but only God can bring this to perfection.

Human art is not a copying of nature, but rather an imitation of the *natura naturans* that forms images, "the world process as it

---

[207] *Beauty in Nature* 2 W VII 127.
[208] *Ibid.*, 128-129.
[209] *Ibid.*, 6, 144-147.
[210] *Ibid.*, 140, 146, 153.
[211] *Ibid.*, 9, 159.

is drawn forward in its aesthetic aspect".[212] Truth and goodness are not enough – or, better, they are both pressing toward embodiment. But only someone who believes in immortality and resurrection can ascribe an ultimate meaning to artistic activity. The one who "reconciles himself (even if only theoretically) to the triumph of an all-destroying material process must treat beauty and, in particular, all that is 'ideal' in the world, as a subjective illusion of the human imagination – as indeed the most consistent minds of this school do".[213] Today there can no longer be a third standpoint between Christian hope and faith and pure materialism. There may have been such in the pre-Christian period, when the ideal had yet to be incarnated, when myth served as the aesthetic anticipation of Godmanhood. The Egyptians were right to organize their culture and art around the idea of resurrection, even if it could in no way be actualised;[214] Plato likewise was right in wishing to let his Eros be creative in the sphere of the Beautiful, even if the content sensed in this could nowhere actually be grasped.[215] A true work of art is simply "the perceptible representation of an object from the perspective of its ultimate condition or (which is the same thing) in the light of the world beyond'.[216]

It is in this context that one must set the *Essay on Eros*, in which the authentic personal love of man and wife appears as the central "theurgic" work of art. Such love aspires to a superhuman wholeness above and beyond the separation and struggle of the sexes in a purposiveness that transcends enslavement to the concerns of the species and of sexuality[217] (with which marital love in its personal core has nothing to do – so little, in fact, that there exists no direct proportionality between sex and Eros).[218] The Western theme of an

---

[212] *The Meaning of Art* 1 W VII 172.

[213] *Ibid.*, 2 W VII 181.

[214] GS 2 W II 223-224: "The Egyptians were above all else artists. The final goal of this art was the vision that it gave of a victory over death, the eternalisation of life, the bringing to life of the dead.... This great religious idea of a general resurrection or restoration of all things is a specifically Egyptian one."

[215] *The Drama of Plato's Life* 22 W VII 318: "[Plato's] theory of love, unheard of in the pagan world, profound and bold, remains unelaborated"; and 320: "The proper activity of Eros can be nothing other than the rebirth or resurrecting of life into immortality."

[216] W VII 194.

[217] RG II 7, 8 D II 159f.

[218] *Sexual Love* 1; W VII 201-211.

androgynous unity in humanity, found from Plato to Dante to Böhme, Novalis and Baader, is thus resumed and brought in classical fashion to its conclusion. And yet this does not imply a process in which the person is transcended; the human being as "the reasoning power of truth" can indeed "infinitely perfect its life and nature without transcending the limits of its human form.... Therein lies the essential distinction between the cosmological and the historical process."[219] The power of Eros is that it can creatively perceive the (objective!) ideality of the personality in the beloved and can work to make this real: Eros as looking up to the ideal ascends; as embodying the ideal in a real beloved human being it descends.[220] Its essential theurgic power lies in the faith by which it "accords unconditional significance" to the beloved, a significance that an empirical and temporal nature cannot as such have. Only he can love who believes in the eternal meaning of his love for this particular finite substance; and this does not occur without a parallel belief in God, immortality and the resurrection, not only of the I and the Thou, which is impossible, but of the whole cosmos. Only in such a context does this love have space and scope.[221] The emotion of love (being "in love") can of course be a prefiguration of Eros, but it first becomes real when realised actively and creatively.[222] The true lover "actually sees something, perceives with his eyes, something other than that which other men see": he sees the ideality that is the true reality; in an inchoate way he sees the beloved person as God sees him, which is indeed the only way God wills to see him. And to let this ideality be true, to make it true, is "the beginning of the visible restoration of God's image in the material world."[223] Here Soloviev, in accordance with the most characteristic concerns of his programme, has allowed the power of (platonic) Eros to merge into the power of the agape of the Sermon on

---

[219] *Sexual Love* 2, art. 1 W VII 213. "To bring into being the true man, the union in freedom of the masculine and feminine principles, to preserve, in both, their formal separateness, while having overcome their essential distinctness and dividedness – this is the proper and most immediate task of love"; art. 3, 1: 272.

[220] *Ibid.*, art. 4, 7 W VII 255.

[221] *Ibid.*, art. 4, 6 251-253.

[222] *Ibid.*, art. 3, 2 229.

[223] *Ibid.*, art. 3, 3 230-231.

the Mount. The Christian, therefore, is obliged because of this to see his neighbour as God the Father sees him in his redeeming Son, and to take this ideal vision as a guide in his actual dealings with others.[224] Soloviev therefore expressly subsumes the model of androgynous Eros under the twofold norm and prototype of God's relation to the world as the divine Sophia, and Christ's to the Church as the incarnate Sophia. This at the same time implies that the individual relationship of syzygy must, because of these prototypes, open itself out into an erotic relationship with the whole of the rest of the world. The person who believes and loves must embrace in his love the whole of humanity and the cosmos, as well as Christ and God, since they are Sophia in the process of coming to be, God's own beloved.[225] It is in this context that Soloviev's most significant poems have their place. His cosmic lyricism is both Christian and erotic in the highest sense just defined; for here he senses and glorifies in all worldly forms only the veilings and hidden revelations of his eternal secret beloved, the divine Sophia. Her eschatological glory he takes on faith alone; but with the eye of Eros he sees into the future, sensing her presence, as he lives out of the cosmic love of God.

But Sophia's apocalyptic unveiling is not the same as the apocalypse of world history. In Soloviev's last years, the lyrical intuition of an eternal presence of love takes on an ever-darker hue, turning to an apocalyptic foreboding of the imminent incarnation of evil in history.[226] And since for Soloviev there is no individual fulfilment without the collective fulfilment of all men and all creatures – "no one has the right to separate his own welfare from the true welfare of all living things"[227] – then the revelation of Sophia too is bound to recede into the collective mystery. Evil, according to the *Three Conversations*, is "not only a natural lack, an imperfection," it is the power of the lie, of seduction, especially in the name of the Good.[228]

The first question to be posed from a standpoint high above the human stage concerns war: is its abolition possible? Is the

[224] *Ibid.*, art. 4, 5 248f.
[225] *Ibid.*, art. 5, 4 268-272.
[226] Text in Ludolf Müller, *Übermensch und Antichrist.*
[227] *Sexual Love* art. 5, 1 W VII 260.
[228] *Three Conversations*, foreword D I 227.

Tolstoyan gospel of nonresistance a correct interpretation of the Sermon on the Mount? Soloviev was as sceptical as Péguy would be not long afterward. Two orders are here being confused with each other. "Why did Christ not employ the power of the Gospel spirit in such a way as to arouse the good hidden in the soul of Judas, Herod, the Jewish high priest – and finally of that impenitent sinner whom we normally overlook when we discuss his penitent fellows. If he forgave his enemies, why – to use your own [Tolstoy's] words – did he not release their souls from the fearful darkness in which they lay? Why did he not conquer their wickedness by the power of his meekness?"[229] But Christianity, after all, is not moral rearmament; it demands a Yes or a No. "In earlier times, Christianity was comprehensible to one, incomprehensible to another; but only our age has succeeded in making it repellent and mortally boring."[230] This moralisation reflects a seriously anti-Christian spirit, for Christ did not come to bring peace, but a sword. Otherwise Christ's disciples would have to "perform greater moral miracles (on the higher level of moral development we have now reached) by their meekness and nonresistance to evil than was possible eighteen centuries ago".[231] Man remains as he is. And, above all, death remains what it always was: "in this respect, there is no cultural advance to be recorded of any kind".[232] What has Christ succeeded in changing on earth? His work was "an astonishing failure". Historically, "in any case, far more evil than good has resulted from it", since Christ's resurrection is, of course, not itself a part of the historical process.[233] "We have only one refuge: the real resurrection... all else is only the condition, the path, the step toward it... and in reality it is still a Kingdom of Death."[234]

The Antichrist will blur the edges of the apocalyptic rift between morality and the cross, between cultural progress and the resurrection of the dead. He will permit Christianity to merge into this synthesis as one positive element. "Christ

---

[229] *First Conversation* D I 206.
[230] *Third Conversation* D I 315.
[231] *Ibid.*, 319.
[232] *Ibid.*, 327.
[233] *Ibid.*, 335f.
[234] *Ibid.*, 338-339.

divided men in terms of good and evil; I shall unite them through the benefits of salvation, which are necessary to good and evil alike. Christ brought the sword, but I bring peace. He threatened the earth with a terrible Last Judgment; but I shall be the last judge, and my judgment is one of grace." Satan fills his son with his spirit; his soul is filled with a glacial abundance of enormous power, courage and effortless skill. He composes a manifesto, *The Open Path to World Peace and Welfare*, an all-embracing programme that unites all contradictions in itself – the highest degree of freedom of thought and a comprehension of every mystical system, unrestricted individualism and a glowing devotion to the general good. He establishes a European union of states, then a world monarchy, satisfies the needs of all the poor without perceptibly affecting the rich and founds an interconfessional institute for free biblical research. He seeks to be elected by the general assembly of the churches as head of the Church (from now on ecumenically united), and receives the approval of the majority. But resistance comes from Pope Peter II, John the Elder, leader of the Orthodox and Professor Ernst Pauli, representing Protestantism: under the pressure of persecution the three churches in this eschatological situation at last unite. Peter's primacy is recognised, and the Pauline and Johannine churches come into the Roman fold. The spokesmen of Christianity are persecuted and killed, but they rise again; the last Christians journey to the wilderness, the Jews raise a revolt and the Christians join with them. They are slaughtered; but then Christ appears, robed in the imperial purple, his hands outspread with the marks of the nails upon them, to rule for a thousand years with those who are his own.[235]

What is important in this story is not its novelistic features, but the fact that Soloviev quite unconcernedly surrenders great parts of his philosophy of cosmic process into the hands of the Antichrist. As regards the *facts* of the process, he has not abandoned a single detail; the one thing he has given up is the idea that the process comes to perfection within history. The harvest of the world is brought home, but not by man; it is brought home by Christ, who alone lays the whole Kingdom at

---

[235] *Ibid.*, 348-380.

his Father's feet.   He is himself the integration of all things. And if we believe ourselves capable of establishing within history some kind of signs of the end – perhaps in the unification of the world or in this ideal seen as the way in which "the whole of humanity gathers itself around an invisible but powerful focus in Christian culture"[236] – even such indications will never suffice to gain an overview of the real course of the historical process as it appears from God's own standpoint.   In this respect, Soloviev humbled himself before the all-conquering Cross.

---

[236] *First Steps Towards a Positive Aesthetic* W VII 350.

PREFACE

Although the name of Vladimir Solovyov (1853–1900) is well known to the English public, and a number of his works have been translated into English, the general spirit and character of his teaching and his personality is known but vaguely and often interpreted erroneously. If I am not mistaken, the chief source of information about him is the English translation of Michel d'Herbigny's French book *Solovyov — a Russian Newman*. Although the author is on the whole well informed, the book contains a number of mis-statements; moreover, in his attempt to sum up Solovyov's spiritual individuality as that of an Orthodox theologian converted to Catholicism, d'Herbigny gives not merely a one-sided but a distorted idea of his general outlook. And Fr. Thomas F. Gerrard's Introduction to the English edition betrays a lack of information and gives a somewhat fantastic account of the subject.[1]

The purpose of the present anthology is to give such a selection of extracts from Solovyov's works as would enable the reader to form a general impression of the entire range of Solovyov's ideas throughout the course of his spiritual development (only the more specialized works on metaphysics, epistemology and theories of ethics have been left out of account). The extracts are arranged in systematic order according to the main subjects, but most sections contain instances of Solovyov's work at different periods of his life.

In making the selection I endeavoured to give material that was not only interesting in itself, but also as far as possible new to English readers. The only extracts from works that have already been translated are those from *Lectures on God-Manhood*, *The Meaning of Love* and *Three Conversations* (*The Story of Antichrist*); all these are given in a new translation. The rest of the material appears in English for the first time.

In my Introduction I am much indebted to an excellent

---

[1] A satisfactory account of Solovyov's life and teachings is given in Peter Zouboff's Introduction to his translation of *Lectures on God-Manhood* (Dennis Dobson, London, 1948).

Russian book by K. Mochulsky, *Vladimir Solovyov*, published by the Y.M.C.A. Press in Paris in 1935 — the best that has been written about Solovyov's spiritual development.

In making up the anthology I have used Solovyov's complete works in ten volumes, second edition, St. Petersburg, 1910–12, and three volumes of *Solovyov's Letters*, St. Petersburg, 1908–13 (these are referred to in the text as *L.*). I have unfortunately been unable to obtain the fourth volume of *Letters* published much later; but all the important material in it is given in Mochulsky's book and is quoted from it.

My thanks are due to the Student Christian Movement Press, and in particular to the editor the Rev. R. Gregor Smith, for accepting my suggestion to publish this anthology.

I also thank Fr. C. Lialin of the Prieuré d'Amay, Chevetogne, and Fr. K. Korolevsky of the Roman Monastery, Stoudion, for kindly giving me information on canonical questions in connection with Solovyov's communion in a Uniate church.

S. L. FRANK

London, 1949

Omissions of one page or more of the Russian text are indicated by one line blank, and of less than one page by dots at the beginning of a paragraph.

INTRODUCTION

WHEN as a young man of twenty-one (in 1874) Vladimir Solovyov defended at the Petersburg University his thesis *The Crisis of Western Philosophy* — a bold challenge to the prevailing positivism of the day — a distinguished Russian historian, Bestuzhev-Ryumin, said: 'Russia may be congratulated upon a new genius.' This judgment proved to be true. Solovyov is unquestionably the greatest of Russian philosophers and systematic religious thinkers. And even from the general European standpoint he must, I think, be recognized as one of the greatest thinkers and spiritual leaders of the nineteenth century. It is hard to find in the recent past a Western religious thinker resembling Solovyov in his type of thought and universality of interests.[1] Solovyov was a philosopher, a theologian, a perfectly original mystic, a man of the 'prophetic' type, a moral teacher, a political thinker, a poet and a literary critic. And all this multiplicity of interests and creative gifts was centred in one religiously-mystical intuition and was the expression and realization of one dominant idea.

I

The first thing that strikes one in all Solovyov's writings and opens out new horizons to the reader, transferring him into a different atmosphere, is the keenness and clearness with which Solovyov sees the invisible — the spiritual world. It has for him the kind of obviousness with which ordinary people perceive the sensuously given world of objects. His apprehension of it sometimes takes the form of concrete vision (as, for instance, his vision of the divine basis of the world, 'St. Sophia', that determined his whole world-conception), but general spiritual insight devoid of any perceptual character is even more characteristic of him. As he said of himself, he 'did not believe the deceptive world' and

[1] The only man akin to Solovyov in spiritual and intellectual make-up and partly even in his ideas is the German thinker of the early nineteenth century Franz Baader — also quite an exceptional type of mind and not sufficiently appreciated to this day.

9

'recognized the radiance of Godhead under the coarse crust of matter'. In one of his letters he says: 'Not only do I believe in everything supernatural, but strictly speaking I believe in nothing else. . . . From the time that I began to think, the materiality that weighs over us has always seemed to me merely a kind of nightmare of the sleeping humanity' (*L.*, I, 33–4). In his theory of knowledge he maintains that the perception of any reality as such is an act of faith and that therefore there is no difference whatever between faith in the existence of God and faith in the reality of the external world. That doctrine — philosophically untenable — is characteristic of Solovyov: he himself really did believe in God as we 'believe' in the reality of the visible world. The dead were as real for him as the living; he speaks of meeting them after death as simply and naturally as we speak of meeting people separated from us by distance; he remained in constant communion with them and insisted that we had duties towards them. As will become apparent later, his whole attitude to church problems was determined by the fact that the one universal Church of Christ was for him not 'an idea', but a living, sensible reality, something like the reality of his native land to the ordinary man; he could not admit the reality of its actual break-up into different denominations. After saying that the sacrament of the Eucharist makes us brothers, he adds, 'and if we kill one another in the name of so-called national interests, we are really and not metaphorically fratricides'. Everything 'ideal' — truth, goodness, beauty — has for him the same living reality. He is a Platonist not only in abstract thought; he is a Platonist because he sees the ideal world and lives in it. He overcomes the dualism of classical Platonism, because for him all the sensuous, empirical world is, as it were, included in the ideal realm and has its true being in it. This is the purport of his basic intuition. The spiritual world in which Solovyov's whole personality is absorbed is not a mere multiplicity of separate, isolated entities and realities interconnected by external relations. In its essential nature it is an all-unity, *tout dans l'unité* (a term coined by Solovyov[1]), and the intuition of that unity determines the whole of Solovyov's world-conception. Humanity and the whole cosmos appears to him as a complete, living organism; the vital force of that organism lies in its intimate connection with God, in its being penetrated by

[1] *Vseyedinstvo*, sometimes translated as 'pan-unity' (Translator).

divine powers; and in that sense cosmic being is itself potentially divine. (In his early youth Solovyov drew his first inspiration from Spinoza.) But this conception is not pantheism; it would be more correct to call it panentheism.[1] To begin with, the all-unity is *concrete*: it does not swallow up the multiplicity of individual entities, but on the contrary provides a basis for it. Universal being is a great organism, embracing and penetrating by its unity the multiplicity of living entities. The world is not identical with God, the creature is different from the Creator; but Solovyov could have said with Nicolas of Cusa that the highest knowledge of God is the knowledge *of the unity of the Creator in the Creator and in the creature*. In its distinction from God, the world is God's 'other'; proceeding from God, it is in its innermost nature akin and near to Him. At the same time Solovyov is keenly aware that the world in its actual state is fallen away from God and therefore broken up into separate and hostile parts — and this constitutes the essence of evil. The world must *become* all-unity — become that which it *is* in the bosom of God who conceived it. All-unity is not merely a theoretical formula explaining the nature of the world, but rather the final end of cosmic development, the task which man must realize. The term 'all-unity' is for Solovyov a battle-cry, a call to work for the world's salvation, which consists precisely in overcoming the hostile dividedness, in freely and lovingly merging all into an all-embracing harmonious unity. The motive of spiritual struggle for the salvation of the world — or, to use a Patristic term, for its 'deification' — is more pronounced in Solovyov's thought than that of contemplative insight.

The intuition of all-unity was centred for Solovyov in a perfectly concrete vision, imparting to it the character of an intimate relation to a living being, to the service of which he devoted his whole life. Solovyov tells the story of this most significant event in his life in a poem called *Three Meetings*. Once in his childhood (in 1862) and twice in his youth (in 1875 and 1876) he had a vision of a heavenly feminine being; he called that being his 'eternal friend'. Solovyov's relation to it was religiously-erotic; he loved it with the same ardour with which many Christian mystics, inspired by the Song of Songs, loved God. He identified it with St. Sophia, the Wisdom of God who is spoken of as a living

---

[1] A term introduced by the romantic German philosopher Krause; Solovyov does not use it.

person in Solomon's Book of Proverbs. He found traces of the
same idea in the tradition of the Eastern Church, especially in
Russian iconography, and sought for the explanation of it in the
mystical philosophy of Jacob Boehme, Paracelsus and Swedenborg. To serve Saint Sophia meant for him to work for the
salvation of the world.

It is impossible to explain in clear logical terms the connection
between this mystical feminine image and the idea of all-unity.
In order to understand it, one must turn to Solovyov's poetry
rather than to his philosophy. This is what he says in describing
his last vision, the fullest and clearest of all (in the Egyptian
desert):

> 'All that was, and is, and ever shall be
> My steadfast gaze embraced it all in one.
> The seas and rivers sparkle blue beneath me,
> And distant woods, and mountains clad in snow.
> I saw it all, and all was one fair image
> Of woman's beauty, holding all as one.
> The boundless was within its form enclosed —
> Before me and in me is you alone.'

It is equally impossible to give a logical explanation or exposition of the metaphysical significance of the idea of Sophia.
Solovyov attempted to do this more than once (see the fragment
from the *Lectures on God-Manhood* and the article *The Idea of
Humanity* in the present anthology, and a more detailed and
carefully thought out — though by no means more clear —
exposition in the third part of *La Russie et l'Église universelle*). He
has not succeeded, because the task he set himself is essentially
unrealizable. Sophia is the divine basis or essence of that which,
as creation, is distinct from God. At every attempt to make it
philosophically more definite, that idea inevitably breaks up into
two, precisely because it stands for an intermediary and connecting link between the Creator and the creature. On the one
hand, Sophia is the ideal world in God, an element in God's very
essence (conceived as an individual living being), and on the
other, it is the living soul of the created world.[1] The difficulty
lies, in the last resort, in the impossibility of explaining in rational

[1] This is why the later attempts to rationalize that idea (by Fr. P. Florensky
and Fr. S. Bulgakov) also fail to achieve their purpose in spite of all their
subtlety.

and logical terms the relation between the Creator and the creature. Our apprehension of it must inevitably remain mystical, i.e. metalogical, and can only be expressed in categories that belong to the realm of 'the unity of opposites' (as in the teaching of Nicolas of Cusa).

At bottom, the idea of Sophia is with Solovyov a mystical intuition and not a metaphysical conception. Solovyov's mysticism is of the gnostically-theosophical type, best represented by Jacob Boehme: in it, mystical contemplation is directed not upon the transcendental essence of God and the heavenly world as distinct from everything created, but upon the mysterious depths of the created world itself — the depths in which it springs from God and is in contact with Him. What is essential in this doctrine of Sophia is not its abstract logical justification, impossible from the nature of the case, but its 'spirit', its concrete religious significance — and that consists in religious love for the world and mankind in its sacred, potentially divine and beautiful primary nature. This leads to the striving to transfigure and 'deify' the world, so that its actual condition should correspond to its essence as conceived by God, proceeding from God, and in that sense divine. This tendency of Solovyov's teaching about Sophia is directly contrary to the doctrine, prevalent in Catholic theology, of the sharp and irreconcilable duality between the 'supernatural' and the 'natural'.

The intuition of all-unity as the standard of truth and goodness is the source of Solovyov's whole teaching: whatever he may be speaking of, he has before him the entrancing vision of divine wholeness, harmony and nearness between the Creator and the creature, and of the loving union in one spiritual organism of all that is separate and mutually hostile in the fallen world. His metaphysics and theory of knowledge, his theology and ecclesiastical policy, his æsthetics and his conception of love, his ethics and political philosophy, consist in the last resort in affirming this universal harmony, and are passionately opposed to all that deviates from it or hinders it. He was an ecumenical peace-maker.

II

The fundamental ideas of Solovyov's philosophy remained unchanged throughout his life, but his spiritual development passed through several stages differing in their general tenor and in the particular interests that prevailed in them (though the *motifs* of each stage are repeated in the others). Solovyov reached intellectual maturity remarkably early: the main features of his world-conception were formed by the time he was twenty-one. Not counting his early youth, or, rather, adolescence, there were three distinct stages in his life.

Vladimir Solovyov was born in Moscow in 1853 and was the son of the famous historian of Russia, Sergey Solovyov; his grandfather, whose memory he venerated, was a priest, and before his death consecrated his eight-year-old grandson to the service of the Church. Solovyov reached adolescence and early youth at the period of political and intellectual unrest that coincided with the epoch of the great social reforms of Alexander II. It was the period when, as Solovyov expressed it later, 'Philaret's catechism' (compulsory in teaching the Orthodox doctrine in schools) 'was suddenly replaced by the catechism of Ludwig Büchner' (the popular German materialist). Brought up in the customs and traditions of the Orthodox Church, Solovyov at the age of fourteen became an atheist, a materialist and a socialist, a passionate advocate of the still prevalent new faith, which he later summarized in the mercilessly ironical formula, 'Man is a hairless monkey and *therefore* must lay down his life for his friends.' His intimate friend from childhood, the philosopher Lopatin, says that he never met anyone who believed so firmly in the quick and final salvation of mankind through a social revolution as did Solovyov in his boyhood. This was at bottom only a naïve form of Solovyov's later faith in the world's final 'deification' and salvation. By the time he was eighteen, he had got over this youthful phase and consciously returned for the rest of his life to the Christian faith. At the university he passed from the study of natural science to philosophy and at the same time attended lectures on theology in the Moscow Theological Academy. In his letters to his betrothed (the marriage did not take place) as a young man of twenty he clearly sets out the programme of his creative work; henceforth and to the end of his life his task will be to raise Christianity from blind traditional faith to the level of rational conviction and thus help to save mankind from evil and perdition (*L.*, III, 56).

The first period of Solovyov's work belongs to the 'seventies. His early books are *The Crisis of Western Philosophy* (1874), *The Philosophical Principles of Integral Knowledge* (1877), *The Lectures*

on God-Manhood (1878) and *The Critique of Abstract Principles*
(1880). Although all these works are concerned with the theological and philosophical justification and interpretation of the
traditional Christian doctrine, his chief interest during that period
was gnosticism and theosophy. In 1875–76 when Solovyov
applied for a travelling scholarship he described his object as the
study of 'the gnostic, Indian and mediæval philosophy'. At the
British Museum he studied almost exclusively the gnostic and
mystical literature about 'Sophia'; he was interested too in
spiritualism, fashionable in England at the time, but was soon
disappointed in it. In the reading-room he had a vision of 'St.
Sophia' (the second in his life). She commanded him to go to
Egypt and promised to show herself more fully to him there.
Solovyov gave up his research work and went to Egypt on the
pretext of studying Arabic. In the desert near Cairo he had the
promised — and the last — vision of Sophia, and soon after returned to Russia. In Petersburg he continued studying the works
of mystics who wrote about Sophia (*L.*, II, 200).

The chief work of that period is *The Lectures on God-Manhood.*
It is the only attempt that Solovyov ever made to give a systematic exposition of his religious and philosophic world-conception as a whole. It takes the form of a strictly logical deduction of
ideas which are shown to be a synthesis of mutually contradictory affirmations. His review of the historical stages of mankind's spiritual development conforms to this scheme. This
method of exposition is partly determined by the influence of
Hegel's dialectics. But for Solovyov it has another and an intimately personal significance: in contradistinction to other mystics,
Solovyov tries, so to speak, shyly to conceal from the reader, and
as it were to stifle in himself, the mystically-intuitive source of his
ideas (revealed in his poetry only), insisting upon their dialectic-
ally-deductive, would-be logically self-evident necessity. This
duality between rationalistic form and mystical content can be
detected in all Solovyov's writings. The task of 'raising faith to
the level of rational consciousness' becomes a logical 'deduction'
of the dogmas of faith (e.g. of the doctrine of the Trinity and of
the Incarnation) as well as of his personal mystical discoveries.
The classical Thomistic distinction between rational and revealed
truths was utterly foreign to Solovyov. The main theme of his
book is the doctrine of God-manhood. The Chalcedon dogma of
the unity of two natures, the divine and the human, in Jesus

Christ, 'without division or confusion', is raised to the level of a philosophical principle embracing the whole of existence. At the same time the generally accepted sharp opposition between the divine and the human is reconciled through the doctrine of Sophia. The whole cosmogonic process, centred in the history of humanity which is the connecting link between God and the world, is the process of the deification of the creature. The image of the perfect God-man Christ is not an object of passive faith, but a call to all creation to become the receptacle of the universal divine Incarnation.

This stage of Solovyov's creative activity, mainly gnostical and theosophical in character, coincided with the brief period of his professorship. The transition to the next stage was marked by a certain event in his life. After the assassination of Alexander II on March 1, 1881, Solovyov delivered a public lecture in which, strongly condemning this crime and all other violent revolutionary action, he called upon the new Tsar to forgive his father's assassins, and by this Christian act initiate the spiritual regeneration of Russia. Alexander III answered this by an order to administer a severe reprimand to Solovyov and by forbidding him to give public lectures for a time. Solovyov thought it necessary to resign both his professorship and his post at the Ministry of Public Instruction, though he was not required to do so. From that time onwards he devoted himself to writing and remained a free lance.

Solovyov's interest was now centred upon the Church, and this coloured the whole of his general outlook. In 1882–84 he wrote *The Spiritual Foundations of Life*, a remarkable instance of instruction in Christian spiritual life, strictly in accordance with the spirit of the Church, but presented in a manner which makes it intellectually acceptable to people who have no church sympathies; this book has preserved to this day its great missionary influence. Another work of that period, *The Jews and the Christian Problem*, is devoted to the religious justification of Judaism as the faith in the incarnation of the divine righteousness on earth. But the central theme of Solovyov's thought and writing is henceforth the problem of the reunion of the churches. His whole character seems to have predestined him to be the champion of this idea. A man whose final criterion of goodness and righteousness was all-unity was bound to feel that the fact of division in the Church of Christ, the receptacle of the Holy Spirit and the organization of the divinely-human life, was a sin and a shocking violation of the moral norm.

In his youth Solovyov was close to the Slavophils who based their social ideals upon the Christian faith; their opponents, 'the Westernizers' were unbelievers, and the only thing that attracted them in modern Europe was its scientific progress and liberal institutions. Solovyov's keen intelligence and moral sense soon detected the contradiction between the fact that believing Christians preached national pride, religious isolation and irreconcilable hostility to the whole of Western Christendom, while the unbelievers defended the universal solidarity of mankind. Solovyov preserved almost to the end of his life the Slavophil faith in the great religious and spiritual vocation of the Russian people, but he early became aware of the tendentiousness of the Slavophil criticism of the Western Church and culture. As a Christian and a champion of universal unity he came to the conclusion that Russia's vocation consisted precisely in her brotherly solidarity with the Western Christian world and in the task of re-establishing the unity of the Ecumenical Church. Beginning in 1881 he devoted himself to studying the history of the Church at first hand. Two years later his new conviction finally took shape. He expressed it in the book *The Great Dispute and Christian Politics*, which led to a rupture, very painful to him, with his Slavophil friends and to accusations of being a 'papist' and betraying the Russian national ideal. His work for furthering the union of the churches was combined with a struggle against Russian nationalism, which was particularly marked at that period.

The idea of the universal Church was connected in Solovyov's mind with the idea of theocracy: in virtue of the universal nature of Christianity, the Christianization of the world was to embrace the whole of social life; the unity of the church, headed by the high-priest, was to be reflected in the political unity of Christendom, headed by a 'king', spiritually (but not politically) subordinated to the high-priest. Solovyov was inspired by Dante's *De Monarchia*. But he introduced one essential and characteristic correction into the mediæval conception: the offices of the 'high-priest' and 'the king' are supplemented in his theocracy by the free office of the 'prophets' who guide the Christian world in the path of the full realization of God's Kingdom. The subject was to have been dealt with in the *History and the Future of Theocracy*, a work planned by Solovyov in three volumes; but only the first volume, *The Philosophy of Biblical Theocracy*, was written in 1886. It is characteristic of Solovyov's optimistic and utopian mood[1] of that period that he did not so much as consider the possibility — or rather, the inevitability — of conflicts between these three services or 'offices'.

Solovyov entered into relations with the Croat Catholic bishop Strossmayer, well known for his work among the Slavs. In 1886 he went to see him at Zagreb (in Croatia) and submitted to him his proposal for the union of the churches. Strossmayer was greatly impressed by him; in recommending Solovyov to the papal nuncio in Vienna and to the papal court, he speaks of him as '*anima pia, candida ac vere sancta*'. Strossmayer arranged for him to have an audience with the Pope Leo XIII in the spring of 1888 (the Pope's jubilee); there are no biographical data to show that Solovyov ever went to Rome or had the audience. In January 1888 Solovyov was asked by Fr. Pierling, S.J., to write in French a short summary of his ideas. This gradually developed into a long book published in Paris in 1889, *La Russie et l'Église universelle*. In connection with this work Solovyov went in the spring of 1888 to Paris where he made friends in Catholic circles, especially among the Jesuits. On the way home he once more and for the last time met Bishop Strossmayer. Solovyov kept spiritually in touch with him for years and had the greatest reverence for him, but the general result of his two journeys left him with a sense of profound disappointment. He was disappointed, not in the idea of the union of the churches, but in the possibility of realizing it in practice and, indeed, in the very conception of theocracy.

Solovyov's actual plan was extremely unpractical. He was strongly opposed to every form of external, official union, and thought that the union ought to be the result of inner spiritual reconciliation and be 'chemical' and not 'mechanical'; but at the same time he dreamed that the reconciliation would be affected through an agreement between the Pope and the Russian Emperor: he assigned to Alexander III the part of Charlemagne! When the Pope Leo XIII acquainted himself with Solovyov's ideas, he said, '*Bella idea, ma fuor d'un miracolo, é cosa impossibile*'

[1] His French pamphlet, *L'idée russe* (1888), begins with the words, 'Universal history is nothing other than the realization of utopias, or, rather, of the one Judæo-Christian utopia of the triumph of righteousness or the Kingdom of God.'

(a beautiful idea but, short of a miracle, impossible to carry out); this verdict was a great blow to Solovyov. But to reckon on the Tsar was sheer madness. Alexander III was a worthy man, but distinctly limited, and a firm believer in the necessity of preserving in all things a *status quo*; quite apart from his personal character, however, not even the autocratic power of the Tsar could change the traditional structure of the Orthodox Church. Instead of realizing his utopia, Solovyov found himself in danger of being arrested and sent into exile for his propaganda (fortunately, the fears proved groundless).

La Russie et l'Église universelle, in which Solovyov's Catholic sympathies reach their climax, is a curious book. It was originally intended as an appeal — unhampered by Russian censorship — to the Western and to the Russian Christians, showing to both sides the possibility and the necessity of church union. It proved in fact to be an unnatural combination of passionate and one-sided polemics against Byzantine hierarchy and the ecclesiastical policy of Byzantine Emperors, a justification of the supremacy of the Roman see, and a profound mystical theosophical treatise. The treatise is hard to understand and highly questionable from the point of view of ecclesiastical tradition, especially as it ends with a bold admonition to Christendom as a whole in the name of 'prophetic spirit'. The first half of the book alienated the Orthodox, the second the Catholics. 'My Jesuit friends', Solovyov said bitterly in 1889, 'abuse me for free-thinking, dreaminess and mysticism' (L., III, 121). It must be admitted that from their point of view they were perfectly right. It was, to say the least of it, inexpedient to include in the appeal for the union of the churches a mystical doctrine of Sophia and an obviously 'heretical' surmise, traceable to Boehme and Schelling, that God created the world out of chaos hidden in His own depths, as well as to urge the Church to renounce 'absolute clericalism' and one-sided dogmatism, and to tell the laity that the sacrament of holy chrysm made every one of them 'equal to bishops and kings' and that their freedom, if rightly used, meant 'sovereign power equal to that of the Pope'. But for Solovyov the call for church union would lose its meaning if he betrayed his 'eternal friend' and said nothing about his faith in God-manhood and the divine basis of the free human spirit. His book merely shows that he was a mystic and a prophet and not a conventional theologian and a judicious church-worker.

In what sense was Solovyov a Catholic at all?[1] There is no doubt that as early as 1883 or, at the latest, 1884 Soloyvov became convinced of the falsity of the usual Orthodox denunciations of Catholicism, and of the essential truth of the three 'new' Catholic dogmas which Orthodox theologians consider questionable or false — *filioque, immaculata conceptio* and *infallibilitas ex cathedra*; he preserved his faith in them to the end of his life, though in the course of years he revised their meaning in accordance with his new religious standpoint. Faith in the divinely appointed head of the Church was inseparably bound up in his mind with his mystical faith in the Church as a divinely human organism. A solemn declaration of this faith, marked 'N.B.', is placed at the end of his introduction to *La Russie et l'Église universelle*:

'As a member of the true and venerable Orthodox Eastern or Græco-Russian Church, speaking not through an un-canonical Synod or officials of the secular Government but through the voice of its great Fathers and Teachers, I acknow-ledge as the supreme judge in matters of religion him who has been recognized as such by St. Irenaeus, St. Dionysius the Great, St. Athanasius the Great, St. John Chrysostom, St. Cyril, St. Flavian, the blessed Theodoret, St. Maxim the Confessor, St. Ignatius and others — namely, the Apostle Peter living in his successors to whom not in vain Our Lord said: "Thou art Peter, and upon this rock I will build my church. Strengthen thy brethren. Feed my sheep, feed my lambs."'

In the dogma of *immaculata conceptio* (which, in his opinion was in conformity with the traditional Russian cult of the Mother of God) Solovyov saw a symbolic ecclesiastical sanction of his mystical faith in St. Sophia, the sacred soul of humanity.[2] His attitude to the *filioque* dogma was more superficial: generally he simply pointed out that it had been accepted by some of the Fathers greatly revered in the Eastern Church such as St. Gregory of Nyssa and St. Maxim the Confessor, and only once he at-tempted to give a purely philosophical — not a theological — proof of it.

[1] For the facts of the case see Appendix I.
[2] In the paper he submitted to Strossmayer he rather pointedly remarks that Thomists and Dominicans in general took a long time to recognize this dogma (*L.*, I, 185).

The chief interest and the main content of Solovyov's religious convictions is not his belief in the Catholic Church *in contra-distinction* to the Orthodox, but his faith in the inviolable and unviolated unity of the universal 'Orthodox-Catholic' Church as a mystical divinely-human reality. To admit that its unity had at any time ceased to exist would be for Solovyov tantamount to admitting that Christ's promise of the Church being invincible had proved false. This attitude is a clear expression of Solovyov's genius: his mystical faith revealed to him the reality hidden under the thousand-year-old layer of errors due to human limitations and sinful passions. The division of the churches took place *de facto*, but is not valid *de jure*. The Eastern and the Western churches as represented by their hierarchs quarrelled, parted and mutually isolated themselves. Solovyov, at the height of his Catholic sympathies, was inclined to put the blame on the Eastern Church — as a reaction against the one-sided view prevalent in Russia; but whoever was chiefly responsible, the only thing that matters is that this sinful human quarrel has not disturbed the real, divinely ordained unity of the Church *embracing both its halves*. This is why Solovyov thought he was entitled to regard himself as belonging to the universal Church and be in brotherly union with its Western part while remaining a member of the Orthodox Church (he emphasizes the fact in his confession of faith, quoted above). As his canonical justification he points out that in 1054 (the year of the final rupture as generally recognized) the papal legates anathematized only the Patriarch Michael Cerularius and 'the adherents of his folly' and not the Eastern Church as a whole, and since that time the Eastern Church has held no Ecumenical Council which alone would have the right to sanction the division. Dogmatic beliefs binding upon the Orthodox were established before the division of the churches and are equally recognized by the Catholics; on the other hand, the Catholic dogmatic 'innovations' are formally justifiable in accordance with the principle of 'dogmatic development' (Solovyov affirms this principle independently of Newman, whose works he had not read). Since the Church is universal, the re-establishment of its unity would not be a subordination of the Eastern Church to the Western or its 'Romanization', but a harmonious combination of both parts in their individual religious character. Solovyov clearly distinguished between the divinely ordained supremacy of the Roman pontiff — the successor

of St. Peter — and the power of the Roman Pope as the patriarch
of the Western, Latin Church.[1]

To ask whether Solovyov was a Catholic in the sense of
belonging to the Roman Catholic Church is as inadequate to the
breadth and boldness of his religious genius as it would be to ask
— *toutes proportions gardées*, of course — whether St. Paul was a
'Judæo-Christian' *or* a 'member' of the Christian Church of the
Gentiles. Solovyov was the first in the nineteenth century to
proclaim the principle of 'Ecumenism'. True, his main interest
was the reunion between Catholicism and Orthodoxy; he
thought that canonically the Protestants had cut themselves off
from the Church; but he believed that in spite of their defection,
they stood for a principle of vital importance to the Church —
the principle of individual freedom of faith, and that their return
to the fold would be a natural consequence of reconciliation between the Catholics and the Orthodox. In later years, as we shall
see, he came to take an even broader view of the subject.

Solovyov found himself in a tragic position after the failure of
his project for church union. His rupture with the Slavophils and
ecclesiastically minded Russians was final: they regarded him as
a papist and a traitor, and he regarded them as men who had
replaced Christian faith by the pride and egotism of narrow
nationalism. But in a deeper sense he was in his whole spiritual
make-up a typical representative of Eastern Christianity, though
he himself was not sufficiently aware of it. He could not become
really intimate with the representatives of the Western Church in
spite of his respect for them and close agreement on questions of
dogma; all personal contact and exchange of opinions with them
invariably ended in a reaction towards Orthodoxy. After his first
visit to Croatia he said in a letter: 'I returned from abroad having
got to know better and seen more clearly both the good and
the bad (Solovyov's italics) sides of the Western Church. My
answer to the attempts at conversion aimed at me personally
was, first of all, . . . to go to confession and communion in the

[1] In the paper he submitted to Strossmayer about the union of the churches
(L., I, 183–90) and in many of his writings of the period (Vols. IV and V)
Solovyov points out that at any rate one, then living, hierarch of the Russian
Church — Platon, Metropolitan of Kiev — openly expressed a similar view
of the relation between Orthodoxy and Catholicism. I happen to know that
later the same point of view was held by the Uniate Metropolitan Andrey
Szepticki.

Orthodox Serbian church at Zagreb. . . . Altogether, I returned to Russia more Orthodox, if one may put it so, than when I left it' (*L.*, III, 189). At that time Solovyov published at Zagreb an article in the Croat language defending the Orthodox Church against the Catholic accusations of heresy. Similarly, during his stay in Paris in 1888, in the hey-day of his Catholic sympathies and friendship with French Catholics, he wrote: 'I am told that Russian newspapers spread rumours about my conversion to Catholicism, and so on. In truth I am *now still further from taking such a step than before*' (*L.*, II, 157).

In the early 'nineties Solovyov went through a profound spiritual crisis; it was complicated by the frustration of his hopes of personal happiness: an unsatisfactory love affair of many years' standing came to an end. He was on the brink of despair. But his spirit was living, and the crisis led to a new period of creative activity which now reached its final depth and enlightenment. The period of ecclesiastically theological thought and struggle was replaced by that of individually mystical faith; new horizons opened out for his Christian thought, and it acquired still greater boldness and breadth. His faith in the truth of Christ and in its final triumph was no longer connected for him with the destinies and the earthly organization of the Church. The main result of this spiritual revolution was that his optimistic, utopian world-conception was replaced by one that might be called tragic and eschatological. His personal connection with the Church and participation in its life grew considerably weaker, though it was not severed. The 'institutional element in religion' — to use Baron von Hügel's term — that occupied a central place in his thought in the 'eighties now receded into the background and lost its interest for him. (This is the essential difference between Solovyov and Newman, to whom, following d'Herbigny, he is generally compared.) There is a remarkable personal confession made by Solovyov in 1895. Writing to an intimate friend (the poet Velichko), he says: 'You and I have not been observing the rules about fasting or going to church and there was nothing bad in it, for all this is not meant *for us*' (*L.*, I, 223).

From theology and ecclesiastical politics he turned once more to philosophy — chiefly to ethics and æsthetics. At that time he came into close contact with the Petersburg circle of agnostic and liberal 'westernizers'; they were alien to him spiritually, but he shared their political sympathies. He became a regular contributor to their magazine, *Vestnik Evropi* (*The European Review*) on political and literary subjects, and was one of the most prominent opponents of the political and religious reactionism of that period. His chief philosophical works during the 'nineties were articles on beauty and on art (1889–90), the essay *The Meaning of Love* (1892–94) — a true work of genius — a system of ethics, *The Justification of the Good*, and a supplement to it, *Morality and Legal Justice* (1895–97). Solovyov was also writing a work on *Theoretical Philosophy*, but it remained unfinished. He translated some of the works of Plato and wrote a remarkable essay, *The Tragedy of Plato's Life*, which throws light on Solovyov's own spiritual development.

All Solovyov's writings of that period hint only indirectly at the radical change in his religious standpoint. It is finally revealed only in the very last thing he wrote, *Three Conversations*, and especially in its epilogue, *The Short Story of Antichrist*, and can be best traced through his letters. Only once did he give public utterance to it, in a paper read in 1891 before a learned society. In religious and conservative circles this paper, called *The Collapse of the Mediæval World-Conception*, produced the impression of a bomb-shell. Solovyov argued that the Church had failed to carry out Christ's chief commandment — to make active love for one's neighbour the basis of social life; this commandment, however, inspires unbelievers who champion freedom and social justice and must therefore, in spite of their unbelief, be recognized as true disciples of Christ. In a letter written in 1892 Solovyov said: 'I am as far from the narrowness of Rome as from that of Byzantium, or of Augsburg, or of Geneva; the religion of the Holy Spirit which I profess is wider and at the same time fuller in content than all particular religions; it is neither their sum nor their extract, just as the whole man is neither a sum nor an extract of his particular organs' (*L.*, III, 44). He now laid special emphasis on 'the privilege belonging, in St. John's words, to every Christian ("ye have an unction from the Holy One, and ye know all things") of judging about church matters in the sense of seeing whether they are in accord with the spirit of Christ' (*L.*, III, 183, 1897). In a note written in 1893 (Vol. VI, 401–10) he decisively rejects 'the path of external, enforced submission, instead of inner self-activity, in matters of faith'; he commends the contention of his old opponent, the Slavophil Yuri Samarin: 'Nothing that is *visible* in the Church is in itself *infallible*, and nothing that *is infallible* in the Church can be *visibly* detected'; he says: 'The dilemma — papism or spiritual freedom — can only be avoided at the cost of fruitless and unworthy compromises with conscience' and he himself accepts 'one of the horns of the dilemma — spiritual freedom'. His friend, the philosopher Lopatin, tells that in those years Solovyov used to say about himself: 'I am supposed to be a Catholic, but as a matter of fact I am more of a Protestant.'[1]

Solovyov not only recognized the futility of his plan of universal theocracy, but came to the conclusion that the very idea of it was mistaken. He drew a clear distinction between the truth of Christ's revelation and its promised final triumph on the one hand, and the earthly historical success of the Church and actual Christianization of the world on the other. His belief in the uninterrupted cosmogonic process of the gradual deification of the world was shattered; the historical development of mankind appeared to him as a tragic conflict between the true Church of Christ, persecuted till the end, and the powers of this world. 'The light shines in darkness.' He retained his faith in the universal Church, but it no longer had for him a visible outline, and was merely 'a little flock' of faithful souls devoted to Christ.

This new standpoint was most clearly expressed by Solovyov in a remarkable letter to a French Catholic writer Tavernier in May 1896.[2]

'*Respice finem*. With regard to this question there are only three indubitable truths, to which God's word bears witness:

(1) The Gospel shall be preached in all the world, i.e. the Truth shall be proclaimed to all mankind.

(2) The Son of man shall find hardly any faith on the earth, in other words, in the last time true believers shall be in a numerically insignificant minority, and the rest of mankind shall follow antichrist.

(3) And nevertheless . . . evil shall be overcome and the faithful shall triumph.'

The conclusion from this is: 'If there can be no doubt that the

[1] Quoted by Mochulsky in his book on Solovyov (in Russian), p. 217.
[2] See Mochulsky, pp. 213–14. This letter is a key to the true meaning of the apparently inexplicable fact of Solovyov's receiving Holy Communion in a Catholic church (in Feb. 1896) at about the same time as it was written. See Appendix I.

truth will be finally accepted only by a persecuted minority, we ought definitely to give up the idea of the external greatness and power of theocracy as the direct and immediate aim of Christian policy. That aim should be *righteousness*.' Pointing out the necessity for the faithful to unite round the traditional centre of unity (papal authority), Solovyov goes on: 'This is all the more practicable because that centre no longer possesses external compulsory power, and therefore everyone may unite with it *to the extent indicated to him by his conscience*. I know that many priests and monks think differently and demand complete submission to ecclesiastical power as to God. *This is an error*; when it is clearly formulated, it will have to be called a heresy. It may be expected that ninety-nine per cent. of these priests and monks will side with antichrist.'

The same mood and the same ideas are expressed in the *Short Story of Antichrist* (1901). In it the union of the churches is supposed to take place only at the end of the world, under the rule of antichrist, and only the faithful minority of Catholics, Orthodox and Protestants will take part in it. As reported by the poet Andrey Bely, who was present on the occcasion of the author reading this story aloud, Solovyov remarked: 'I have written it to express my final view of the church problem.'[1]

During the last five years of his life Solovyov had a foreboding of the world-troubles to come. In 1894, at the first and scarcely perceptible signs of unrest in China, he wrote a poem called *Panmongolism* picturing the invasion of Russia by Mongolian hordes. Divine retribution for her sins will overtake Russia — 'the third Rome', as the Slavophils loved to call her — she will fall like Byzantium, 'the second Rome'. (Solovyov's prophecy in this particular form has not so far been justified, but it is remarkable that eleven years after it an apparently incredible fact took place: the mighty Russian empire suffered defeat from the small Japanese nation, and in another twelve years came the downfall of the five-hundred-year-old Orthodox Russian monarchy itself.)

From 1897 Solovyov's prophetic premonition of the approaching world-catastrophe expressed itself as the expectation of the speedy end of the world and of the coming of antichrist. In June 1897 he wrote to his friend Velichko: 'Something is preparing,

[1] See the biographical sketch by S. M. Solovyov (the philosopher's nephew) in the introduction to the sixth edition of *V. Solovyov's Poems* in 1915.

someone is coming. You can guess that by "someone" I mean antichrist. The approaching end of the world is wafted to me as a kind of clear, though elusive breath — just as a wayfarer feels the sea air before the sea itself comes into sight' (*L.*, I, 232).

The subject of the *Three Conversations* is the overwhelming power of evil threatening the world and the necessity for waging a stern and unyielding struggle against it. Solovyov's argument was chiefly directed against the good-natured Tolstoyan attitude of 'non-resistance to evil' under the mask of Christianity. 'The historical drama is over, and only the epilogue remains, though it may, as with Ibsen, be drawn out into five acts' — those are the concluding words of the last note he wrote (Vol. X, 226, June 1900).

In his preface to the *Three Conversations* Solovyov wrote that he was hastening to publish the book, for he was 'conscious of the not too far distant image of pale death'. This too proved prophetic. He wrote those words at Easter 1900, and on July 31st he died after a short illness in the country house of his friends, the Trubetskoys, near Moscow, having made his confession to an Orthodox priest and received communion. Before death he prayed for the Jewish people. His last words were: 'Hard is the work of the Lord.'

Two ikons were placed on his grave in Moscow by an un-known admirer: a Greek ikon of the Resurrection with the inscription Χριστός ἀνέστη ἐκ νεκρῶν, and a Catholic ikon of Our Lady, inscribed *In memoria aeterna erit justus.*

III

What is the significance of Solovyov's ideas and his whole spiritual outlook at the present day? He was a nineteenth-century thinker; for the greater part of his life he shared the faith in continuous progress that was so characteristic of that century and that now, after the experience of the last fifty years, is rejected by all thinking people. True, Solovyov gave it a deeper, religious meaning of faith in the cosmic and universally historical process of the 'deification' of the world, i.e. of the gradual incorporation in it of the divine power and righteousness. But that too sounds to us now like a Christianized version of the Hegelian idealism or, in other words, as another optimistic illusion of the nineteenth century.

Solovyov's other ideas, which appeared bold and original at
the time, betokening a new spiritual era, share the fate of all new
ideas: once they have been generally recognized they seem, if
taken in the abstract, self-evident and therefore not original.
This is the case, for instance, with Solovyov's religious 'Ecumenism', unknown in the nineteenth century, but widely
spread in our own day, or with his conception of Christianity as
the ideal of mankind's integral regeneration, including its social
life. That idea, occasionally met with in the nineteenth century,
had not, I think, been worked out so fully by anyone before
Solovyov, but at present it is the favourite subject of popular
Christian thought. Finally, we are likely to underrate Solovyov's
highest achievement, won by him at the cost of intense spiritual
struggle — the combination of unwavering faith in Christ's truth
with a keen and sober awareness of the tremendous power of evil
persisting till the end of the world; for in our tragic era this
awareness forces itself, as it were, upon believing Christians, or at
any rate upon the more sensitive among them.

But in the first place it should be remembered that all those
new, though now fairly familiar ideas still meet with obstinate
resistance from the inert mass-mind. Such facts as the domination
of communism — this evil distortion of the eighteenth- and nineteenth-century ideas — and the prevalence in the Christian world
of narrow confessionalism and passively moral piety remote from
life compel us to recognize Solovyov, with his intellectual genius
and profound spiritual fervour, as still one of the leaders in the
struggle for the true, responsible Christian faith. Besides, a genius
has the privilege of never growing old: the original expression,
coloured by the depths of his own spirit, which he gives to his
ideas imparts to them an abiding force and significance, even
though their abstract content may cease to be new. And Solovyov
was both a genius proclaiming truths new to his generation and a
prophetic spirit aware, through some mysterious religious apprehension, of things to come — not, of course, in concrete detail,
but in their general spiritual meaning. A prophet's vision of the
future is more profound than ordinary people's sober apprehension of it when it has become the present and thus remains a
source of spiritual guidance to later generations.

But apart from these general reflections, the whole content and
spirit of Solovyov's religious world-conception holds indeed a
certain new message, especially for the Western world, the

significance of which can hardly be exaggerated. The eschatological standpoint characteristic of his last writings is, of course,
in itself not new to Christian consciousness. That 'the whole
world lies in wickedness', that Christ's revelation does not
promise the victory of the good over evil within the confines of
'this world' and that we must live in the expectation of the end
of the world and the final triumph of Christ, is a belief that has
formed part of Christianity from the first, though it has been
largely forgotten by the Western Christians during the recent
centuries. But it has usually led to monastic detachment from the
world, to contempt for it and often even to indifference to earthly
wrongs and earthly human suffering. In Solovyov we find quite
a new and different attitude which henceforth should be predominant in Christian consciousness: he combines a bitter awareness of the power of evil, unconquerable till the end of history,
and the foreboding of trials to come with a keen sense of the
Christian's responsibility for the world's evils and insistence upon
active struggle for Christ's truth in every domain of human life.
Solovyov preaches a *heroic* Christianity which has no need of
optimistic illusions for carrying on its arduous moral activity and
unwavering struggle against evil. When the ideal of the theocratic structure of society ceased to satisfy him, there grew up in
his heart and mind a kind of grand synthesis between the spiritual
attitude of the first Christians, the mediæval faith in the Church
as the spiritual guide of mankind and the humanitarian faith of
modern times. True, he did not definitely formulate this synthesis; he called it his religion of the Holy Spirit. It points the
way which Christian thought must follow — the way which
Péguy sought after him and to which the most sensitive minds of
our day are unconsciously drawn.

This synthesis finally sums up Solovyov's primary religious
and philosophical intuition which he faithfully preserved throughout his life — the idea of God-manhood. Two spiritual forces
have been struggling against each other in the history of European
peoples since the Renaissance: faith in God and faith in man.
Speaking generally and therefore of course schematizing the
manifold variety of the traditional Christian thought, one may
say that its main tendency — most clearly expressed by St.
Augustine — was to magnify God at the expense of belittling
man. Therefore when at the epoch of the Renaissance there
sprang up an ardent faith in the great vocation and the creative

power of man — a faith which, of course, was born of Christianity and could only find its justification in it, it took the form of rebellion first against the ecclesiastical tradition and then against God. All the tragic history of modern Europe down to our own day is overshadowed by this fatal misconception. Faith in the freedom of the human spirit and its inalienable rights, a passionate appeal to secure to man conditions of life befitting his great dignity, become the inspiration of the unbelievers, their battle-cry in the struggle against Christian faith. In virtue of its inner contradiction this non-religious and anti-religious humanism was bound to degenerate into sheer demonism and therefore into a new, unheard-of enslavement and disintegration of the human spirit; the latest expressions of it are national-socialism and communism. But the *truth* of humanism is the Christian truth, not sufficiently understood or revealed in moral practice.

Christian thought has long been disturbed by a vague consciousness of this contradiction. As early as the nineteenth century, and especially in our time, there have been continuous attempts to overcome the humanist rebellion *from within* by sanctioning all that is legitimate in its claims. But the 'Christian democratic' and 'Christian socialist' movements remain inwardly weak because they are of the nature of a compromise. They lack the spirit of ardent faith that can move mountains. This spiritual flame can burn up only when its deepest religious and dogmatic source is recognized — when the Christian revelation is seen to be a new revelation not only about God but also *about man*. This 'Christian humanism' was indicated by thinkers like Nicolas of Cusa, Erasmus and St. Francis de Sales. Faith in man might have developed within the bosom of the Christian Church itself, and then the whole social and spiritual history of Europe might have followed a different and more harmonious course. But this was not destined to be.

The significance of Solovyov is to have once more faced this decisive problem in all its depth and importance, and it is in this respect that his creative work is a great — perhaps the greatest — contribution of the Russian religious spirit to the shaping of man's destiny. He understood Christianity as the revelation of the universal principle of God-manhood. He was conscious of the indissoluble bond between faith in Jesus Christ as God, and faith in man. The greatness and holiness of God is *ipso facto* the greatness and holiness — indeed, potential divinity — of His creature man (and of all the world). The triumph of the divine power and truth in Christ's resurrection is the beginning and the token of the real victory over all servitude and humiliation of man, including victory over death. This is not a dogma of passive faith, but the aim of man's universal creative activity. The boldest hopes and creative aspirations of the human spirit — fatal or meaningless apart from God — are justified and, indeed, are binding for man as a being rooted in God, as a recipient of God's power and holiness. It will not be an exaggeration to say that this central idea of Solovyov's religious philosophy — whatever we may think of it as a system — shows the spiritual path which alone can lead humanity out of its present impasse.

S. L. FRANK

I

GOD AND MAN

1

GOD, THE DIVINE BASIS OF CREATION AND MAN

CHRISTIANITY has a content of its own, and that content is solely and exclusively Christ. In Christianity as such we find Christ, and Christ only — this is a truth very often uttered but very little assimilated.

At the present time there are many people in the Christian world, especially among the Protestants, who call themselves Christians, but believe that the essence of Christianity is Christ's teaching and not His person. They say: we are Christians because we accept Christ's teaching. But in what precisely does His teaching consist? If we take His moral teaching developed in the Gospels and wholly reducible to the precept 'love thy neighbour as thyself' (and it is on the moral teaching that emphasis is laid), we are bound to admit that this precept is not as such exclusively characteristic of Christianity. Far earlier than Christianity, the religious doctrines of India — Brahmanism and Buddhism — preached love and mercy not only for human beings but for all that lives.

Nor can the specific content of Christianity be found in Christ's teaching about God as the Father, as a pre-eminently loving and merciful Being, for that conception too is not peculiar to Christianity. The name of father was always given to the chief gods of all religions, and in one of them, namely in the Persian, the supreme God was conceived not merely as a father, but as an all-merciful and loving father.

If we consider the whole of the theoretical and moral content of Christ's teaching as expounded in the Gospels, the only thing that will be new in it and specifically different from all other religions is Christ's teaching about Himself, His speaking of

Himself as the living, incarnate truth: 'I am the way, the truth and the life; he that believeth on me hath everlasting life.'

Thus, if the characteristic content of Christianity be sought in the teaching of Christ, we must admit that it is to be found in Christ Himself.

What, then, are we to think? What appears to our reason under the name of Christ as the life and the Truth?

The eternal God forever realizes Himself in realizing His content, i.e. in realizing all. That 'all', in contradistinction to the living God as absolutely One, is plurality — but plurality as the content of the absolute unity, as dominated by unity, as reduced to unity.

Plurality reduced to unity is a whole. A real whole is a living organism. God as a Being that has realized its content, as a unity containing all plurality, is a living organism.

. . . The elements of the divine organism, taken together, embrace the fulness of being; in that sense it is a universal organism. But universality does not prevent it from being perfectly individual — on the contrary, it logically implies individuality.

We call (relatively) universal an entity which as compared with others contains a greater number of different specific elements. Clearly, the greater the number of particular elements that form part of it, the greater is the number of combinations in which each of those elements enters, and the more each of them is conditioned by the others; hence, the connection between all of them is the stronger and the more indissoluble, and so is the unity of the organism as a whole.

Further, it is clear that the greater the number of elements in an organism and the number of combinations between them, the less likely it is that the same combination of elements will be found in another organism, and the more original and *specific* that organism will be.

Further, since every relation and every combination necessarily implies *distinction*, the more elements an organism contains, the more distinctions are present in its unity, and the more distinct it is from all other organisms; in other words, the greater the multiplicity of elements reduced to unity, the more the principle of unity asserts itself and consequently the more individual the organism is. So from this point of view, we again come to the conclusion that an entity's universality is in direct ratio to its individuality: the more universal it is, the more individual, and therefore an absolutely universal being is absolutely individual.

Accordingly, a universal organism expressing the absolute content of the divine principle is pre-eminently a unique individual being. That individual being or the realized expression of the absolute living God is Christ.

In every organism there are necessarily present two unities: on the one hand, there is the unity of the active principle which reduces the multiplicity of the elements to itself as one, and on the other there is the multiplicity as reduced to a unity, as a definite image of that active principle. We have the producing unity and the resultant unity, or unity in itself as a principle and unity in manifestation.

In Christ's divine organism the acting, unifying principle, the principle which expresses the unity of absolute being is obviously the Word or Logos.

The second kind of unity, i.e. the resultant unity, is in Christian mystical philosophy called Sophia. If we distinguish the absolute as such, i.e. as absolute being, from its content, essence or idea, we shall find the direct expression of the first in the Logos and of the second in Sophia, which is the expressed or realized idea. Just as an entity, though distinct from the idea of it, is at the same time one with it, so the Logos, though distinct from Sophia, is inwardly united to her. Sophia is God's body, the matter of the Deity permeated by the principle of divine unity.[1] Christ who realizes or bears in Himself that unity as an integral divine organism, universal and individual at the same time, is both Logos and Sophia.

To speak of Sophia as an essential element of the Deity does not, from the Christian point of view, mean introducing new gods. The conception of Sophia was always present in Christianity and indeed it is pre-Christian. In the Old Testament there is a whole book ascribed to Solomon which is called Sophia. It is non-canonical, but in the canonical book of Solomon's *Proverbs* the same idea of Sophia (under the Jewish name Hohma) is worked out. It says there that Sophia existed before the creation of the world (i.e. of the natural world). God possessed her in the

[1] Such words as 'body' and 'matter' are used here, of course, only in their most general sense, as relative categories, free from the specific ideas which are applicable to our material world, but are utterly unthinkable in respect of the Deity.

beginning of His way, i.e. she is the idea which He has before Him as Creator and which He realizes. In the New Testament the same term is used in direct relation to Christ (by St. Paul).

The conception of God as an integral being, as a universal organism presupposing the multiplicity of entities which compose that organism, may seem to conflict with the absoluteness of the Deity and to introduce nature into God. But in order that God may differ absolutely from our world, from our nature, from the visible reality, it is essential to recognize in Him His own special eternal nature, His own special eternal world. Otherwise our conception of the Deity will be poorer and more abstract than our idea of the visible world.

The negative line of development in religious consciousness always took the form, first, of so to speak purifying the Deity from all actual determinations and reducing it to a pure abstraction and then getting rid of this abstract Deity altogether: religious consciousness passes into atheism.

If the whole fulness of actuality, and therefore, necessarily, of plurality, be denied to the Deity, positive significance will inevitably be ascribed to the plurality and actuality of *this* world. Only a negative significance will be attached to the Deity and it will gradually be rejected altogether, for if there is no other absolute reality, no other plurality and fulness of being, this world of ours is the only reality: the Deity has no positive content left to it. It is either identified with this world, this nature, which are regarded as the direct and immediate content of the Deity, and we end in naturalistic pantheism for which this finite nature is all, and God is only an empty word; or — and that is more consistent — the Deity as an empty abstraction is simply denied, and we have frank atheism.

And so God as an integral being possesses both unity and plurality — a plurality of substantival ideas, i.e. of potencies or powers with a specific, definite content.

These powers, each of which has a definite content of its own, variously related to the contents of the others, necessarily constitute different secondary wholes or spheres, but all form one divine world.

... The reality of that world, which is infinitely richer than our visible world, can obviously be fully accessible only to those who actually belong to it. But since our natural world is, inevitably, closely connected with that divine world (what the nature of the connection is will appear later), since there is not and there cannot be any impassable gulf between them, separate rays and reflections of the divine world must penetrate into our reality constituting all the ideal content, all the truth and beauty which we find in it. As belonging to both worlds man can and must through intellectual contemplation be in touch with the divine world, and while still dwelling in the world of struggle and anxious confusion, enter into communion with the serene images abiding in the realm of glory and eternal beauty. This positive insight, incomplete though it be, into the reality of the divine world is particularly characteristic of poetic genius. Every true poet must penetrate to 'the native land of flame and word' so as to borrow from it the archetypes of his creations and the inner enlightenment called inspiration which enables us to find even in our natural world colours and sounds for the embodiment of ideal patterns.

The divine or eternal realm is not a puzzle to our reason. As the ideal fulness of all that is and the realization of truth, goodness and beauty, it appears to reason as something essentially *normal*. As absolute norm that realm is logically necessary to reason, and if reason as such cannot prove its existence as a *fact*, this is simply because reason is not in itself an organ for the cognition of facts. The reality of facts is obviously cognized only through actual experience; but speculative reason clearly perceives the ideal necessity of the divine realm and of Christ as its absolutely universal and therefore absolutely individual centre possessing the whole fulness of it. It is only in that eternal sphere that reason can find the absolute standard by comparison with which it recognizes our natural world of fact as something conditional, transitory and not normal.

It is not the divine eternal world that is a puzzle for reason, but this natural, actually given world; the task of reason is to explain its unquestionable but unintelligible reality.

This task obviously consists in deducing the conditional from the unconditional, that which, as such, ought not to be from the unconditionally binding — in deducing contingent reality from the absolute idea, the natural world of phenomena from the divine reality. Such deduction would be an impossible task if the two opposite terms, one of which is to be deduced from the other, had not something to connect them — something that belongs equally to both spheres and therefore forms the transition from one to the other. This connecting link between the divine and the natural world is *man*.

Man includes in himself every kind of contradiction, all reducible to the one great opposition between the unconditional and the conditional, between the absolute and eternal essence and the transitory phenomena or appearances. Man is both divine and insignificant.

I have already said that it is necessary to distinguish a twofold unity within the wholeness of the divine Being: the active or producing unity of the Word's divine creativeness, and the produced or the realized unity. Similarly, in a particular organism in the natural world we distinguish the active unity, the principle that produces and maintains the organic wholeness and is the living and active *soul* of the organism, and the unity produced or realized by that soul — the unity of the organic *body*.

In the divine being — in Christ — the first or the producing unity is Deity as such, God or Logos as an active power, and in that unity Christ is essentially divine; but the second, the produced unity, to which we have given the mystical name of Sophia, is the principle of humanity — the ideal or the normal man. In that unity Christ participates in the human principle and is man, or, as the Scripture puts it, Second Adam.

Thus, Sophia is the ideal, perfect humanity eternally contained in the integral divine Being or Christ. Since in order to exist really and actually God must manifest His existence, i.e. must act in another, the existence of that other is thereby made necessary; and since temporal categories are not applicable to God, and all that we say of Him presupposes eternity, the existence of the 'other', in relation to which God manifests Himself, must necessarily be recognized as eternal. That 'other' is not *absolutely* 'other' for God (this would be unthinkable), but is His own expression or manifestation, in relation to which God is called the Word.

But this manifestation or inner revelation of the Deity, and consequently, the distinction between God as the Logos and God as the primary substance or Father, necessarily presupposes that in which the Deity is revealed, or in which it acts, and which exists in the Father substantially or in a latent form and is revealed through the Logos.

Consequently, if we are to conceive of God as being from all eternity the Logos or acting God, we must presuppose the eternal existence of real entities receptive of divine action — we must presuppose the existence of the world as subject to the divine activity, as *making room* within itself for the divine unity. The world's own 'produced' unity — the centre of the world and at the same time the circumference of the Deity — is humanity. All actuality presupposes action, and action presupposes a real object of action, i.e. a subject receptive of the action; hence, the actuality of God, based upon divine action, presupposes a subject receptive of that action — presupposes man — and does so *eternally* since God's action is eternal. It cannot be urged against this that the eternal object of God's action is the Logos, for the Logos is the same God, but God as manifested, and manifestation implies the presence of the 'other' in relation to which or for the sake of which God manifests Himself, i.e. implies man.

It is obvious that in speaking of man or of humanity as eternal we do not mean the natural man or man as an empirical fact.

. . . We have neither the need nor the right to limit man to the given, visible reality. We are speaking of the ideal man who is not any less concrete or real — indeed, is incomparably more concrete and real than the visible manifestation of human beings. There lies within our own selves an infinite wealth of content and power hidden beyond the threshold of our present consciousness; only a certain part of it crosses the threshold, never exhausting the whole.

In the words of an ancient poet, 'it is in us, and not in the stars of heaven or in depths of Tartarus that the eternal powers of the cosmos dwell'.

Though man as an empirical fact is temporary and transient, in his essence he is of necessity eternal and all-embracing. What, then, is the ideal man? To be actual, he must be one and many; hence, he is not only the abstract universal essence of all human entities, but a universal and at the same time individual being actually containing in himself all those entities. Every one of us, every human being, is essentially and actually rooted in the universal or absolute man and has a part in him.

Just as the divine powers form one complete, absolutely universal and absolutely individual organism of the living Logos, so all human entities form a complete pan-human organism, both universal and individual, which is the necessary realization and receptacle of the first, as the eternal body of God and the eternal soul of the world. That organism, i.e. Sophia, in its eternal being inevitably consists of a multiplicity of elements of which it is the real unity; consequently, each of these elements, as a necessary component part of the eternal divine humanity, must be recognized as eternal on the absolute or ideal plane.

And so in speaking of humanity being eternal we mean by implication that each separate human entity is eternal. If it were not, humanity itself would be a fiction.

It is perfectly obvious that to regard man as merely an entity that arises in time, is created at a definite moment and does not exist before physical birth, means to identify man with his phenomenal appearance, with his manifested being which really does begin with physical birth. But then it also disappears at the death of the body. That which only appeared in time, must disappear in time also; an infinite existence *after death* does not logically tally with nothingness *before birth*.

As a natural being or appearance, man exists solely in the interval between physical birth and physical death. It is only possible to admit that he exists after death if it be recognized that he is not merely a being which lives in the natural world, that he is not merely an appearance, but is also an eternal intelligible essence. In that case, however, it is logically necessary to admit that he exists not only after death but also before birth, since an intelligible essence is from its very meaning not subject to our temporal forms which apply to appearances only.

2

THE ESSENCE OF
CHRISTIANITY

THOSE to whom Christianity is a living religion attach
. . . absolute and essential meaning not to this or that constituent element of it but only to the single spiritual principle
which forms them into one definite whole and imparts relative
force and value to each of them. True, genuine Christianity is not
a dogma, or hierarchy, or liturgy, or morality, but the life-giving
spirit of Christ really, though invisibly, present in humanity and
acting in it through complex processes of spiritual growth and
development. This spirit is embodied in religious forms and
institutions that constitute the earthly church — its visible body
— but *transcends those forms*, and is not finally realized in any one
given fact. Traditional institutions, forms and formulae are
necessary to Christian humanity, just as a skeleton is necessary to
the organism of the higher animals, but in itself the skeleton does
not constitute a living body. A higher organism cannot exist
without bones, but ossification of the walls of the arteries or the
valves of the heart is a sure sign of approaching death.

. . . All are agreed that true, genuine Christianity is that which
was preached by the Founder of our religion. But what exactly
did He preach? If quotations from the Gospels are picked to suit
one's own taste, many different answers will be given to that
question. Some people will find the essence of Christianity in
non-resistance to evil, others in obedience to spiritual authorities
('if they have kept my saying, they will keep yours also'), the
third will insist on belief in miracles, the fourth on the separation
of the divine from the secular, and so on. The arbitrarily chosen
texts are equally arbitrarily abridged, for if read in full and in the
context they do not yield the required meaning. Leaving these
exegetic extremes aside, I would only say that the many views as
to the essence of Christianity, different as they are, but equally

justifiable (for each of them is based upon some Gospel text), cannot possibly express the real essence of Christianity; at best, they are particular aspects of the doctrine which are as many as are the separate sayings of Christ handed down to us. The true meaning of these particular truths and their real significance can only be understood and estimated through their relation to the one central idea of Christianity. And that idea cannot be defined by mechanically appealing to the letter of separate texts, but requires the use of some more reasonable method. The Gospels must contain a direct indication of what Christ Himself and His immediate disciples recognized as the essence of His teaching. After all, they do speak of Christ's teaching in its totality and express the idea of Christianity as a whole. How, then, is it described? Is it called the teaching about non-resistance, or about spiritual authorities, or about miracles, sacraments, the Trinitarian dogma, redemption and so on? No; all those points are to be found in the Gospel, but the Gospel itself, the good news of Christ, proclaims itself in a different way. It does not designate itself as the Gospel of non-resistance, or of hierarchy, or of miracles, or of faith, or even of love: it invariably recognizes and calls itself *the Gospel of the Kingdom* — the good news of the Kingdom of God. The word of truth sown by the Son of Man is 'the word of the Kingdom', the mysteries revealed by Him are 'the mysteries of the Kingdom', His true followers are 'the sons of the Kingdom', and so on.

Thus, undoubtedly, the central idea of the Gospel, according to the Gospel's own testimony, is the idea of the Kingdom of God. Almost all Christ's words are directly or indirectly concerned with making it clear — the parables addressed to the multitude, the esoteric conversations with the disciples, and the prayers recorded in the Gospels to God the Father. All the texts bearing upon this, taken together, show that the Gospel idea of the Kingdom is not confined to the conception of God's power over all that is — power that belongs to God as Almighty and All-sustaining. That power is an eternal and unchangeable fact, while the Kingdom preached by Christ is something that moves, approaches, comes. It has different aspects. It is within us, and yet it is manifested outwardly; it grows in mankind and in the whole world through a certain objective organic process, and it is also taken by a free effort of our will. This may appear contradictory to those who worship the letter, but to those who have the mind of Christ it is all included in one simple and all-embracing definition according to which the Kingdom of God is the complete realization of the divine in the naturally human through the God-man Christ, or in other words, it is the fulness of the natural human life, united through Christ with the divine fulness.

The perfect union of the Deity with humanity must be mutual; if one of the terms disappears, there is no union, and if it loses its freedom the union is not perfect. The inner possibility, the fundamental condition of the union with the Deity is thus to be found in man himself — the Kingdom of God is within you. But the possibility must become an actuality, man must manifest the Kingdom of God hidden within him, and in order to do that he must combine a deliberate effort of his free will with the secret action of the divine grace within him — 'the Kingdom of heaven suffereth violence and the violent take it by force'. Without personal effort the possibility will remain a possibility, the token of the future blessings will be lost, the germ of the true life will die down and perish. Thus the Kingdom of God, perfect in the eternal divine idea ('in heaven') and potentially present in our nature, is at the same time of necessity something that is being *accomplished* for us and through us. In this aspect of it, it is our work, a task set for us to carry out. This work and task cannot be confined to the separate individual existence of particular people. Man is a social being, and the highest work of his life, the final end of his efforts is not confined to his personal destiny, but is to be found in the social destinies of mankind as a whole. Just as the general inner potency of the Kingdom of God must for its realization necessarily become an individual moral achievement, so the latter, if it is to attain completion, must inevitably enter into the social movement of all humanity and form part, in one way or another, at a given moment and under given conditions, of the general divinely-human process of universal history. The Kingdom of God is the union of divine grace with man, not as shut up in his own selfhood but with man as a living member of the cosmic whole. Such a man finds the Kingdom of God not in himself only, but also in the objective course and structure of the Revelation, in the actual manifestations of the Deity in past and present humanity, and in the ideal anticipation of other, more perfect manifestations in the future. In all this, no doubt, there is something fated, predetermined, independent of each man's personal will, and yet individual freedom is preserved, for everyone is free to use or not to use *for himself* the universal religious heritage of mankind, to enter or not to enter with his own living powers into the organic development of the Kingdom of God. In any case, the latter is not confined to the subjective moral world of separate individuals, but has its own objective reality, its own universal forms and laws, and develops through a complex historical process in which separate persons play partly an active and partly a passive part. Hence the vital significance of the visible church as a formal institution symbolizing, and to a certain extent realizing, the universal whole in which separate persons participate, into which they enter, but which is certainly not formed by an arithmetical summation of them or their mechanical mass. The collective divinely-human process presupposes and includes our personal moral acts, but is not made up of them — and it is its objectively organic and super-personal (though not impersonal) character that renders possible the *suddenness* (to us) of its final results, directly indicated in the Gospel. Of course, this suddenness is merely relative and perfectly compatible with the continuous and predetermined development of the divinely-human organism; in purely physical development, too, inwardly prepared critical moments manifest themselves outwardly with the same kind of suddenness. A seed that has filled out and germinated in the ground suddenly thrusts out its shoot above the surface, and a ripe fruit falls to the ground as suddenly; in a similar way the chief phases of God's Kingdom come suddenly, but *in the fulness of time*, i.e. as necessarily prepared by the foregoing process. The suddenness does not therefore exclude but, on the contrary, presupposes the active participation of individual forces in the general development of the Kingdom of God.

Thus the apparent contradictions between the inward and the outward character of God's Kingdom and between the gradual and the sudden realization of it disappear of themselves with the true understanding of the case. As existing for us, the Kingdom of God must be our own spiritual state, namely, a state of inner union with God. Such union reached its individual perfection in the person of the God-man Christ, and revealed itself in Him as super-individual. A true *union with another* cannot be merely a subjective state; the union of the whole man with God cannot be merely personal. The divine or heavenly Kingdom cannot be simply a psychological fact: it is, first and foremost, the eternal and objective truth of positive universal unity. Such unity is latent in the natural man too — in the social character of his life, in the all-embracing nature of his reason; it is present, but not realized, set as a task, but not given as a fact. The fulness of existence perfectly united with God through the Son of Man is the absolute ideal, the realization of which began and continues in the world's history as humanity's common and universal task; all work for it unconsciously and involuntarily, but to participate in it freely and consciously is the morally social duty of every enlightened Christian. In this aspect of it the Kingdom of God is constituted not by a simple act of the soul's union with God, but by a complex and all-embracing process — by the spiritually-physical growth and development of the all-inclusive divinely-human organism in the world. Like all organic growth it presupposes not merely quantitative continuity (implied in the crude idea of accumulating the requisite number of righteous souls for the heavenly Kingdom) but also qualitative discreteness of forms and degrees. Although the higher of those forms necessarily presuppose the lower, and are prepared by them (in the order of genesis), they cannot possibly be wholly deduced from the lower and therefore appear as something new and miraculous.

Once the central idea of true Christianity has been defined, it is easy to detect and show up various counterfeits of it prevalent at the present day. We will note only the most important and the most pernicious of them.

Since the Kingdom of God comes not as a *Deus ex machina*, but is conditioned by the cosmic and historical divinely-human process in which God acts only with and through man, the view that man plays a merely passive part in the divine work must be recognized as a crude counterfeit of Christianity. It is said that man's whole duty with regard to the Kingdom of God consists, on the one hand, in slavishly submitting to the given divine facts (in the visible church) and on the other in waiting inactively for the future final revelation of the Kingdom of glory — and meanwhile devoting all his activity to pagan and secular interests which are not regarded as in any way connected with the work of God. For appearances' sake the view in question is supported by the argument that God is everything and man is nothing. But in truth this false humility is rebellion against God, for He loved and magnified humanity in Christ, from whom Christians must not sever themselves: 'to them gave He power to become sons of God'. Sons of the kingdom of freedom are called to conscious and independent co-operation in the work of the Father. The fact that some of them are not yet spiritually of age must be taken into consideration, but not raised to the rank of a final and universal principle.

The champions of this counterfeit Christianity compare God's activity in gathering together and building up His Kingdom — that is, His participation in the growth and development of the divinely-human organism — to the manifestations of His omnipotence in the phenomena of nature and events of cosmic life. But in doing so they involve themselves in an inner contradiction which betrays the fallaciousness of their position. If they think that they must not actively interfere in the destinies of God's Kingdom because it is dependent upon His will, they must not interfere in anything, for everything depends upon God's will. And yet they devote all their energies and enthusiasm to arranging all kinds of secular affairs, personal, national and so on. Why this difference of attitude? Why do they consider it necessary to help the Almighty God so zealously in their insignificant little affairs, but do not want to help Him in His great work? Clearly because they are interested in their own concerns but not in His. God's work is not *their* affair and so they do not care about it. But Christianity wholly consists in the fact that God's work has become the work of man also. This unity between God and man *is* the Kingdom of God, which comes only in so far as it is realized. Obviously those pseudo-quietists preach a false Christianity. They serve mammon the more actively in practice, the more passively they submit themselves, in theory, to another Master. His greatness and holiness are to them merely a convenient pretext for not thinking of Him at all.

This counterfeit Christianity is generally connected with denying all progress and development in the Christian religion. It is a fact that many believers in evolution adopt a one-sided and mechanistic interpretation of it, excluding the action of the higher power and all teleology; it is also a fact that many preachers of historical progress understand by it man's endless increase in perfection without God and contrary to God. From this an obviously absurd conclusion is hastily drawn that the very ideas of development and progress are somehow atheistic and anti-Christian. In truth, however, those ideas are specifically Christian (or, more exactly, Judæo-Christian); they were first brought into men's minds by the prophets of Israel and the

Evangelists. Both the Eastern and the Western paganism in its highest expressions — Buddhism and Neo-platonism — put absolute perfection completely outside the historical process which was for them either an endless and purposeless series of accidental changes or a gradual change for the worse. Only the Christian (or, what is the same thing, the Messianic) idea of the Kingdom of God gradually revealing itself in the life of mankind gives meaning to history and determines the true conception of progress. Christianity reveals to mankind not only the ideal of absolute perfection but also the way to attain it, and therefore it is essentially progressive. Consequently, every view which denies this progressive element in Christianity is a counterfeit concealing a pagan attitude under a Christian guise. Its purpose — not, of course, always a conscious one — is to draw men away from God's work and to confirm them in the bad worldly reality abolished by Christ, who overcame the world. Meanwhile, the supposed Christians are attempting, though vainly, to wrest from Christ His victory, by doing their best to support secular laws and institutions which have nothing in common with the Kingdom of God. There is no place for such a conservative attitude in true, genuine Christianity, to which both conservatism and radicalism as such are essentially foreign. From the standpoint of the Christian religion neither the preservation nor the destruction of any secular institutions can *in itself* be of value. If we care about building up the Kingdom of God, we must accept that which is worthy to serve our cause, and reject that which is opposed to it. We must be guided in this not by the dead criterion of some abstract *-ism* but, in accordance with St. Paul, by the living criterion of the mind of Christ — if we have it in us; and if we have not, we had better not call ourselves Christians. In truth those who bear that name must be concerned, not with preserving and strengthening *at all costs* the existing social forms and groups in secular Christianity, but with regenerating and transforming them in the Christian spirit as far as possible and actually bringing them into the sphere of God's Kingdom.

And so, the idea of the Kingdom of God necessarily brings us (that is, every sincere and conscientious Christian) to the duty of doing what we can for realizing Christian principles in the collective life of mankind and transforming all our social institutions and relations in the spirit of the higher truth. In other words, it leads us to *Christian politics*. At this point we come across a fresh counterfeit of Christianity or, rather, to a new modification of the old anti-Christian reactionism in a Christian mask. Christian politics, they say, is a *contradictio in adjecto*, Christianity and politics can have nothing in common: *My Kingdom is not of this world*, etc. But the fact that Christ's Kingdom is not of this world by no means implies that it cannot act in the world, gain possession of it and rule it.

... In accordance with sound logic it follows, on the contrary, that just because Christ's Kingdom is not of the world but *from above*, it has a right to possess and govern the world. It must be one or the other: societies that call themselves Christian must either renounce that name, or they must recognize it as their duty to harmonize all their political and social relations with Christian principles, i.e. to bring them into the sphere of God's Kingdom — and this is precisely in what true Christian politics consist.

If, as the champions of pseudo-Christian individualism assert, all social and political institutions are alien and even contrary to Christianity, true Christians ought to live without any such institutions. But this is an obvious absurdity disproved by their own life and activity. If, however, social and political forms of life cannot be abolished (for that would be equivalent to abolishing man as a social and political being), and if, on the other hand, they are as yet far from embodying Christian principles, it clearly follows that the task of Christian politics is to perfect these forms and transmute them into realities fit for the Kingdom of God.

3

THE IDEA
OF HUMANITY

FROM the philosophical and historical standpoint we are
. . . bound to recognize in the French Revolution something
of value which justifies it and gives it its ideal significance and
attractive force — namely, the declaration of the *rights of man*.
Speaking generally, this was nothing new, since all human rights
are contained, of course, in the power given to men to become
the sons of God, as proclaimed in the Gospel (John i. 12). But,
speaking purely historically, the declaration of the natural rights
of man was new not only with regard to the ancient and the
mediæval world but also to Europe after the Reformation, whose
champions, just like their opponents, completely forgot that man
had inalienable rights. The French Protestants who suffered from
the dragonnades of Louis XIV could not protest against them on
the ground of principle, for so far as the most essential of human
rights was concerned, the freedom of religious convictions, that
king was of one mind with their own teacher and law-giver
Calvin, though more powerful and less resolute than the latter.
Calvin at the first opportunity calmly burnt at the stake an
innocent and distinguished man for disagreeing with him about
the Trinitarian dogma.

The principle of human rights was extremely important and
new for the whole world at that time.

. . . The two sides of the French Revolution — first, the declaration of the rights of man, and then their unheard-of systematic violation by the revolutionary powers — are not a merely
accidental contradiction, not merely an inability to realize the
principle in practice. No, a profound foundation for this duality
is contained in the declaration itself, owing to the addition of one
single word: the rights of man and *citizen*. At first sight it seems

an innocent and even a reasonable addition. Human rights cannot
be realized without civic rights. At the historical level reached
long ago every man is, among other things, a citizen, just as he is a
member of a family, of his church, his party, school and so on.
All these partial definitions are very important, but there is
nothing 'self-defining' in them, nothing which *in itself* could be
the basis of essentially inalienable rights. The conception of the
rights of man was valuable just because it indicated something
inalienable from the subject of rights — something unconditional, from which all the demands of justice could be deduced
with the inner necessity of formal logic. But the pernicious terms
'civil' and 'citizen', confusing the categories and putting the
conditional on the same level with the unconditional, spoiled the
whole thing.

. . . Being a citizen is in itself merely a positive right which
may, as such, be taken away without any inner contradiction.
But being a man is not a conditional right — it is an essentially
inalienable property; it alone, as the primary basis of all rights,
can make them inalienable in principle and unconditionally condemn their violation or arbitrary limitation. So long as the determining principle is one — the rights of *man* — the rights of all
are secure and inviolable, for it is impossible to declare that men
of such and such a race, or religion, or class are not human. But
as soon as we put alongside of the natural primary basis of all
rights an artificial one, citizenship, there open up wide possibilities of declaring this or that group of men to be in a special
position as citizens, or rather, as *not*-citizens, and of depriving them
of all human rights under the pretext that those rights belong to
citizens only. Thus raising 'citizenship' into an *independent*
principle alongside of 'humanity' proves to be fatal to the universality of civic rights. The French Revolution has the merit of
extending civic rights to large groups of people who had been
half or altogether deprived of them in pre-revolutionary France
— to the serfs, to the Protestants and the Jews. But by giving up
the pure and clear principle of building the work of liberation on
its unconditional ground (the dignity of the human being as
such) and by adding to it the conditional and indefinite conception of 'a good citizen', the revolution opened the door to all
kinds of savagery in the future. And indeed during the revolutionary period itself all those multitudes of human victims,
drowned, massacred and guillotined, suffered not, of course,

because they ceased to be human beings, but because they were declared to be bad citizens, bad patriots, 'traitors'.

... The two principles, 'man' and 'citizen', were put side by side, with no connection between them, instead of the second being subordinated to the first; and naturally the lower, as more concrete and obvious, proved to be the stronger. In practice it soon replaced the higher, and afterwards swallowed it up altogether — for executing a citizen inevitably meant killing the man as well.

The savagery of the revolutionary terror rested, in principle, on the declaration of rights — namely, on the addition of the words 'and citizen'; but that addition could not have been due either to an accidental mistake or to a direct evil intention — it must have had some inner basis or meaning. And indeed it followed from the just and natural, though falsely understood and (owing to historical conditions) wrongly applied feeling that man taken as an isolated individual was *insufficient* to be *actually* the unconditional bearer of human rights — he could not make them real.

The best people responsible for the great revolution understood, or at any rate felt, the inner infinitude and autonomy of the individual human being, but they also understood, or felt, that in itself man's infinite significance is merely a *possibility*, and that to make it actual the individual must have something added to him — something actually higher and more powerful than himself. What, then, is this fuller reality bestowing actual fulness of life on the individual? Classical antiquity that had long been idealized owing to the intellectual reaction against mediæval theocracy pointed to *citizenship*, the state, the fatherland; the only change introduced in the course of modern history was that the idea of the highest political whole came to be associated with the people or the nation instead of with a city. National patriotism, which first powerfully asserted itself in the fifteenth century on semi-religious grounds in the person of Joan of Arc, became more and more 'secularized' in the succeeding centuries, and was finally established in its purely secular and even pagan form by the French Revolution.

It is only as the citizen of his state, the son of his fatherland, that the individual was supposed to become fully and really a man. Auguste Comte is the first to deserve the honour and merit of

not being satisfied with this clear and well-looking conclusion.
For a man who believes in the Heavenly Father there is, of course,
no special honour or merit in refusing to replace Him by earthly
fatherland; but Comte did not believe in the one Almighty God.
Nor did he believe in the absolute significance of the human individual as such; but in seeking for his real complement he did not
stop at the collective whole which exists concretely and obviously
and is recognized by all — he did not stop at the national unity.
He was one of the first and the few to understand that the nation
in its actual empirical reality is essentially relative, and that although it is always more powerful and physically longer-lived
than an individual, it is by no means always more valuable in the
spiritual sense. Who, for instance, came nearer to the true fulness
of human dignity — Socrates in his righteousness and outer
impotence, or the Athenian state in its inner unrighteousness
triumphing over him through brute force? And if, in spite of his
lofty personal dignity, even Socrates taken in his separateness was
not a complete or perfect man, if he too needed completion, it
was certainly not from his city state or his people — who merely
filled him a cup of poison — but from something other than it.

It is a still greater merit and glory of Comte's that he indicated
more clearly, fully and decisively than any of his predecessors
that 'something other' — the collective whole which in its inner
essence, and not merely externally, surpasses every individual
man and actually completes him, both ideally and really: he
indicated *humanity* as a living positive unity embracing us, as
pre-eminently 'the Great Being' — *le Grand Être*.

The idea of humanity would have been neither new nor interesting if Comte meant by that term an abstract generic notion, or
the actual totality of human units.

What he had in mind, however, was not an abstract notion and
not an empirical aggregate, but an actual living being. With the
courage of genius he went further and said that an individual man
by himself or taken separately is merely an abstraction and that in
reality he does not and cannot exist. And of course Comte was
right.

No one denies the reality of the elementary terms of geometry
— point, line, surface and, finally, volume or a stereometrical
figure, i.e. a geometrical body. All this really exists and we
operate with it all both in science and in life. But in what sense

do we ascribe reality to those geometrical elements? If we think at all clearly, we see that they exist not in their separateness, but solely in definite relation to one another and that their reality entirely consists in this relatedness.

The whole is prior to its parts and is presupposed by them. This great truth, obvious in geometry, retains its full force in sociology as well.

. . . The reality of the component parts cannot be denied, but they are real only in their connection with the whole — taken separately, they are mere abstractions. According to his connection with the whole, a separate individual — the sociological point — may have far more significance than many families, nations and even races, and the same thing may be true of a geometrical point: the centre of a sphere, a single point, is far more important than all other points, and even than all the lines, in that body; and thus, for example, the person of Socrates in its great universal meaning immeasurably excels not only the line of his family but the whole surface of the Athenian city-state. And yet he could have had no actual existence at all apart from his family and his state, which in its turn could not exist by itself apart from the life of humanity.

According to a true and profound remark of Comte's, all the sophisms advanced by unsystematic or reactionary thought against the real being of humanity are self-destructive. They presuppose the standpoint of exclusive individualism which cannot be consistently thought out; the very language in which they are expressed reveals their absurdity, since language is unquestionably something supra-individual.

'The Great Being' contains in itself (not as a sum but as a living unity or actual wholeness) all beings that freely co-operate in perfecting the world-order.

. . . In so far as the Great Being cannot be observed by the outer senses or be the subject of mathematical calculations, it is, according to Comte, an object of faith, but of faith necessarily connected with the whole of scientific knowledge.

Humanity as a full and living reality is recognized by Comte as a positive fact to which the whole system of scientific knowledge

can be finally reduced. 'Careful study of the world-order', he
says, 'reveals to us the pre-eminent existence in it of a real Great
Being which, as destined continually to perfect that order and
make it conform to itself, represents in the best possible way its
true nature. This indubitable Providence, the arbiter of our fate,
necessarily becomes the common centre of our feelings, thoughts
and actions.'

The Great Being of Comte's religion, in addition to its complete reality, power and wisdom which make it our Providence,
has another permanent characteristic: it is a feminine being. This
is not a metaphor or a personification of an impersonal idea, as
in classical mythology which represents virtues, arts and sciences
in the form of women. Comte's own words make it sufficiently
clear that the Great Being was no abstract idea for him. He clearly
distinguished between humanity as the sum of national, family
and personal elements (that was *humanité* with a small *h*) and
Humanity as the essential, actual and living principle of the unity
of all those elements (*Humanité* with a capital *H* or *le Grand Être*).
And in this main sense Humanity though collective in its make-up
is in itself more than a collective noun and has an existence of
its own.

An analogy at once suggests itself between Comte's religion of
humanity represented by the Great Being of feminine gender,
and the mediæval cult of the Madonna. A curious coincidence
should also be noted. At the very time when in Paris Comte was
proclaiming his religion which exalts the feminine, affective
principle in human nature and morality, in Rome the thousand-
year-old cult of the Madonna found its theological culmination
in the dogmatic definition by Pope Pius IX about the Immaculate
Conception of the Blessed Virgin (1854).

. . . But the ancient cult of the eternal feminine has one historic
expression about which Comte could not have known anything
whatever and which nevertheless lies closer to the heart of the
matter and to his ideas.

A thorough Westerner, Auguste Comte would have been very
much surprised at being told and shown that the idea formulated
by him as the *Grand Être* had been expressed with particular certainty and vividness, though without any clear understanding, by
the religious inspiration of the Russian people as early as the

eleventh century. The central conception of his 'positive religion' stands for the aspect of Christianity that had ages before been keenly felt, if not clearly apprehended, by the Russian mind; and that feeling or presentiment, though scarcely thought out, at once found for itself an appropriate artistic expression.

If Comte had happened to visit a certain derelict old town in Russia he would have seen with his own eyes a true image of his *Grand Être*, more complete and exact than those he had seen in the West.

. . . The most remarkable thing about it is that the actual subject of the picture is represented *together* with the figures of beings that are akin to it and are generally confused with it — but is represented in such a way that it is completely distinct from them and no confusion is possible.

The centre of the chief ikon in the ancient Novgorod cathedral (of the times of Yaroslav the Wise[1]) is occupied by a peculiar feminine figure in royal vestment, seated on a throne. Facing it and slightly bending towards it are, on the right, Our Lady of the Byzantine type, and, on the left, St. John the Baptist; Christ with uplifted arms is seen to rise above the seated figure, and above Christ there is the heavenly world represented by several angels surrounding the divine Word symbolized by the book of the Gospels.

Who, then, is the chief, central and royal figure, manifestly distinct from Christ, and from Our Lady, and from the angels? The ikon is called the ikon of Sophia, the divine Wisdom. But what does that mean? As early as the fourteenth century a certain Russian nobleman asked this question of the archbishop of Novgorod, but received no answer — the archbishop said he did not know. And yet our ancestors worshipped this mysterious being as the Athenians once worshipped 'the unknown god', built Sophian temples and cathedrals, appointed the day and the order of church service for celebration, in which Sophia, the divine Wisdom, approximates now to Christ, now to Our Lady, thus not admitting of complete identification either with Him or with Her — for, clearly, if the Wisdom were Christ, she could not be Our Lady, and if she were Our Lady, she could not be Christ.

Our ancestors did not receive this idea from the Greeks, for in

[1] Eleventh century.—*Ed.*

Byzantium, according to all the testimony in our possession, the divine Wisdom, ἡ Σοφία τοῦθεοῦ, was either taken to mean the general abstract property of the Deity or was synonymous with the eternal Word of God, the Logos. The ikon of Sophia in Novgorod has no Greek prototype — it is the work of our own religious creativeness. Its meaning was unknown to the four-teenth-century bishops, but we can divine it now.

This great, royal and feminine Being, which is not God, not the eternal Son of God, not an angel, not a saint, but receives homage both from the last representative of the Old Testament and the progenetrix of the New, is no other than the true, pure and perfect humanity, the highest and all-embracing form and the living soul of nature and of the universe, united to God from all eternity and in the temporal process attaining union with Him and uniting to Him all that is. There is no doubt that this is the real meaning of the Great Being, partly felt and understood by Comte, and fully felt but not at all understood by our ancestors, the pious builders of Sophian temples.

... The founder of the 'positive religion' understood by humanity a being which becomes absolute through universal progress. And humanity is indeed such a being. But Comte, like many other thinkers, failed to see that an absolute which is be-coming in time presupposes an absolute which eternally is, or else the process of 'becoming' absolute (from being not-absolute) would be a self-transformation of the lesser into the greater, or the appearance of something from nothing, i.e. pure nonsense. There is no need to raise the philosophical problem of the rela-tivity of time in order to see that one can only become absolute through assimilating that which eternally and essentially *is* absolute. With the instinct of truth Comte ascribed a feminine character to the Great Being. As standing midway between the relative and the absolute, as participating in both, it is by nature the principle of duality, ἡ ἀόριστος δυάς of the Pythagoreans — the most general ontological definition of femininity. Humanity is the highest form in and through which all that is becomes absolute — the form of union between material nature and the divine. The Great Being is universal nature as *receptive* of the divine — this is another reason for ascribing a feminine character to it.

It is clear that true humanity, as the cosmic form of the union of material nature with the Deity, or the form in which nature is receptive of the Deity, is inevitably deified humanity and deified matter. It cannot be *simply* humanity, for that would mean a receptacle without a content, form without matter or an empty form.

The Great Being is not an empty form but an all-embracing divinely-human fulness of the spiritual and material, divine and created life, revealed to us in Christianity. Comte's conception of the true Great Being was incomplete and not fully thought out or expressed, but he implicitly believed in its completeness and bore witness to it in spite of himself. But how many believing Christians, both past and present, have never known, or wanted to know, this very essence of Christianity which, though only half understood by him, inspired wholehearted devotion in the godless infidel — Comte!

4

THE COLLAPSE OF THE MEDIÆVAL WORLD-CONCEPTION

By the term 'mediæval world-conception' I designate, for shortness, the historical compromise between Christianity and paganism — the half-pagan, half-Christian order of thought and of life that grew up and became predominant in the Middle Ages, both in the Romano-Germanic West and in the Byzantine East.

Usually both the opponents and the champions of the mediæval world-conception take it for Christianity itself, or at any rate believe that the connection between them is as indissoluble as that between content and form. I think it is useful and important to make it clear that far from being identical with Christianity, the mediæval world-conception is in some ways the very opposite of it. That will help to show that the failure of the mediæval order of thought is due not to Christianity, but to the distortion of it, and that this failure presents no danger whatever to true Christianity.

I

The essence of true Christianity is the regeneration of mankind and the world in the spirit of Christ, the transformation of the kingdom of this world into the Kingdom of God (which is not of this world). This regeneration is a long and complex process; it is with good reason that in the Gospel itself it is compared to the growth of a tree, the ripening of the harvest, the leavening of bread and so on. But, of course, the Christian regeneration of humanity cannot be merely a natural process or take place of itself by means of unconscious movements and changes. It is a spiritual process ('verily, verily I say unto thee: except a man be born of water and the spirit he cannot enter into the Kingdom of

God'); it is necessary that humanity itself should take part in it with its own powers and consciousness. The fundamental and essential difference between our faith and other Eastern religions, especially Islam, is that Christianity, as a divinely-human religion, presupposes divine action, but requires at the same time activity on the part of man. In this sense the realization of the Kingdom of God depends not only upon God but upon us as well, since clearly the spiritual regeneration of humanity cannot take place apart from man himself, cannot be simply an external fact; it is a *work* entrusted to us, a *problem* which we must solve. It is equally clear that we cannot at once, by a single act, even grasp the whole significance of that problem, to say nothing of solving it. Even an individual is not converted and regenerated all of a sudden. Take Christ's immediate disciples. They, if anyone, had every chance of rapid and complete spiritual regeneration; and yet we see no such regeneration throughout the Saviour's earthly life, and not, indeed, until Pentecost. They remain such as they were. Christ's coming deeply affected them. His spiritual power attracted and attached them to Him, but it did not regenerate them. They believed in Him as in a fact of higher order and expected that He would establish God's Kingdom *as also an external fact*. It is precisely with reference to them — the elect, the salt of the earth — that we can best see how small is the significance of faith in the Divine as an external supernatural fact. It is certainly not accidental that the famous sixteenth chapter of St. Matthew places side by side the greatest praise of Peter for his fervent confession of the true faith and the words addressed to the same Peter: 'Get thee behind me, Satan; thou art an offence unto me: for thou savourest not the things that be of God, but those that be of men.' That means, one may have the most zealous, fervent and right faith, and yet not have the Spirit of God but resemble Satan — for it is said in another passage of the New Testament that 'the devils also believe and tremble'. The more fervent and uncompromising are the external expressions of such faith, the more contrary it is to the Spirit of Christ and the less inner power and stability there is in it. It is with good reason, too, that the Gospels tell the story of how that same fervent disciple struck off the ear of the high priest's servant in defence of his Master and then that same night denied Him thrice. To ascribe these defects of Peter's faith to his personal character is the same as to put the whole blame — as we generally do — for pseudo-Christian fanaticism and violence on to the Roman Catholic Church of which St. Peter is considered to be the prototype. But something similar is told in the Gospel about Christ's beloved disciple John — the prototype, as some people think, of our Eastern Orthodoxy:

'And John answered and said, Master, we saw one casting out devils in thy name; and we forbade him, because he followeth not with us. And Jesus said unto him, Forbid him not: for he that is not against us is for us.

'And it came to pass, when the time was come that He should be received up, He steadfastly set his face to go to Jerusalem, and sent messengers before His face: and they went, and entered into a village of the Samaritans, to make ready for Him. And they did not receive Him, because His face was as though He would go to Jerusalem. And when His disciples James and John saw this, they said, Lord, wilt thou that we command fire to come down from heaven and consume them, even as Elias did? But He turned and rebuked them, and said, Ye know not what manner of spirit ye are of. For the Son of man is not come to destroy men's lives but to save them. And they went to another village' (Luke ix. 49–56).

If faith were the chief thing, there could be, one would think, no stronger faith than that of men who are prepared at once, without the slightest doubt, to bring down fire from heaven; and yet, with such apparently great faith, James and John did not know the spirit of Christ, and they did not know it just because they believed above all in His external miraculous power. Such power was there, but it was not the essential thing.

II

Only after an external parting did the spirit of Christ inwardly possess and regenerate them. It also took possession of that first commune of the faithful in Jerusalem who in the Acts of the Apostles are said to have had one heart and one mind. But the Church in the broad sense, Christian mankind as a whole, had not yet attained to its Pentecost; its relation to Christ was as external as was that of the apostles during His life on earth — it too had not yet learned to think in God's way or to know of what spirit it was. The more widely the teaching about the new, spiritual Adam spread in the pagan world, the more resilient and resistant the old carnal Adam proved to be. The apostle's Epistles to the different churches are distinctly *denunciatory* in character; in those first Christian communities special spiritual gifts co-existed with crying offences (see St. Paul's Epistles to the Corinthians).

The well-established and widely prevalent conception that the pre-Constantine epoch was a period of ideal purity and the golden age of Christianity can only be accepted with considerable reservations. There was, of course, a difference, but there was no complete contrast between the first three centuries and those that followed. Speaking generally, even at that time the majority of Christians regarded the Kingdom of God in a purely external way and awaited it as a miraculous cosmic catastrophe which might take place any day. But however crude such an attitude might be, the expectation of an impending end of the world on the one hand and the still more immediate possibility of martyrdom on the other kept the Christians of that day at a relatively high spiritual level and did not allow practical materialism to gain the upper hand. Of course, persecutions were not a matter of everyday occurrence. There were no absolutely universal persecutions throughout the Roman Empire; widely spread persecutions lasted a very short time: most persecutions were local and accidental. But there were Roman laws on the strength of which Christianity could be persecuted as a criminal offence against the state, and consequently the *possibility* of martyrdom menaced Christians always and everywhere and imparted a tragic and purifying character to their lives. The important advantage of the early ages as compared with the later was that Christians could be and sometimes were persecuted, but could not in any case be persecutors. Altogether it was far more dangerous than advantageous to belong to the new religion, and therefore as a rule only the best people embraced it with sincere conviction and enthusiasm. Even if the life of the Church in those days was not wholly permeated by the spirit of Christ, the highest religious and moral motives predominated in it. There actually existed amidst the pagan world a truly Christian community, far from perfect, but at any rate governed by a different and a better principle of life.

From this point of view the end of persecutions and the official recognition of the new religion as, first, having full rights, and then as the dominant religion of the state certainly made an important change for the worse. Under Constantine the Great and

Constantius pagan masses adopted Christianity wholesale not from conviction but from slavish imitation or self-interest. There appeared a type of feigned Christians, hypocrites, that had not existed before. It multiplied further when under Theodosius and, finally, under Justinian paganism was legally suppressed and every subject of the Græco-Roman Empire, with the exception of a scattered handful of half-tolerated Jews, was compelled to be a Christian under the threat of severe penalties. Between this newly formed type of Christians by compulsion and out of fear, and the remaining type of true Christians by profound conviction there were, of course, many gradations of superficial and indifferent Christians. But they were all without distinction covered by the general organization of the Church as a formal institution in which all the categories of inner worth were effaced and confused. The former truly Christian community was merged with the mass that was Christian in name but pagan in reality. The overwhelming majority of superficial, indifferent and feigned Christians not merely preserved in practice pagan principles of life under a Christian name, but tried in every way — partly instinctively and partly consciously — to establish the old pagan order beside Christianity, to perpetuate and legalize it, deliberately ruling out the problem of renewing it from within in the spirit of Christ. That was how the first foundations were laid of the compromise between Christianity and paganism which determined mediæval thought and life.

III

I am not speaking of the *actual* compromise between the absolute truth and our reality. The whole of our life, past, present and future, right to the end of history is, at each given stage of it, an actual compromise between the higher ideal principle that is being realized in the world and the material environment which does not correspond to it. When the ideal is fully realized there will be an end of all compromise, but it will also be an end of history and of the whole world-process. While there is any imperfection in the world, that means there is a compromise between the opposing principles, for imperfection is nothing other than an actual *concession* of the higher to the lower. True striving after perfection merely demands that the ideal principle should penetrate deeper and deeper into the environment which is opposed to it and possess it more and more fully.

If there is struggle and victory, effort and improvement, if the absolute ideal is not rejected or forgotten but remains the inner inspiration and the final end of action, compromise with the existing environment is merely an external necessity and not an inner falsehood. It implies no dual faith to reckon with bad reality as a fact does not mean to believe in it; to make temporary concessions to it in small things in order to abolish it finally in the large does not mean to worship it. Curing disease may perhaps also be a compromise, and straight-laced moralists denounce it; but Christ has sanctified it by His example.

When, however, the pagan world accepted Christianity, it was a question not of the inevitable compromise with facts, but of compromise with principles. The majority of the new converts wanted everything to remain as before. They acknowledged the truth of Christianity as an external fact and entered into certain formal and external relations with it, but only on condition that their life should be pagan as before, that the secular kingdom should remain secular and the Kingdom of God, being not of this world, should remain outside the world, without any vital influence upon it, i.e. should remain as a useless ornament, as a mere appendix to the secular kingdom. But surely Christ came into the world in order to save it and not to enrich secular life by a few novel ceremonies. By His death and resurrection He saved the world in principle, at the root, at the centre, but it is only together with mankind that He can spread that salvation to the whole circumference of human and cosmic life and realize the principle of salvation in the whole of our reality, for no one can be really saved without his own knowledge and consent. True salvation is regeneration or a new birth; but new birth presupposes the death of the old false life — and no one wants to die. Before deciding to accept true salvation as its own task, its own heroic endeavour, the pagan world wanted to try the easy, cheap salvation, salvation through dead faith and works of piety — *works* and not work; outer performance was meant. But true Christianity, however, is first and foremost *work* — the work of life for humanity; works come later. But work is difficult, and works are easy; and the easiest of all is abstract faith in incomprehensible objects, i.e. in one's own verbal confession of such faith. It was in this form that Christianity was accepted by the masses.

3

Of course, even in the first three centuries Christianity was not clearly and definitely recognized as a morally-historical, universally human task, but all the same it was then a life-long work for all: to prepare oneself for martyrdom and for the impending end of the world was not easy. But now martyrdom ceased altogether, and the end of the world receded more and more into the background. There was no occasion either to die for Christ or to prepare for His second coming. Both His first and second coming — the centre and the end of the cosmic process — lost their vital significance, became an object of abstract faith. The limits between the divine past and the divine future moved far apart, and human life which should be an active continuation of the one and an active preparation for the other, retained all its material senselessness and inertia. To preserve that pagan life as it was, merely anointing it with Christianity from outside — that was the real desire of those pseudo-Christians who had no need to shed their own blood, but had already begun to shed the blood of others.

It is the essence of religion that its truth is not abstractly theoretical, but is affirmed as the *norm of reality*, as the law of life. If, for instance, I believe not merely verbally but in fact in the Trinity of Godhead as a religious truth, I must understand and accept its vital moral meaning. All our dogmas have such a meaning, and at first this was clearly felt in the Christian world, even if not fully understood.

IV

I will not expound here my view of the vital significance of the fundamental truths of Christianity and more especially of the truth of the tri-unity of Godhead and the divinely-human nature of Christ. . . . The point at issue can be explained by reference to another, a more simple religion. The doctrine of Islam is rather poor in content, but that limited religion is fully realized in the life of the Moslem world. The conception of God as a single *exclusive power* is distinctly one-sided, but it determines the whole Mohammedan order of life: to the one despot in heaven there corresponds one despot on earth. Theoretical denial of the freedom of will and, generally speaking, of the independence of the human principle is in full harmony with the fatalism and quietism characteristic of the Moslem attitude to life.

The Christian teaching in contradistinction to Islam contains the fulness of truth. But that truth is not completely realized (and indeed cannot be till the end of the world) and, besides, the actual task of realizing it is rejected by the pseudo-Christians — who thus reject the very meaning of Christianity. The meaning of Christianity lies in transforming human life in accordance with the truths of faith. This is what justifying faith by works means. But if that life was left under the old pagan law, if the very idea of radically transforming and regenerating it was set aside, the truths of the Christian faith were thereby deprived of their meaning and significance as norms of reality and the law of life, and retained only their abstractly theoretical content. And, since that content is not understandable to many, the truths of faith became binding dogma, i.e. conventional symbols of ecclesiastical unity and obedience to spiritual authorities. But at the same time it was impossible to abandon the idea that Christianity is the *religion of salvation*. And so the illegitimate union of the idea of salvation with church dogmatism gave birth to the monstrous doctrine that the only means to salvation was faith in dogma, and that apart from it one could not be saved. Fortunately, besides the dogma there still remained the sacraments as a kind of addition to them. Although the true meaning of sacraments was partly forgotten and partly undeveloped, this essential element of Christianity had at any rate the advantage of being universally accessible. The most rabid champion of right belief could not expect a baby correctly to confess the dogma of the union of the two natures in Christ without division or confusion, or to anathematize Nestorius or Eutyches. For a baby baptism was sufficient. And what if the baby died before it was baptized? Then there was nothing for it — all was over, there was no salvation. Tender souls invented for such babies various limbos at the portals of hell. As to the conscious unbelievers and heretics, they were inured to the eternal torments of hell by means of temporal torments beforehand. To this terrible extent did the apostles' successors carry out the prophetic words of Christ: 'ye know not what spirit ye are of'!

V

And yet in the midst of this perverted Christianity there were men who did not substitute the dead and mortifying dogmatism for the living and life-giving truth; there were men for whom

Christianity remained their life-work. Without such true Christians the mediæval system could not have persisted so long or manifested the spiritual life which we actually find in it. Why, then, did they not save and regenerate it? They did not and could not save the Christian *society*, the Christian *world*, because in spite of all their righteousness and holiness they mistakenly believed that individual souls alone could and ought to be saved. They attained their purpose: they saved their own and many other souls, while the world from which they had severed themselves and escaped remained out of reach and followed its own course.

From the time that the truly Christian community of the first centuries was dissolved in the pagan environment and took its colouring from it, the very idea of sociality disappeared from the minds of even the best Christians. They left public life entirely to ecclesiastical and secular authorities, and set themselves solely the task of individual salvation. They had, of course, the excuse that the authorities too were Christian in name and therefore could and ought to impart a Christian character to public life. But the point is that all authorities are first and foremost *conservative* and do not undertake of their own initiative any radical changes — except in such unusual cases as that of Peter the Great. A government is after all the progeny of society and is organically connected with it, and if the society of the Græco-Roman Empire and of Romano-Germanic Europe was predominantly pagan in character the state had no incentive to trouble about ordering public life in a Christian spirit. That task, of course, belongs more to the province of the ecclesiastical authorities; but in the West the Church was so busy defending its rights against the state that it forgot more and more about its duties, and in the East it had no independent position at all. The contrast between the *paganism of the cities* and the *Christianity of the desert* was particularly marked in the East. With the sole exception of St. John Chrysostom the preaching of the Eastern ascetics was not concerned with any Christian reforms of social life. Not a single definite demand for that is to be found in the whole of Byzantine history. It is not surprising that the state and its laws remained as pagan as the social customs and morals. It is not surprising that the Code of Justinian is at bottom the code of the pagan Roman Empire merely seasoned with Christian phrases. In the West things were slightly better. There were striking instances of striving for a Christian social morality, beginning with the protest of St.

Martin of Tours and St. Ambrose of Milan against the institution of capital punishment and ending with the activity of Gregory VII. But, on the whole, here too the church authorities' efforts in this direction were not sufficiently insistent and successful to counteract the effect of examples set by those same authorities in quite the opposite direction.

VI

In limiting the work of salvation to personal life, pseudo-Christian individualism was bound to renounce not only the world in the narrow sense of society and public life, but the world in the broad sense of material nature as a whole. In its one-sided spiritualism the mediæval world-conception came into direct conflict with the very basis of Christianity. Christianity is the religion of divine incarnation and the resurrection of the flesh, but it was transformed into a kind of Eastern dualism rejecting material nature as an evil principle. And yet material nature as such cannot be an evil principle: it is passive and inert — it is a feminine element receptive of this or that spiritual principle. Christ cast seven devils out of Mary Magdalene and animated her with His Spirit. But when the pseudo-Christians excommunicated the cosmic Magdalene from the spirit of Christ, evil spirits naturally took possession of her. I am referring to the way black magic and all kinds of devilry flourished at the end of the Middle Ages and at the beginning of modern history. The spirits were raised, but the exorcisms did not work. The pseudo-Christians, who in their dogmatism somewhat resembled the believing devils, and in their false spiritualism lost the actual power of the spirit, could not imitate Christ and the apostles, and used the very opposite method. Christ and His disciples cast out devils to heal the possessed, and these put the possessed to death in order to cast out devils.

VII

While pseudo-Christians have been denying the Spirit of Christ in their exclusive dogmatism, one-sided individualism and false spiritualism, while they have been losing it in their life and activity — what has become of that Spirit itself? I am not speaking of its mystical presence in the sacraments of the church, nor of its individual action upon the souls of the elect. Can it be that humanity *as a whole* and its history have been forsaken by the Spirit of Christ? What in that case can be the source of the social, moral and intellectual progress of the last few centuries?

The majority of men who are responsible for that progress disdain the name of Christians. But if nominal Christians have been faithless to the cause of Christ and almost ruined it, if it could be ruined, why should not nominal non-Christians, denying Christ in words, serve His cause? In the Gospel we read about two sons; one said 'I am going' and did not go, another said 'I am not going' — and went. Which of the two, Christ asks, did the will of the Father? It is impossible to deny that the social progress of the last centuries was carried on in the spirit of justice and humanity, i.e. in the spirit of Christ. Take the abolition of torture and cruel executions; the cessation, at any rate in the West, of all persecution of heretics and dissenters; the abolition of serfdom and feudal bondage — if all these Christian reforms were made by unbelievers, so much the worse for the believers.

Those who feel horrified at the thought that the Spirit of Christ acts through men who do not believe in Him, are wrong even from their own dogmatic point of view. When an unbelieving priest correctly celebrates the liturgy, Christ is present in the sacrament in spite of the celebrant's unbelief and unworthiness, for the sake of the people who need it. If the Spirit of Christ can act through an unbelieving priest in a sacrament of the Church, why can it not act in history through unbelieving agents, especially when the believers drive it away? The Spirit bloweth where it listeth. Its enemies may well serve it. Christ who has commanded us to love our enemies can certainly not only love them Himself but also know how to use them for His work. And nominal Christians who pride themselves on having the same kind of faith as the devils should call to mind another thing in the Gospel — the story of two apostles, Judas Iscariot and Thomas. Judas greeted Christ with words and with a kiss. Thomas declared his unbelief in Him to His face. But Judas betrayed Christ and 'went and hanged himself', and Thomas remained an apostle and died for Christ.

The unbelieving promoters of modern progress acted for the benefit of true Christianity, undermining the false mediæval world-conception with its anti-Christian dogmatism, individualism and spiritualism. They could not injure Christ by their disbelief, but they have injured material nature which many of them were championing. Against the pseudo-Christian spiritualism which regards nature as an evil principle, they put forth another equally false view that nature is lifeless matter and a soulless machine. And earthly nature, as though offended by this double untruth, refuses to feed mankind. This is the common danger which ought to unite the believers and the unbelievers. It is time that both recognized their solidarity with mother-earth and saved it from deadness, in order to save themselves from death as well. But what solidarity can we have with the earth, how can we have a moral relation to it, when we have no such solidarity, no such moral relation to one another? The progressive unbelievers are trying — as best they can — to create such a solidarity, and to some extent they have succeeded. Those who call themselves Christians do not believe in their success, spitefully find fault with their efforts and resist them. It is easy to blame other people and to hinder them. Try to do better yourselves, to create a living, social, universal Christianity. If we are Christians not in name only but in deed, it depends upon us that Christ should rise from the dead in His humanity. Then the historical Thomas too will reach out his hand and touching this truly risen body of Christ, cry out joyfully: 'My Lord and my God!'

II

THE CHURCH
OF CHRIST

1

THE UNION OF
THE CHURCHES

(a) THE GREAT DISPUTE
AND CHRISTIAN POLITICS

THE Christian Church in the historical sense is the combination of two constituent principles: the Eastern, consisting in passive devotion to the Deity, and the Western, affirming the independence of man. The Church equally needs both: mankind must voluntarily and therefore independently carry out the will of God which it recognizes as supreme. In so far as it forms part of the Church, mankind must, in the first place, *believe* in the superhuman truth revealed to it and, secondly, *act* so as to embody that truth in its human world.

The ideal of the Church is not to merge these two different activities into one, but to *harmonize* them. That ideal, given in the person of the God-man, has been fully realized by Him alone; humanity is only on the way to the Kingdom of God and may, and actually does, disturb the balance between the divine and the human activity in one direction or the other. The human activity in the Church may either prove too weak, bringing stagnation and inertia into church life, or manifest itself too strongly, distorting the divine work through the admixture of human passions and interests. On Christian ground humanity is menaced on the one hand with the immobility of the East and on the other with the vanity of the West. In Christianity both the historical East and the historical West have found their highest truth, but before they are fully penetrated by that truth and reborn in the new humanity — the universal Church — they have temporarily stamped Christianity itself with their one-sidedness. The peoples of the East and the West, united by the Church, soon began to differ in their interpretation of it. Both the East and the West interpreted it in their own way, and instead of trying to find in each other a corrective of this one-sidedness, each held to its own particular interpretation, regarding it alone as true and unconditionally binding; thus theoretical difference of opinion, accompanied by ill-will, became in the end actual rupture.

The life of the Church as a *divinely-human* body is made up of two elements: the given divine truth, and the human activity conformable therewith. Those two aspects of the true religion are closely interconnected, for the same divine grace that was active in the original revelation of the truth guides mankind in the further realization of that truth on earth. But divine grace cannot act by compulsion: in penetrating the human will, it does not destroy that will — just as a ray of sunshine, penetrating through the atmosphere, does not destroy the air, but only lights and warms it. In this way there is always preserved in God's work the difference between divine and human action.

The East, orthodox in theology and unorthodox in life, understood Christ's divinely-human nature, but could not understand the divinely-human significance of the Church; it wanted to have only the divine in the Church and not the divinely-human. The Church was for it simply something holy, given from above in a final form, preserved through tradition and accepted through piety. And indeed this is the first thing about the Church; but for the East it was both the first and the last: the whole truth of Christianity, represented by the Church, was taken to be *above* man and *prior* to him. But Christianity is the truth of God-manhood, i.e. of the inner union of the Deity with humanity as a whole. Therefore the Church, having a superhuman *foundation*, cannot be limited to that divine foundation, but must include the whole edifice of human life. The Church or the Kingdom of God must not remain *merely* above us, be merely an object of our veneration and worship — it must also be within us as the ruling force and the free life for all humanity. The Church is not only holiness, but also power and freedom. Without this tri-unity of holiness, power and freedom there is no true life in the Church. To affirm religious freedom alone, while rejecting the holiness of church tradition and the authority of the spiritual power, means to erect the roof of a building that has neither foundation nor walls. On the other hand, to hold fast to the basis of the true religion in the church tradition, forgetting its purpose, the free divinely-human communion, and the chief means to that end, the organization of the spiritual power, means to give up building the walls and the roof in the joy of possessing a secure foundation. That was the position in which the Christian East found itself owing to its one-sided conception of the Church — with the surest foundation, but with no walls or arches. Attaching itself wholly to the divine basis of the Church, it forgot about its completion in humanity. But if the Church is founded, that does not mean it is completed, or that we have nothing to do for its completion. The Church is permanent and unchangeable independently of us, and at the same time it is built up by us, changeable and moving. That which unchangeably abides in the Church — the unbroken succession of holy orders, the eternal truth of the dogma, the active power of the sacraments — all this directly relates to God and demands nothing but recognition and acceptance from man. On the contrary, all that moves and changes in the Church, all that is gradually and historically built upon its divine foundation, directly relates to man and requires his independent activity. The combination of both these aspects in the Church is necessarily implied by its divinely-human nature. As the true body of the God-man Christ, the Church must unite, as He does, the divine and the human, without division or confusion. The human element in Christ — His rational will — submitting itself always and in all things to the will of the Father, through this self-renunciation gains mastery over His material nature, heals, transfigures and resuscitates it in a new, spiritual form. In like manner in the Church the holiness of God, acknowledged by human reason and will, must, through the self-renouncing work of individuals and nations, be brought into the whole constitution of mankind, into the whole of its natural life and through this into the life of the whole world, bringing it healing, transfiguration and resurrection. In Christ, divinity was not a passive object of worship and contemplation for His human consciousness, but was inwardly united with His human will and acted through it, regenerating His physical nature. Likewise in the Church its divine essence or holiness must be not merely revered and worshipped but, united with the practical powers of man, must actively penetrate through them into all the elements of the world so as to sanctify and spiritualize them. The divine principle of the Church must not merely abide and be preserved in the world but *rule* the world. The Church, being permanently and unchangeably holy, must at the same time be an active power.

This spiritual power of the Church guides humanity and leads the world to its final end, i.e. to the union of all in one divinely-human body in which all the forces of creation actively manifest in themselves the one Deity.

The holiness of the Church given in the revelation and preserved in tradition (priesthood, dogmas, sacraments) is the beginning, the spiritual power connected with this holiness is the means, and the free divinely-human life is the end or purpose of God's work.

The Church as the union of the divine and the human thus has two aspects, the absolute and the relative. In its divine aspect the Church as holiness preserved by tradition is absolutely stable and unchangeable (the static element in the Church, $\sigma\tau\alpha\sigma\iota\varsigma$) in its human aspect, on the contrary, the Church has a relative and practical character, is mobile and changeable (the dynamic element in the Church, $\kappa\iota\nu\eta\sigma\iota\varsigma$).

. . . On the stable foundation of church tradition the free forces of humanity must move under the general guidance of spiritual authority. The second, the human, aspect of the Church — its mobile, practical element — also has two opposite poles: authority and freedom.

When the ecumenical power, rooted in tradition and watchful over the holy heritage of the Church, guides men's free activity to the realization of the Kingdom of God; when individual men, piously devoted to the unchangeable holiness of the Church and obedient to the authority of the spiritual power, voluntarily consecrate themselves under its guidance to the service of God's cause, freely directing all their energies to it; when, subordinating their human wills to the will of God, they gain mastery over material nature and transfigure it—then only will religion and the Church appear in their full significance as the harmonious interaction of the divine and the human, as the true sojourn of God in men and men's free life in God.

This ideal balance between the divine and the human contained in the Church from the very first was, in its further history, disturbed in both directions — in the East, in favour of the static divine basis of the Church, in the West in favour of its human element on both its poles: first, of power (Papism), and then of freedom (Protestantism).

It has already been mentioned that in the East the Church was understood and preserved mainly as holiness abiding in tradition — in its static element. That was in keeping with the general spiritual character of the East which always had a leaning for the absolute alone and was sceptical and indifferent with regard to the relative movement of life and practical historical tasks. Though such an interpretation of the Church corresponded to the one-sidedness of the East, it did not correspond to the fulness of Christianity. Early Christianity which represented that fulness in an embryonic form knew nothing of such a one-sided conception of the Church: it appeared only when the Eastern (Greek) and the Western (Latin) churches became differentiated from each other, and that did not happen before the fourth century, the time of Constantine the Great. During the early centuries at the time of the apostles and martyrs, under the power of a pagan Empire and in the absence of external unity, all Christian churches from Mesopotamia to Spain were in complete inner union.

. . . Beginning with the fourth century, the inner solidarity between the parts of the Church weakened although Christians increased in numbers and were no longer persecuted.

. . . That process was furthered by the important political change that took place in the fourth century. The same Emperor who liberated the Church and made it rich and powerful transferred the capital of the Empire to the East, to Byzantium, making that city one common centre for the whole of the Christian East, which had no such centre before; he thus definitely helped the segregation of the Eastern Church.

. . . Having become a new Rome for the state, Byzantium aspired to be a new or a second Rome for the Church. As early as the end of the fourth century there appears the fatal rivalry between the see of Byzantium, the representative of Eastern Christianity, and the see of ancient Rome, representative of the Christian West. But the division of the churches was delayed for a few centuries by the struggle against heresies. During that period, from the fourth century till the ninth, with the deterioration of moral life in the Christian world, its best spiritual powers were centred upon the Christian *doctrine*; the main interest was to formulate the orthodox dogma attacked by the heretics. For this purpose religious thinkers and seers of the East needed the help of the Western primates, who were for the most part men of firm will and authoritative action. In this way the predominance of religious interest limited the cultural and political rivalry between the churches and preserved their unity. It always happens that when men disinterestedly serve a noble cause and whole-heartedly devote themselves to it, they achieve at the same time other useful results, often quite involuntarily. So in this case the prevalence of a lofty and disinterested striving to define and affirm the pure truth of orthodoxy against heresies served at the same time to maintain church unity between East and West.

That unity was particularly important when, in the struggle between orthodoxy and heresy, the imperial power sided with the latter. It will be remembered that a great many Byzantine emperors patronized various heresies, and some of them actually originated them (Heraclius was responsible for the monothelite heresy, Leo the Isaurian for iconoclasm). Meanwhile the Byzantine hierarchs were dependent upon the emperors.

Under such circumstances it was natural that men to whom the cause of orthodoxy was precious above all things greatly valued the significance of the hierarchical centre which preserved its independence from the heretical emperors and combined the religious advantages of chief apostolic see with those of political freedom. In their struggle against heresies all the leaders of orthodoxy in the East, from Athanasius the Great (persecuted by the Arians) down to Theodore the Studite (persecuted by the iconoclasts), looked to the West and found in orthodox Rome defence and support. Great importance attaches to the very fact that during all that period of dogmatic struggle the Roman see was never occupied by a heretic (with the sole and very doubtful exception of the Pope Honorius). It may therefore be well understood that Ecumenical Councils and the greatest teachers of the Eastern Church affirmed in the strongest possible terms the high significance and authority of the Roman see.[1] On the other hand, Rome in its turn needed the spiritual powers of the East. Orthodox and independent, it was surrounded by Germanic barbarism and soon lost its wealth of intellectual culture; in the second half of the seventh century Pope Agathon testified that in the Roman Church it was difficult to find two or three learned clerics skilled in dialectics. Thus Rome in its struggle against

[1] St. John Chrysostom, the blessed Theodoret, St. Maxim the Confessor, St. John Damascene, St. Theodore the Studite and many others; also the Third, Fourth, Sixth and Seventh Ecumenical Councils.

heresy (which at that time was its main interest too) could not dispense with the help of Greek theologians.

. . . At that glorious epoch, then, the spiritual forces of the Eastern and the Western churches, united in the common cause of affirming the orthodox dogma against a common enemy, heresy, were in constant friendly interaction and completed each other. Practical Rome gave refuge to the religious thinkers of Greece, and Eastern theologians found support in the authority of the Roman pontiffs; Roman legates were present at Greek Councils, and Eastern monks were the allies of Western hierarchs.

Beginning with the ninth century the situation definitely changed. The heresies had run full circle; the fundamental dogma of Orthodox Christianity was clearly defined and finally established by the joint efforts of the East and the West, of Councils and Popes, of theological thought and hierarchical authority. Byzantium, which had been the playground of all the heresies in turn, celebrated at last the triumph of orthodoxy — there was no further reason to preserve the spiritual bond with the Western Church and it was severed. The dogmatic interest of orthodoxy, all-important to the Greek Christians, was satisfied by the definitions of the seven Ecumenical Councils, and, undisturbed by new heresies, no longer needed the authoritative support of Rome; national hostility and hierarchical rivalry had now the field to themselves. On the other hand, when the German barbarians were finally won for the Church, and their chief ruler received the imperial crown in Rome, foundations were laid for a new Western civilization and culture, making the Christian West independent of the Christian East. Their former common task — the establishment of dogma — was over, the unity of higher interests was gone; antagonism and rivalry, no longer restrained by this higher unity, became predominant, and the division between the churches took place.

It is not my purpose here to tell how it happened and repeat the sad story of Photius and Cerularius — nor to discuss whether Byzantium or Rome was more to blame; I will confine myself to pointing out that to a certain extent both parties were at fault. The Christian East, right in its unwavering piety, right in its steadfast devotion to the holy orthodox faith of the Fathers, unfortunately forgot that the holy tradition of the Church, which it defended so zealously, was only the foundation and the beginning of God's work, and that if one always thinks of the beginning alone and looks backwards only, the purpose of the work cannot be attained and finally disappears from view. Jealously guarding the basis of the Church — the holy tradition — the Orthodox East did not want to build anything on that basis. In this it was wrong. Holy tradition is the first and most important thing in the Church, but one must not stop at that: strong walls and a free summit are needed. The walls of the Church are a regularly organized and unified ecclesiastical authority, and the summit is free spiritual life.

That summit was forgotten by the Roman Church also. While the East wholly devoted itself to preserving the sacred *beginnings* of the Kingdom of God, Rome, being essentially practical, cared above all things about *the means* of attaining God's Kingdom on earth. The first and most important means or condition for it is the unity of spiritual power, and so Rome put its whole soul into the task of uniting and strengthening that power. This task was in keeping with the nature of the Roman genius. In its distinctive historical character Christian Rome was the same as pagan Rome, being representative, as the latter was, of the principle of *will* or practical reason, expressing itself objectively as law and authority. But in paganism that principle had no real content and consequently found its final embodiment in the senseless tyranny of the Cæsars; Christianity gave it a fulness of meaning, and applied it to God's work on earth. Christian Rome, having the same force of imperious human will as pagan Rome, wholly devoted it to building up the Church and creating a world-wide theocracy; it came forward everywhere with its authoritative decision and firm action.

The nature and direction of its activity were the source both of great strength and of great danger for Rome. The danger was to forget the purpose of God's work on earth while struggling for power as the chief means or condition of that work, and imperceptibly to replace the end by the means. It was easy to lose sight of the fact that spiritual power only serves to prepare and lead mankind to God's Kingdom in which there no longer is any power or domination. The contemplative East sinned by not thinking at all of the practical means and conditions of carrying out God's work on earth; the practical West erred in thinking of those means first and foremost and making them the end of its activity. Christianity is neither an object of mere abstract contemplation nor is it simply a practical task. The chief trouble, however, was not that the East was too contemplative and the West too practical, but that neither had sufficient Christian love. In the absence of love, mutual understanding disappeared, and with it the possibility of knowing and correctly gauging one's relative merits and weaknesses; consequently East and West could no longer help and complete each other within the wholeness of the universal Church.

The Orthodox East rightly prides itself on its unwavering faith. But, in the words of the greatest teacher of faith, 'though I have all knowledge and *all faith*, so that I could remove mountains, and have not love, I am nothing'. The Western Church is renowned for many works and self-sacrificing labours throughout the world. But the same apostle who 'laboured more abundantly than they all' testifies that 'though I bestow all my goods to feed the poor, and though I give my body to be burned, and have not love, it profiteth me nothing'.

In the mutual relations of the Eastern and the Western churches from the ninth century onwards one may find, on both sides, everything except that love which 'suffereth long and is kind, envieth not, vaunteth not itself, *seeketh not her own*'. Indeed, if in Rome and Byzantium they were not seeking their own, there would have been no division of churches.

The true fundamental cause of all human deeds, small and great, private and of universal importance, is the human will. In the present case, whatever might have been the ostensible reasons and contributing circumstances, the division of the churches could finally have taken place only because both in the East and the West they were determined to have nothing more to do with each other. The most important factor in all this was the deep inner hostility between the church people of the East and West. There was a *desire* for separation, and the separation took place. Its real cause is unconsciously expressed in the decision of the Constantinople Synod in 1054 anathematizing the papal legates and the whole of the Western Church: 'Certain impious persons', it says, 'came from the darkness of the West into the realm of piety and this God-protected city from which as from a source the waters of pure doctrine flow to the ends of the earth.' The real misfortune of the Roman legates was that they came from the West; the real cause of the break was not *filioque* and not 'the unleavened bread' but the ancient culturally-political antagonism between East and West, which blazed up afresh with the decline of the Christian principles that abolished their hostility.

After the final division of the churches, the Byzantine and the Latin one-sidedness, no longer held in check by the restraining influences of ecclesiastical communion, developed to the full. From the eleventh century onwards history is once more concerned not with mankind made one in Christ, but with the isolated East and the isolated West; and the isolation was fatal to both. Secluded in its complacent piety Byzantium divided its spiritual life between mystical contemplation in monasteries and dialectical arguments in theological schools; having lost all practical force of action and resistance it surrendered to the alien power of Islam. The isolated West in its anxious activity developed strenuously and exclusively the human (Roman) principle which lay at the basis of it. The result of this strenuousness and exclusiveness was that although human activity in the West served in the first instance the cause of God (in the Catholic Church), that cause (universal theocracy) was for the most part interpreted in an external and formal way; spiritual authority was bound up with material power, and inner religious truth was subordinated to the hard and narrow legal forms that aroused protest and discontent. The unsatisfactory character of Christian activity incited and justified an anti-Christian movement of thought. Just as the solitary religious contemplativeness of Eastern Orthodoxy proved helpless against the living force of an alien faith, so the solitary religious activity of Western Catholicism was helpless against thoughtful disbelief. The holiness of God's Church was preserved in both the separated halves of the Christian world, but the realization of this holiness in the life of mankind when its powers were divided proved impossible or perverted. The pious quietism of Byzantium, not supported by the authoritative energy of Rome, gave the Christian East into the power of an anti-Christian religion; the jealous love of power and active strength of Rome, no longer softened by the influence of the contemplative East, could not preserve the Christian West from the false ideas of anti-Christian enlightenment.

. . . The great dispute between the Christian East and the Christian West, from its beginning down to the present day, can be reduced to the following question: has the Church of God a definite practical task in the human world, the fulfilment of which necessarily requires the union of all its forces under the banner and the power of a central ecclesiastical authority? In other words, the question is, should the Church represent on earth the active Kingdom of God and, consequently, should it be one and centralized? A kingdom divided against itself shall not stand, but the Church, according to the Gospel promise, shall stand till the end, and the gates of hell shall not prevail against it. The Roman Church definitely answered that question in the affirmative; it dwelt chiefly upon the practical task of Christianity in the world, upon the significance of the Church as the active Kingdom or City of God (*civitas Dei*), and stood from the first for the principle of central authority which visibly and practically unifies the earthly activity of the Church. Therefore the abstract question of the significance of central authority in the Church becomes a concrete historical question as to the significance of the Roman Church. The real subject of the great dispute was that church, its ideas and its deeds.

The principle of ecclesiastical authority or of spiritual power, represented mainly by the Church of Rome, has a threefold expression and raises a threefold question. To begin with, in the Church's own realm, it may be asked what must be the relation of the central spiritual power to the representatives of local national churches; secondly, there is the question of the relation of the Church to the state, of the spiritual to the secular power, and thirdly, of the relation of the spiritual power to the spiritual freedom of the individual — the question of the freedom of conscience. Roman Catholicism both in its history and its doctrine answered this threefold question clearly and resolutely.

... The Roman Church equally demands absolute submission from local churches and their bishops, from the state and all secular powers and, finally, from each individual Christian. It insists upon the necessity of threefold submission: ecclesiastical, political and personally-moral. It is well known that this triple demand called forth a triple protest. The ecclesiastical absolutism of Rome was resisted by Byzantium, and to this day the whole of the Orthodox East remains firmly opposed to it; the political absolutism of the Roman throne met with armed opposition from secular powers, kings and nations, who are still carrying on a bitter and successful struggle against papacy, having passed from the defensive to the offensive; finally, the moral absolutism of the Roman Church, demanding absolute submission from the individual conscience and reason, was challenged by German

Protestantism and rationalism to which it gave birth, and to this day the free forces of the personal spirit are opposed to the demands of ecclesiastical authority.

Rome strove to unite the heterogeneous elements of humanity, but only succeeded in uniting them in their common hostility to itself and to its claims. What different forces, what different men gathered together in the course of history under the common banner of opposition to papal authority! Photius and Luther, Emperor Frederick II and Mark of Ephesus, Melanchthon and Henry VIII! In view of such many-sided and apparently successful resistance to Roman Catholic claims, in view of the obvious decline and humiliation of papal power, it becomes very easy to answer the absolute claims of Rome by an absolute rejection of them, and to condemn papacy unconditionally.

In order to be just to the Roman Catholic Church we must first of all discriminate between the *purpose* it sought to gain in the course of its history, and the *methods* it pursued.

In the ecclesiastical sphere as such the Roman Church, as already pointed out, stood for the principle of visible unity, centralized power, supreme authority. To form a correct judgment on this subject we must distinguish three questions in it: (1) Is central power necessary in the visible Church at all? (2) On what grounds is that power claimed by the Roman See? (3) What use did it make of it?

The answer to the first of these questions entirely depends upon whether we recognize that the Christian Church has a practical task in history and admit that, having a firm and unchangeable foundation, it is a moving historical power which has to act and struggle in the world — in short, whether we recognize the earthly Church as the Church *militant*. For practical action and struggle it is essential to have unity and complete solidarity among the active forces, to have a supreme central authority, a proper hierarchical order and a strict discipline.

Authority, order, discipline — what low words as compared with the spiritual and divine essence of the Church! 'The Church', people say, 'is not an authority, but truth, just as Christ is not an authority, and God is not an authority.' Yes, in their absolute essence God and Christ and the Church are *only* the truth; but humanity does not live by absolute essence only, and truth is for it conditioned by authority. Christ did not say about Himself that He was *only* the truth: He said, 'I am the way, the truth, and the life'. When He made Himself manifest on earth He not only taught and enlightened men, not only testified to the truth abiding in Him, but also asserted His authority. It is significant that the Evangelist lays special stress upon the fact that Christ spoke and acted as one *having authority*, which distinguished Him from other people.

. . . The forces that rage against Christianity are not susceptible to the pure truth itself, for they are rooted in the impure ground of human passions and vices. In so far as it faces those enemies — the dark and evil forces of cosmic and human nature — the Church is, and is called, the *army* of Christ and as such it should act in unity, have a central power and discipline.

This brings us to the second question: why should Rome, the Roman episcopal see, have a central significance for the universal Church? To begin with, because no other church has ever had such significance. One or the other: either the Church must not be centralized at all, must have no unifying centre whatever, or that centre must be in Rome, for no other episcopal see can possibly be regarded as having the same importance for the universal Church.

. . . But *how* did the Roman Church interpret and express that significance?

The necessity for a unifying centre (*centrum unitatis*) and for a leading authority in the earthly Church follows not from the Church's absolute and eternal essence, but from its temporary condition as the Church militant. Hence it is clear that the privileges of the central spiritual power cannot extend to the eternal foundations of the Church. The first of these foundations is the grace of consecration, i.e. the power handed down from the apostles to ordain others to a sacred office, and in this respect the bearer of central power, let us say the Pope, can have no advantage whatever over other bishops. He can have power over them not as one bishop over others but only as the chief ruler of the Church over other, subordinate rulers; in the terminology of Latin theologians, the priority of the Pope refers not to *potestas ordinis* in which he is completely equal to other bishops, but only to *potestas jurisdictionis*, i.e. to ruling and teaching in the Church. So far as holy orders are concerned, the Pope is only a bishop among other bishops. As to the second basis of the Church — the sacraments, with regard to performing them the Pope can have no priority over simple priests: in this respect he is only a priest among other priests.[1] Finally, with regard to the third basis of the Church — the revealed truth of Christianity — the Pope can have no priority whatever over a simple layman. The exclusive possession and management of Christ's truth no more belongs to the Pope than to the least of laymen; just as any other man, the sovereign pontiff has no right to proclaim any new revelations or new truths not contained in the divine revelation given to the Church as a whole.

. . . Thus, papal power does not touch upon the eternal foundations of the Church and can only give the bishop of Rome the privileges of sovereign guidance of the Church's earthly affairs, for better directing and applying social and individual forces to the needs of God's work at any given time. The superhuman holiness of the Church, given to us through the revelation and preserved through tradition, is not subject to any man — neither to Cæsar nor Pope: the latter can govern only the human side of the Church, its temporal militant organization.

For this reason, to call the Pope the head of the Church is, in any case, inexact. To begin with, the Church in its indivisible wholeness can have only Christ for its head; but even apart from this, and having in mind only the visible part of the Church, i.e. the earthly humanity that forms part of it, it is easy to see that this humanity, or the visible Church throughout its historical existence, embracing many centuries in the past and in the future, cannot possibly have for its head the person of the Pope, i.e. the mortal man who happens to occupy the papal throne at a given moment; for in that case the historical Church as a whole would have as many heads as there have been, and as there will be, Popes — which would deprive it of any unity in time. The long series of pontiffs does not as such present any kind of unity, nor does the so-called See of St. Peter, if it is merely a place occupied by one Pope after another. If it is to have a unifying significance for the Church at different places and different period of time, it must be St. Peter's See in a real sense, i.e. we must recognize that the real guide of the earthly Church throughout its historical existence is one and the same mighty and immortal spirit of the leading apostle, mysteriously connected with his tomb in the eternal city and acting through the whole succession of Popes,

---

[1] All the sacraments except that of ordination are meant.

who thus acquire unity and solidarity with one another. Thus the visible Pope is an instrument, often very imperfect and sometimes altogether worthless, through whom the invisible guide of the Church carries on his activity and directs the historical affairs of the earthly Church at any given epoch; so that every Pope is not so much the head of the Church as its leader at a particular historical moment. But if during his time of office he succeeds in guiding the temporal affairs of the Church in accordance with its eternal principles, if he is a pure and worthy instrument of the Eternal High Priest and His chief apostle, then Christians directly perceive through him that which is greater than he, and recognize in him their true leader and head. So in the past both the Western and the Eastern churches heard the apostle Peter in the speeches of Pope Leo the Great and solemnly proclaimed him to be the head of the Orthodox Church of Christ.

It is clear then that the central authority of the Pope has a conditional and subservient significance. Like all ecclesiastical power, that authority is merely a morally practical means, conditioned by a mystical reality, for carrying on God's work on earth, or for directing the temporal life of mankind to its eternal purpose.

... If the sovereign pontiffs' authority has a mystical religious basis, it needs no external support, no outward defences, no formal legal documents. Proceeding from faith, it must inspire confidence. That is its only support — the trustful devotion of the masses which know nothing about the alleged formal rights of papacy. A few mysterious words in the Gospel and one tomb in Rome — this is the true foundation of all papal rights and privileges. This alone cannot be taken away from them. This was all that the founders of papal power — Leo and Gregory — relied upon. They had no need of Isidore's decretals, or of political rivalry with kings and emperors, or of crusades against heretics. The higher their conception of their authority and the more they believed in its power, the less they troubled about such methods of strengthening it. They did not make it their purpose to command kings and nations, but when it was necessary, they did so — and met with no resistance. The authority of the Roman See was never greater and more universally recognized than under those artless Popes.

There were many worthy representatives of the papal system in later centuries also, but there is no doubt that after the separation of the churches and parallel to the development of Byzantism in the East, there appeared in the West a different and impure current of ideas and actions which might be called popery in contradistinction to the papal system in its true significance. There appeared a jealous, anxious attitude to the pontifical authority, a desire to base that power upon external, formal law, to provide juridical grounds for it, to stengthen it by clever politics, to defend it by the force of arms. The Church militant becomes a church at war. Instead of calm, confident strength there is effort and straining, instead of zeal for the faith and the Church there is jealous concern for its own supremacy, spiritual loftiness is transformed into carnal haughtiness; in short, all the characteristics of the highest spiritual service are replaced by those of material domination.

The spirit of popery that possessed Roman Catholicism naturally showed itself in the relations between the Church and the state, the spiritual and the temporal power. In this domain the papal system stands for the idea of theocracy; popery perverts this idea by imparting to theocracy the character of compulsory domination. Justly protesting against this distortion, people generally reject at the same time the very idea of theocracy. When this is done by unbelievers or by enemies of Christianity, their position is understandable. If God does not exist or if He is merely an abstract idea, or an absolutely unfathomable and unapproachable force that has no positive relation to our world, any kind of theocracy is either deception or foolishness. But from the truly Christian point of view, the idea of theocracy is a necessary consequence of the belief in the divine incarnation and in the bond between the earthly and the heavenly realities in the Church.

If there exists on earth a special union of God's servitors in the order of succession, if there exists on earth a special authority entrusted from above with exceptional powers and promised exceptional help in guiding and governing Christian humanity, there cannot be any doubt that all other powers and authorities in the world and all social forces must be subject to this sacred and plainly divine authority.

In the words of St. John Chrysostom, just as the soul excels the body, so pontifical power is higher and more excellent than the royal.

. . . This essentially was the view not only of John Chrysostom but of all the great Fathers of that great epoch. There was no difference in principle about it between the Eastern and the Western churches; the latter, simply, was in a better position for giving practical expression to the general ecclesiastical theory.

. . . There can be no two equally self-subsistent and absolute principles in the life of man; he cannot serve two masters. People speak of complete delimitation and separation between the civil and the ecclesiastical domain. But the question is, whether the civil domain, secular affairs, may from their very nature be *completely* independent, and have the same kind of absolute self-subsistence that essentially belongs to divine realities. Can man's secular interests be separated from his inner, spiritual ones without damaging both? Such a division between the inner and the outer principles, such a separation of the soul from the body is precisely what is called death and decay. The outer, temporal life of man and of mankind is life only in so far as it is not separated from eternal ends, is not posited merely as such, but affirmed as a means and transition to life eternal. Therefore all the interests and affairs of this temporal existence must be merely the means and instruments for the eternal, spiritual interests and tasks, must in one way or another be conditioned by the eternal life and the Kingdom of God; and as soon as the state and society have acknowledged themselves Christian, such a theocratic point of view becomes morally binding upon them.

Accordingly, both logical consistency and obedience to the voice of the universal Church compel us to admit the truth of the theocratic idea, i.e. of the idea that the supreme authority in the Christian world belongs to the spiritual and not to the secular power. But this theoretical admission leads to a practical question: how is the spiritual power to use its supreme authority, how is it to guide the Christian nations' social life? The Orthodox East has given no definite answer to this question, for the despotism of the Byzantine state soon crushed the development of theocracy in the Greek Church. In the West the true realization of theocracy by the best representatives of papacy, beginning with Leo the Great and Gregory VII (and partly even Innocent III) was hindered and spoiled by their successors' wrong theocratic policy, which consisted in governing the world by worldly means alone. Reducing the Church to the level of the state, and the spiritual power to the level of the temporal, that policy not merely distorted the true nature of theocracy but actually undermined the external power of the Popes. The real strength of theocracy lies entirely in its religious, superhuman character. The Church can overcome all other, lower powers of the world only because it contains something which those lower forces lack. The strength of spiritual authority lies in its religious privilege — the privilege of specially serving the cause of God. It is only because of this religious privilege that all the world's powers must be subordinated to the spiritual authority. But when that authority forgets its religious character and in order to subjugate the world uses the means of secular politics — intrigues, diplomacy, armed force — it thereby renounces its religious privilege.

. . . And in that case the spiritual authority can have no lasting success; for as one of many secular powers, it cannot be stronger than all the others and therefore is bound to be overcome by them sooner or later.

Mediæval Popes were wrong not in asserting the superiority of the spiritual over the secular power (they were perfectly right in this), not in maintaining that the civic or political sphere is the lower, but in transferring the purpose of their activity to that lower realm, in acquiring its character and employing its means. The fault of popery is not that it has exalted, but that it has humiliated papal power.

Secular politics should indeed be subordinated to the ecclesiastical, though not through the assimilation of the Church to the state, but, on the contrary, through the state gradually becoming more and more like the Church. Secular reality must be made into the image of the Church — and not that image lowered to the level of secular reality. It is not the high priests who must become kings, but kings must rise to religious and moral union with the true high priests. The Church must attract and draw to itself all secular forces, and not be drawn into and entangled in their blind and immoral strife. In assuming the form of the state the Western Church deprived the real state of its spiritual support, deprived secular politics of their highest purpose and inner meaning. This is the sin of popery against the Christian state. It is guilty of a still greater sin against individual freedom.

Universal truth, given to the Church forever, and in the order of time determined for all through the authority of the spiritual power, is morally binding upon every individual mind. In subordinating himself voluntarily to the universal Church, the individual completes and heals his limitations by the fulness and wholeness of the incarnate God-manhood. Without such subordination, completion and healing the individual can neither know nor create truth. In view of the given and salutary truth, *absolute* freedom to err, and equality between truth and falsehood are as inadmissible in the Church as the freedom to do evil or the enjoyment of full civic rights by a criminal is inadmissible in the state. The followers of Pontius Pilate may repeat his ironical question 'What is truth?' and regard all beliefs and opinions as having the same value and import. The followers of Jesus Christ should know what is truth and what is error and cannot regard them as having equal value or treat them in the same way. Being in possession of Christ's truth, the Church is morally bound to protect its children against the temptations of error. For this purpose it can use three ways of counteracting error, or rather can use three different degrees of counteraction: denunciation, condemnation, excommunication. Through this it fulfils its duty of preventing the dissemination of error, lest one of those little ones should be offended, Spiritual power cannot go beyond excommunication. The very fact that a person is excommunicated puts an end to the Church's jurisdiction over him: he ceases, as it were, to exist for the Church.

. . . Forcing people to join the Church by threats, imprisonment and torture was an attempt to enslave man's conscience and will — a mad and fruitless attempt, but all the more revolting on that account. The free moral act of subordinating the individual mind and will to the universal truth was thus replaced by the effects of physical weakness. In exacting submission by external means, ecclesiastical authority sought to deprive man of the power of moral self-determination. By addressing itself not to man's moral powers but to his physical weakness the Church lost its moral superiority over individual minds and at the same time roused their just opposition. In this way ecclesiastical authority provoked an enemy stronger than itself and prepared for itself the most painful blow of all. Henceforth the sovereign rights of the Church were rejected not only on national and political, but on more profound, moral grounds. Hitherto nations and kings had rebelled against Rome, now *man* rose against it. This last and most formidable rebellion against Roman power is called Protestantism.

The protest, springing from the self-consciousness of human personality, struck at the very heart of popery. Popery itself depended upon the forces of the human element in the Church. In the historical activity of the Popes the human element came forward in the name of power or authority; in Protestantism it came forward in the name of religious freedom and the sovereign rights of personal conscience.

The whole significance of Protestantism is not, of course, confined to this protest of religious conscience against the tyranny of the spiritual power that had forgotten its spiritual character. But the inmost essence and the vital nerve of Protestantism was precisely this moral motive.

It is the merit of Protestantism to have resolutely proclaimed the religious freedom of the individual and the inviolability of personal conscience. But that freedom must be truly religious; the inviolable rights must belong really to conscience, and neither religion nor conscience allows man to make his personal opinion the standard of truth and his arbitrary will the standard of righteousness. No doubt the capacity or possibility of apprehending the divine is hidden in the depths of the human soul, and is present in every separate individual. But if this possibility is to be realized, man must through a moral act of self-renunciation overcome his actual limitations and voluntarily surrender to the universal truth that is independent of him. Without this, the striving of the human soul for the divine remains a mere subjective impulse, fruitless and ineffective. Protestantism was bound to come to this sad end through denying that the significance of the universal truth of the Church is binding upon the individual.

With regard to ecclesiastical authority in particular, the error of Protestants was not to have confined themselves to denying its *compulsory* power. Having justly rebelled against external compulsion, they refused to recognize the inwardly binding moral authority of the universal Church. Man must submit to it not out of slavish fear or dead inertia, but out of Christian humility, consciousness of his personal insufficiency, love for the common cause which requires unity and, finally and most of all, out of firm faith in the Christian truth. That truth cannot remain merely subjective and be abandoned to the play of personal views and opinions. The human representatives of the spiritual power violated the Christian truth in demanding compulsory submission; the Protestants violated it equally by refusing voluntary submission to it.

All that has been said above reveals an instructive and important meaning in the historical vicissitudes of Roman Catholicism. The papal system champions the unity of the Church militant through the centralization of the spiritual power, and there is truth in its claim. But on the strength of that truth popery strove to suppress the independence of the local churches, and that was its first wrong. The division of the churches has shown that *the Church cannot be united by compulsion*.

Further, the papal system claims that the state and secular society must be subordinated to the power of the Church called to rule the world in the name and by the power of Him who overcame the world; and there is truth in that claim. But popery strove for world domination over secular principalities and powers not by the free power of the spiritual man who overcame the world, but through carnal and slavish compulsion, and that was its second wrong. And in answer to it, the triumph of secular power in the whole of Christendom has shown that *the Church cannot dominate the world by compulsion*.

Finally, the papal system claims that the spiritual power of the Church is called to guide all men in the path of salvation and that every man is bound to submit to and obey the sovereign power of the Church — and this claim is true. But popery strove to coerce man's conscience into submission, to force its authority upon his mind by external means. This was its third wrong, and in answer to it Protestantism came into being, showing that *man cannot be saved by compulsion*.

Such is the relative justification of the division between the churches, of the struggle of the secular power against the Popes and of the Reformation.

But the justification is relative only, and the results of those three movements are entirely negative.

The deplorable state of the Christian world has but one cause, and there is but one way out of it. In spite of all the differences between them, all historical movements in Christianity have one common feature, which lies at the root of the matter. All these movements champion certain *rights*: the rights of the central ecclesiastical authority, of the local churches, of the secular power, of individual thought and reason. Now the moral attitude in which a man or a collection of men thinks in the first instance of their rights is contrary to the spirit of Christianity, does not come from God and is utterly fruitless for God's cause.

True Christian life will begin only when all free forces of humanity, laying aside their questionable claims and turning to their unquestionable duties, will voluntarily and conscientiously set to work upon all that mediæval popery tried to achieve by violence and compulsion. That will be the end of the great dispute and the beginning of Christian politics.

The free union of mankind in the Church of Christ is the aim of Christian politics. That aim cannot be attained so long as the actual image of the universal unity on earth — the visible Church — remains in division. Therefore the first task of Christian policy is the re-establishment of church unity. But in order that this task should be truly Christian, it must proceed from religious and moral motives and be guided by them. The aim must be the spiritual union of ecclesiastical communities, and all the rest must be merely a means to that end. Hitherto, however, in the historical attempts to reunite the churches, the union was as a rule merely a means towards the ends of secular politics. For the Byzantine emperors church union was a diplomatic means to support their tottering empire.

. . . It will be remembered that the emperors twice succeeded in persuading or forcing the Byzantine hierarchs to make a formal union with the Western Church (the Lyons Union in 1275, and the Florentine in 1439); but in both cases the *enforced* agreement could not last more than a few years — a clear proof that in church matters a union based upon rational considerations of self-interest and the instinct of self-preservation, without any real feeling or moral will — a purely external and enforced union — cannot endure. In the domain of religion people cannot be ruled by external and artificial conditions; the actual conditions of their religious life are in the last resort determined by their own will.

. . . Equally ineffective and far more harmful for the Church were the later attempts aimed at joining separate parts of the Eastern Church to the Western. The greatest harm is done to the cause of church union when that union is replaced by the romanization of the Eastern Christians.

In spite of the absence of a vital, practical connection between its parts, of strict unity and order in its organization, and the inertness and inactivity that results therefrom, the Eastern Church has an inner religious stability owing to which it preserves both the essential oneness of its principles and its ecclesiastical individuality. To take the Christian East to pieces as the fanatics of Romanism dream of doing is impossible, for that East has an inner spiritual bond, it has its own ecclesiastical idea, its own general principle. In the Middle Ages this was understood in the West; thus, the great Pope Innocent III expressed the idea that the Eastern Church represents the purely spiritual aspect of Christianity and is pre-eminently the church of the Holy Spirit. Whether this be so or not, there can in any case be no doubt about the Eastern Church having a character and significance of its own. It is an essentially necessary and inalienable part of the universal Church in its fulness.

The Orthodox East can never be converted to Romanism, for in that case the universal Church would become the Roman Church, and Christianity would lose its specific significance in human history. We know that in history Christianity appeared as the union and inner reconciliation of the Eastern and Western culture in and through the truth of God-manhood. Therefore if one of these cultures submerged the other and became exclusively predominant, the very nature of the historical mission of Christianity would be perverted. It would then cease to express and embody in world-history the idea of God-manhood.

In order rightly to understand and formulate the task of Christian politics, positive Christianity or the visible earthly Church must be considered in its two main aspects — in its abiding foundation, and in its practical activity in the world.

To begin with, the Church is the living, mystically-real bond between man and Christ as the principle of God-manhood. This bond is permanent and the same for all; it expresses the union between the divine and the human, and is determined by conditions which in no way depend upon the arbitrary will of individuals, but are universal or catholic in character. Those conditions are as follows: first, the recognition of the divinely-human power in the church hierarchy proceeding from Christ through apostolic succession (the way of Christ); secondly, the confession of the divinely-human faith, i.e. of the orthodox dogma of the true and perfect Godhead and true and perfect manhood of Christ in accordance with the definitions of the Ecumenical Councils (the truth of Christ); thirdly, participation in the divinely-human life through the sacraments as the first

4

beginnings of the new spiritual corporeality and gracious life (Christ as life in us). All men who fulfil these conditions — i.e. who acknowledge the *fatherly* authority of the apostolic hierarchy, who confess the *Son* of God and the son of man and take part in the gracious gifts of the Holy Spirit — belong to Christ's Church on earth; they are in the Church and the Church is in them. This is true of us, Eastern Orthodox, and of Western Catholics.

Thus, in considering the Church from this point of view we must admit that the essential, fundamental unity of the universal Church as the divinely-human bond of men with Christ through the succession of holy orders, faith and sacraments is not in the least affected by the apparent separation between ecclesiastical communities owing to their particular beliefs and ordinances. Whatever the relations between those communities and their attitude to one another may be, if their mystically-real bond with the Head of the Church, Christ, is the same, they are one in Christ and form one indivisible body of Christ. The one holy, catholic and apostolic Church essentially abides both in the East and in the West, and shall abide forever, in spite of the temporal hostility and division between the two halves of the Christian world.

. . . The division and struggle between the Christian East and the Christian West follows not from their church principles as such, but only from their temporal negative attitude which has to do merely with the historical manifestations of the Church and not with its true religious essence.

And so first of all it must be recognized that both Eastern and Western Christians in spite of all the disagreements between our ecclesiastical communities go on as before being members of the one indivisible Church of Christ, and that the division between the churches has not altered their relation to Christ and to His mystical grace. In this respect we need not trouble about reunion, for we are one already.

But our visible historical and social separation is all the more sad, all the more painful and unnatural that it is in direct contradiction to our essential, purely religious or mystical unity. Although the first, fundamental aspect of the Church consists in the divinely-human union of men with Christ, and that union is not disrupted by the divisions within Christendom, yet the Church must embrace that Christendom in its actual historical life — and this is the second and pre-eminently human aspect of the Church;

it has to be clearly distinguished from the first, but is correlated to it. For the Church is not *only* the divinely-human basis of salvation for individual men, but also the divinely-human structure (οἰκονομία) for the salvation of this world. The mystical oneness of human communities in Christ must find expression in their actual brotherly union with one another. The first is given from above and does not directly depend upon ourselves; the second must be our own achievement. Humanity must not only accept the grace and truth given in Christ, but also realize that grace and truth in its own personal and historical life, freely growing into the 'measure of the stature of the fulness of Christ'. But this stature of the *fulness* of Christ is impossible when the Christian world is so divided that its two main parts do not *complete* each other.

From this point of view the union of the churches is the first and most important task of practical Christian activity or of what I call Christian policy.

But this task will remain an empty dream or even a source of fresh evils until we recognize the essential unity of the Eastern and the Western churches as fundamentally indivisible parts of the body of Christ. Before visibly entering into brotherly relations with the Western Church, we must recognize our already existing though invisible brotherhood in Christ. If there were no such brotherhood, if the Western Church were *outside* the mystical body of Christ, it would be impossible honestly to speak about agreement and reconciliation and there could only be either conversion or an immoral compromise.

And yet in all former practical attempts at reunion, attention was paid least of all to the essential unity of both churches in Christ. They wanted to unite, though not on the ground of the indissoluble unity given from above in the ever-living truth, but on other, purely human and therefore false grounds. The Eastern and the Western churches appeared as two completely separate mutually alien bodies, and each side felt at bottom that it alone (apart from the other) contained the fulness of the universal Church and was the *whole* body of Christ. Such an attitude inevitably made the apparent union either an impossible attempt at conversion or an immoral compromise.

. . . In truth, however, the Eastern and the Western churches are not radically separate bodies, completely alien to each other, but merely *parts* of the one true body of Christ — the universal

Church, and only in virtue of this each of them has the right to call itself a church.

... The problem is not to create one universal Church which already exists in reality, but simply to make the visible manifestation of the Church conform to its real nature.

Each of the two churches already is the universal Church, though not separately from the other but in unity with it. This unity exists as a fact, for both churches are in fact embraced by the divinely-human bonds of holy orders, dogmatic tradition and sacraments. But it is the spirit of the God-man Christ, and not our spirit that acts in and through those formative bonds. The unity of the two churches exists in Christ and in His gracious activity, but it must also be realized in and through our own actions. The essential unity of the universal Church, hidden from our eyes, must become manifest through the visible reunion of the two ecclesiastical communities divided in history, though indivisible in Christ.

... The so-called division of the churches, i.e. the violation of the brotherly union between the church people of the East and the West, naturally follows from the false view adopted by each of these main parts of Christendom in recognizing itself separately as the whole and appropriating to itself alone the whole fulness of the Church universal. That is the source both of the self-satisfied alienation of the East, and the self-confident proselytizing of the West. 'Only *my* church is the true universal Church', says the Orthodox East, 'and so I do not care in the least about the West so long as it leaves me alone.' This is, so to speak, *defensive* conceit.

'Only *my* church is the true universal Church', says the Roman Catholic West, 'therefore I must convert the Eastern Christians to my own true path.' This is *aggressive* conceit. But in reality the universal Church is free from exclusiveness; it abides both in the East and in the West and is that which *sanctifies* both East and West, that which united the Christian nations in their infancy, and in the name of which they must unite again in order to attain the full stature of Christ.

When this is recognized, mutual condemnation will be replaced by mutual justification.

... If I am asked what in the first place must we *do* for the union of the churches, I will say that we must first of all reconsider once more all the main points of dispute between them, not for the sake of polemics or denunciation as hitherto, but with the sincere desire fully to understand the opposite side, to do it full justice and, in so far as we ought, to agree with it. This desire, this peaceable attitude, is, I repeat, the one thing needful, and all the rest shall be added unto us.

There shall be added not only the visible union between the Eastern and the Western churches, but also the reunion of the Protestants to the Church. Our free and moral reconciliation with the Catholic principle of authority will deprive that principle of the compulsive and external character by which the Protestant movement was called forth.

When we, the Orthodox and the Catholics, who abide in the unity of the body of Christ, become aware of that mystical unity and are moved to confirm it by the moral bond of love and communion, then the Protestant principle of freedom will find its true application and occupy a high position in the completion of the Church, for that completion is *free theocracy*.

Then the truth of God-manhood *given* to us in its inner essence will also prove to be our own *work* and find embodiment in actual human life. Then the constitutive principles of East and West, reconciled and made one in Christianity, but again divided in the Christians, will be reunited in them and create a universal divinely-human culture. The Eastern principle of passive devotion to the divine and the eternal, and the Western principle of man's independent activity (through power and through freedom) will be harmonized and justified in the free and active service of the divine truth by all the powers of man.

(b) THE CHURCH AS THE UNIVERSAL ORGANIZATION OF THE TRUE LIFE

The Church is the universal organization of the true life. We can tell what the true life is because we know well what is the *false* life which we live. Its essential falsity consists not in the fact that we put before us some delusive ends — this need not be the case; the essential falsity of all natural life is that while destroying the being of others it cannot preserve its own: it devours its past and in its own turn is devoured by its future, and is thus a perpetual transition from one nothingness to another. We find a clear expression of this characteristic in the continuous change of generations. The old generation, the fathers, the representatives of the past, wholly give their life, in accordance with the law of nature, to the new generation which also cannot keep it, but in becoming the present, is crowded out by the future generation and so on *ad infinitum*. Such unceasing handing on of death from one generation to another under the mask of life is obviously a false existence, and the infinity of this process is a 'bad' infinity.

In contradistinction to it, the true life is one which in its present preserves its past and is not cancelled by its future but reverts in it to itself and to its past. This is the true and really infinite life; in it the first (the beginning, the past) is not deleted or replaced by the second (the continuation, the present), and the third (the end, the future) is merely the perfect unity of the first two.[1]

There is no such true life in natural humanity, the law of which is the endless and meaningless succession of generations, ceaseless patricide and self-immolation. The true life must be realized in spiritual humanity, i.e. in the Church. The life of the Church is half-way between the divine and the natural. In the divine eternal life there is no time at all, no difference between past, present and future; in the natural life, devoured by time, that difference exists, but is deceptive, for it is continually being destroyed: every future moment, before it has had time to become the present, passes into the past in order to disappear altogether. In the life of the Church, however — the divinely-human life — the fulness of eternity must be realized through the difference between the three forms of time which do not indefinitely replace, but definitely complete one another. The abiding connection between these forms of time means the realization of love, and the distinction between them is the condition of freedom.

The ideal of an all-inclusive church, universal brotherhood, and the perfect kingdom of grace and truth, love and freedom, is the future of the Church. Its beginning is actually present among us here and now, but only in the prophets. What, then, must we do to make that future completely real — to make the prophecy

[1] Just as the bad infinity (*schlechte Unendlichkeit*) of our natural earthly life may be represented by a straight line stretching out indefinitely without beginning or end, so the infinity of the true life has from of old been represented by a circle, i.e. a line that returns to itself, is closed or completed in itself.

come true? Are we to destroy for the sake of it the present and the past of the universal Church? That would be in keeping with the law of the natural life in which the future generation comes into its own by crowding out its fathers. But it is not so in the Church, in the divine humanity. In it all the three forms of time are equally essential to one another, and the fulness of the all-embracing Church consists in their inner, spiritually-organic union based upon love and truth.

The past is represented in the Church by priesthood, by the spiritual fathers, the redeemers of original sin, the elders (πρεσβύτεροι). In the universal Church, i.e. in the family of all nations and in the general all-human brotherhood, there must be international priesthood united in the common *father* or universal high-priest, for the unity of a family depends upon having the same father. Brothers are one not of themselves, but merely as the sons of one. We all have one Father in heaven, and many brothers in heavenly glory. But in speaking of universal brotherhood of peoples on earth, and not of angels, earthly fatherhood is presupposed as the reflection and the instrument of the heavenly.

If priesthood represents the past of the Church, its *present* is the people, the state. Division into nations and states is the actual condition of the Christian world. From the religious point of view it is indisputable that this division cannot be the final and predominant form of life for mankind, but must be subordinated to a higher principle, although national freedom and political spheres of activity should be preserved. But we cannot get rid of the *exclusiveness* of the present state, cannot pass from national separatism to the universal brotherhood of nations, without first entering into the relation of true sonship to the principle of the international (or supernational) unity and recognizing the *fatherly* all-uniting authority of ecumenical high-priesthood.

'It becometh us to fulfil all righteousness.' Christ, the representative of the *royal* house of David, the founder and the only true Head of the Kingdom of God in humanity, considered it His duty to fulfil all righteousness through an act of obvious submission to John, the son of the priest Zacharias of the tribe of Aaron — not as to the prophet of repentance (that had nothing to do with Christ Himself), but as to the last representative of the true Old Testament priesthood.

We are the people of the present, a royal priesthood. As to our future, it depends on whether we follow the example of the

Eternal King who, free from all sin (which we certainly cannot say of ourselves either personally or as a nation), did not hesitate, for the sake of fulfilling all righteousness and actually restoring true life to humanity, to give due honour to the sinful representative of the ancient priesthood of Aaron. When we too perform the action corresponding to His and re-establish in all righteousness our spiritual bond with the past of the universal Church; when clearly and consciously by a free moral effort of the national spirit we put ourselves into the relation of true sonship to the universal fatherhood, then only will the perfect all-embracing brotherhood of all nations, living by love and free unanimity, become possible. It is the ideal and the future of the universal Church and at the same time our true national ideal.

Then there shall be manifested the highest, free unity of the Church, based not only upon tradition and habit or abstract intellectual conviction, but upon moral and spiritual achievement. The universal Church will appear to us no longer as a lifeless idol or an animate but unconscious body, but as a self-conscious, morally free being, bringing about its own realization — as the true bride of God, as creation united to Him in a full and perfect union and completely receptive of the Deity — in short, as the divine Wisdom, Sophia, to whom our ancestors with wonderful prophetic feeling built temples and altars without yet knowing who she was.

Moscow, the feast of the Annunciation of Our Lady, 1887.

2

THE JEWS AND THE
CHRISTIAN PROBLEM

THE relations between Judaism and Christianity during the
many centuries of their co-existence present one remarkable
feature. The Jews have always and everywhere regarded Christianity and behaved towards it in accordance with the precepts of
their religion, in conformity with their faith and their law. The
Jews have always treated us in the Jewish way; we Christians, on
the contrary, have not learned to this day to adopt a Christian
attitude to the Jews. They have never transgressed their religious
law in relation to us; we, on the other hand, have always broken
the commandments of the Christian religion in relation to them.
If the Jewish law is bad, their obstinate loyalty to that bad law is,
of course, regrettable. But if it is bad to be loyal to a bad law, it is
far worse to be disloyal to a good law, to an absolutely perfect
commandment. We have such a commandment in the Gospel.
It is perfect, and for that very reason extremely difficult. Special
help, however, is given to us — the help of grace which does not
abolish the law, but gives us the strength to fulfil it. Consequently, if we first reject that help and then refuse to fulfil the
Gospel commandment because we find it difficult, we have no
excuse. The point is not whether the Gospel commandment is
difficult, but whether it can be fulfilled. If it cannot, why should
it have been given? In that case, the Jews are right in blaming
Christianity for having introduced into the world fantastic ideas
and principles which can have no practical application. But if
the Gospel commandment is practicable, if we can stand in a
Christian relation to all, including the Jews, we are entirely to
blame if we fail to do so.

Instead of sincerely repenting of this, we look for a scapegoat.
It is not our fault — it is the fault of the Middle Ages with their
fanaticism, it is the fault of the Roman Catholic Church. But in

our own day persecution of Jews has begun in countries that are not Catholic. In this case the blame is shifted from us on to the victims themselves. Living among us, the Jews treat us in Jewish fashion; clearly, we must treat them as pagans do; they do not want to love us — clearly, we ought to hate them; they cling to their isolationism, do not want to be merged with us, do not recognize their solidarity with us, but, on the contrary, try in every way to profit by our weaknesses — clearly, we must exterminate them.

True, persecution of the Jews and more or less candid justification of such persecution are not at present common in Europe; on the contrary, speaking generally, the Jews are not merely tolerated, but have actually succeeded in occupying a dominant position in the most advanced nations.

. . . But this domination of the Jews actually confirms my contention that Christendom has never regarded them in a Christian way. Modern tolerance, compliance and even submission to the Jews do not spring from Christian feeling and conviction. On the contrary, they are due not to the breadth of our religious beliefs, but to the absence of them and to our complete indifference in matters of faith. It is not Christian Europe that tolerates the Jews, but a faithless, decadent Europe that has lost its vital principles. Jews live not by our moral strength, but by our moral or, rather, our immoral weakness.

Enlightened Europe need not throw the blame on the fanaticism of the Dark Ages or boast of its own tolerance. Religious tolerance is good on the part of believers when it springs from the fulness of faith, from the consciousness of a superior moral strength; but on the part of an unbeliever tolerance is merely an expression of his unbelief. If Christianity and Judaism and idolatry are all one to me, I simply cannot contrive to be intolerant in matters of faith, and there is no merit in my tolerance. However far from Christian perfection religious fanaticism may be, it is nevertheless a moral force, though crude and undeveloped and therefore easily abused. In any case it is something positive, while religious indifference shows an absence of warmth and animation and is the moral freezing-point, the cold of spiritual death.

. . . And so with respect to Judaism the Christian world hitherto has on the whole shown either unreasonable zeal or impotent and decrepit indifference. Both these attitudes lack the truly

Christian spirit and fall short of the Christian idea. As early as the thirteenth century, however, we find individual attempts on the part of outstanding thinkers and public men of Christendom to adopt a different and truly Christian relation to Judaism.[1] Although these attempts led to no visible results, they constitute the beginning of the true solution of the Jewish problem, foretold by St. Paul in the Epistle to the Romans (ch. xi).

In the old days the Jews lived by faith and hope in the *promised* divine humanity; at present they live by protest and hostility against the unrecognized Messiah, the God-man, the first-fruits of divine humanity on earth; the Jews of the future will live a full life when in regenerated Christianity they find and recognize the image of perfect God-manhood. This hope is most firmly founded upon the word of God. Jehovah chose Israel, made a covenant with it, gave it promises. Jehovah is not a man or a son of man and neither deceives nor repents of His promises. A part of the Jewish people rejected the first coming of the Messiah, and is suffering heavy retribution for it, but only for a time, since God's word cannot be broken; and that word of the Old Testament, decisively confirmed in the New by the Apostle of the Gentiles, says clearly and indubitably 'all Israel shall be saved'.

The Jews who clamoured for Christ to be crucified cried: 'His blood be on us, and on our children.' But that blood is *the blood of redemption*. And surely the clamour of human malice is not strong enough to drown the words of divine forgiveness: 'Father, forgive them; for they know not what they do.' The bloodthirsty crowd gathered on Calvary consisted of Jews; but the three, and afterwards five, thousand who after St. Peter's preaching were baptized and formed the first Christian Church were Jews also. Annas and Caiaphas were Jews, but so were Joseph and Nicodemus; Judas who betrayed Christ to be crucified, and Peter and Andrew who were crucified for Christ belonged to the same race. Thomas who disbelieved in the resurrection was a Jew, and he did not cease to be one after he believed in the risen Christ and said to Him, 'My Lord and my God!' Saul, the cruel persecutor of Christians, was a Jew, and Paul who was persecuted for Christianity

[1] It is only fair to note that in the Middle Ages the higher representatives of the Church, and in particular the Popes, adopted a relatively humane attitude to the Jews and some of the Popes actually patronized them, for which they were bitterly blamed by their contemporaries.

and 'had laboured for it more than any' remained a Jew of the Jews. And, what is most important of all, the God-man Christ, betrayed and killed by the Jews, was Himself according to the flesh and to His human nature a pure-bred Jew.

In view of this striking fact, does it not seem strange that *in the name of Christ* we should condemn all Jewry to which Christ Himself indisputably belongs? And it is particularly strange on the part of those of us who, though they have not directly renounced Christ, do not in any way express their connection with Him.

If Christ is not God, the Jews are not more guilty than are the Greeks who killed Socrates. But if we acknowledge Christ as God, we must acknowledge that the Jews are a *God-bearing* race. For the death of Jesus the Romans as well as the Jews are to blame; His birth belongs solely to God and to Israel. It is said that the Jews are always the enemies of Christianity; but the anti-Christian movement of the last few centuries is headed not by Jews, not by Semites, but by Christians of the Aryan race.

I

Why were the Jews predestined to give birth to the God-man, the Messiah or the Christ?

In so far as God is the source of all destiny, destiny is absolutely free. But God's freedom must not be conceived after the fashion of human arbitrary will or partiality. True freedom does not exclude reason; in accordance with reason, such free choice or destination, being God's *relation* to a certain object, corresponds not only to the character of the chooser but also to that of the chosen. The national character of the Jews must *condition* their election. In the course of four thousand years that character had sufficiently defined itself and it is not difficult to discover and indicate its particular features. But, moreover, it is necessary to understand them in their totality and mutual interconnection. No one will deny that the Jewish national character has an integral unity and is all of a piece. And yet we find in it three main peculiarities which, apparently, do not harmonize with one another but are mutually contradictory.

In the first place, Jews are deeply religious and devoted to their God to the point of self-sacrifice. They are a people of the law and the prophets, martyrs and apostles 'who through faith subdued kingdoms, wrought righteousness, obtained promises' (Heb. xi. 33).

Secondly, the Jews have a highly developed self-feeling, self-consciousness and self-centred energy. Israel as a whole, every Jewish family and every member of it, are permeated through and through by the feeling and consciousness of their national, family and personal self and strive in every possible way to express it in action, steadily and indefatigably working for themselves, for their family and for Israel as a whole.

Finally, the third distinctive feature of the Jews is extreme materialism (in the broad sense of the term).

... Their practical materialism, i.e. the predominance of utilitarian and mercenary motives in their activity from the time of the exodus from Egypt down to the stock-exchanges of modern Europe, is too well known to need comment.

Thus the character of this extraordinary nation manifests to an equal extent the strength of the divine principle in the religion of Israel, the strength of human self-assertion in the national, family and personal life of the Jews, and, finally, the strength of the material element which colours all their thoughts and deeds. But how are those conflicting elements combined in one living individuality? What connects the religious idea of Israel with the human, active self-assertion of Jewry and with Jewish materialism? It would seem wholehearted devotion to the one God ought to nullify, or at any rate weaken, both the intensity of human self-assertion and the attachment to material goods. Again, a strong development of the human principle — humanism in one form or another — ought, one would have thought, on the one hand to counteract the superhuman authority of religion and on the other to raise the human spirit above gross materialism.

... It seems equally clear that the predominance of materialistic views and strivings is incompatible with either the religious or the humanistic ideals. In the Jews, however, all this exists side by side, without in the least destroying the integrity of the national character. In order to solve this riddle, we must not dwell upon the abstract ideas of religion, idealism and materialism *in general*, but must consider more carefully the peculiarities of Jewish religion, of Jewish humanism and of Jewish materialism.

Believing in God as One, the Jews never thought that man's religious task was to merge himself in God and disappear in His all-embracing unity. And indeed they did not attribute to God a negative and abstract all-unity or indifference. In spite of certain mystic ideas of the later Kabbalists and the pantheistic philosophy of Spinoza who was a Jew, they always saw in God not the infinite emptiness of the universal substratum, but the infinite fulness of a being that has life in itself and gives it to others. The living God, free from all external limitations and determinations but not diffused in general indifference, defines Himself and appears as a perfect personality or an absolute Self. In accordance with this, religion ought to be not the annihilation of man in universal divinity, but personal interaction between the divine and the human self. Precisely because the Jewish people were capable of such a conception of God and religion they could become God's chosen people.

The living God made Israel His people, because Israel too made the living God their own. Their forefather Abraham, living among the heathen and not having yet received a direct revelation of the true God, was not satisfied with the worship of false gods, so attractive to all other peoples. The worship of the elemental and demoniacal powers of nature was abhorrent to the Jewish soul. The progenitor of Israel could not believe in what was lower than man and sought for a personal and moral God, faith in whom would not be humiliating to man; and this God manifested Himself, and called him and gave promises to his seed. The same thing that brought Abraham out of the land of the Chaldees, brought Moses out of Egypt.

. . . Having severed themselves from paganism and risen, through their faith, above Chaldean magic and Egyptian wisdom, the progenitors and leaders of the Jews became worthy of the divine election. God chose them, manifested Himself to them, made a covenant with them. The treaty of alliance or the covenant of God with Israel is the centre of the Jewish religion. It is a unique fact in the world's history, for in no other nation did religion take the form of a treaty or covenant between God and man as two beings which though unequal in power are akin morally.

This high conception of man in no way detracts from God's greatness, but on the contrary allows it to manifest itself in all its force. In the independent moral being of man God finds a worthy object for His action; otherwise He would have nothing to act upon. If man were not a free personality, how could God manifest His *personal* being in the world? In so far as a self-existent and self-determining God, reigning over the world, excels the impersonal nature of cosmic phenomena, the sacred religion of the Jews is higher than all the naturalistic and pantheistic religions of the ancient world. In those religions neither God nor man preserve their independence: man is the slave of unknown and alien laws, and the Deity in the last resort (in the artistic mythology of the Greeks) proves to be the plaything of human imagination. In the Jewish religion on the contrary both sides are equally preserved throughout — both the human and the divine. Our religion begins with the *personal relation* between God and man in the Old Testament, in the covenant of Abraham and Moses, and is established by the closest possible *personal union* between God and man in the New Testament of Jesus Christ in whom both natures abide without division or confusion. These two covenants are not two different religions but only two stages of one and the same divinely-human religion, or, to use the language of German philosophy, two moments in one and the same divinely-human process. This one true, divinely-human, Judæo-Christian religion follows the straight royal road between the two extreme errors of paganism in which man is either engulfed by the Deity (in India), or the Deity itself becomes the reflection of man (in Greece and Rome).

The true God who chose Israel and was chosen by it is the strong God, the self-subsisting God, the holy God. The strong God chooses a strong man capable of struggling with Him; the self-subsisting God reveals Himself only to a self-subsisting personality; the holy God unites Himself only to the man who seeks holiness and is capable of active moral achievement. Human weakness seeks God's strength, but it is the weakness of the strong man: a naturally feeble man is incapable of strong religious feeling. Similarly, a man with a weak, colourless personality and undeveloped self-consciousness cannot rightly understand the truth of God's self-subsistence. Finally, God's holiness will always be something external and alien to a man whose freedom of moral self-determination is paralysed, who is incapable of spiritual initiative, of moral heroism and of attaining holiness; such a man will never be 'a friend of God'. Hence it is clear that the true religion which we find in the Jewish people does not exclude, but on the contrary actually demands the development of free human personality, of its self-feeling, self-consciousness and independent activity.

Israel was great in its faith, and for great faith great spiritual powers are needed. The energy of the free human principle finds its best expression in faith. There is a widespread fallacy that faith suppresses the freedom of the human spirit, while positive knowledge increases it. But in reality the contrary is true. In faith the human spirit transcends the limits of the given, actually present fact and affirms the existence of objects which do not *compel* his recognition — he recognizes them freely. Faith is an achievement of the spirit that finds evidence of things unseen. The believer does not passively wait to be affected by external objects, but boldly goes forward to meet them; he does not slavishly follow after events, but anticipates them — he is free and independent.

. . . The present and the obvious *insists* on being recognized, but the power of the spirit lies in divining the future, in recognizing and declaring the secret and the hidden. This is why the highest energy of the human spirit manifests itself in the prophets of Israel not in spite of their faith but in virtue of it.

This combination of the most profound faith in God with the greatest intensity of human energy has been preserved in later Judaism too. How strikingly it is expressed, for instance, in the concluding Paschal prayer for the coming of the Messiah:

'Oh may He who is most mighty soon rebuild his house; speedily, speedily, soon, in our days; O God! rebuild it, rebuild it, O God! rebuild it, rebuild thine house betimes! Oh, may He who is the supreme, the greatest and most exalted, soon rebuild his house; speedily, speedily, soon, in our days; O God! rebuild it, O God! rebuild it, rebuild thine house betimes. May He who is all-honoured and all-worthy, most immaculate and merciful, soon, rebuild his house; speedily, speedily, soon, in our days; O God! rebuild it, O God! rebuild it, rebuild thine house betimes. May He who is most pure, the sole God, soon rebuild his house; speedily, speedily, soon, in our days; O God! rebuild it, rebuild thine house betimes. May He who is the all-powerful, the omniscient and all-ruling, soon, rebuild his house; speedily, speedily, soon, in our days, O God! rebuild it, O God! rebuild thine house betimes. May He who is the most glorious and elevated, the God of strength, soon, rebuild his house; speedily, speedily, soon, in our days; O God! rebuild it, O God, rebuild it, rebuild thine house betimes. May He who is the redeemer, the all-righteous, the most holy, soon, rebuild his house, speedily, speedily, soon, in our days, O God! rebuild it, O God! rebuild it, rebuild thine house betimes. May He who is the most compassionate, the Almighty, all-potent, soon rebuild his house, speedily, speedily, soon, in our days, O God! rebuild it, O God! rebuild it, rebuild thine house betimes.' [1]

This characteristic prayer, expressive of the sincere faith in the God of Israel and the insistency of human will directed to Him, has another important peculiarity: the supplicants do not want their God to remain beyond the world. Seeing in Him the ideal of all perfection, they urgently demand that this ideal should be incarnate upon earth, that the Deity should express itself outwardly and visibly, should create a temple for itself, a material abode of its power and glory — and do so at once, as soon as possible. This impatient striving to embody the divine on earth supplies the guiding thread for the understanding of Jewish materialism and also the explanation of the present position of Israel.

In speaking of materialism, three kinds of it should be distinguished: the practical, the scientifically-philosophical and the religious. Materialism of the first kind directly depends upon the prevalence in the people concerned of the lower side of human nature, on the predominance of animal impulses over reason, of sensual interests over the spiritual. In order to justify in himself such dominance of the lower nature a practical materialist begins to deny the very existence of all that transcends that lower nature, of all that cannot be seen or touched, weighed or measured. In raising this denial to the rank of a general principle, practical materialism passes into theoretical or scientifically-philosophical materialism. The latter, through rationalistic analysis, reduces all existence to elementary material facts and systematically denies all truths of the divine and spiritual order. Just as practical materialism has always existed wherever there were morally crude people, so theoretical materialism has persisted through the whole history of philosophy, assuming various forms.

... Neither of these two kinds of materialism is especially characteristic of Judaism. Practical materialism in its pure form is very seldom met with among real Jews: even their notorious cupidity is sanctified by a higher purpose — the glory and

[1] Quoted from the *Service for the First Nights of Passover*, translated by Rev. A. P. Mendes.

enrichment of Israel as a whole. Scientific and philosophical materialism did not spring from Semitic ground either, but grew out of the Græco-Roman and, afterwards, of the Romano-Germanic culture; only through the prism of that culture can the Jews assimilate materialistic philosophy, utterly foreign to their own national spirit. Their national spirit, however, was always characterized by a third, special kind of materialism, radically different from the first two; I have described it, for short, by the rather inadequate term 'religious materialism'.

The Jews true to their religion, while fully recognizing the spiritual character of the Deity and the divine nature of the human spirit, could not and would not separate those higher principles from their material expression, from their external bodily form and their entire and final realization. A Jew expects every idea and ideal to have a visible and tangible embodiment and produce beneficent results; he will not recognize an ideal that cannot subdue reality and be incarnate in it; he is capable of accepting the highest spiritual truth and is ready to do so, but only on condition that he can see and feel its actual effect. He believes in the unseen (for all faith is faith in the unseen), but he wants it to become visible and manifest its power; he believes in the spirit, but only in the spirit that penetrates everything material and uses matter as its veil and its tool.

Not separating the spirit from its material expression, Jewish thought did not separate matter from its divine and spiritual ground; it did not recognize matter in itself or ascribe significance to substantial being *as such*. The Jews did not serve or worship matter. On the other hand, being strangers to abstract spiritualism, they could not consider matter with the remoteness and indifference, and still less with the hostility with which Eastern dualism regarded it. They saw in material nature not the devil and not the Deity, but only the unworthy abode of the divinely-human spirit. Practical and theoretical materialism submit to material facts as to a law; dualism turns away from matter as from an evil; the religious materialism of the Jews made them pay the greatest attention to material nature — not in order to serve it, but in order to serve the God on high in and through it. They had to distinguish in it the pure from the impure, the holy from the vicious, in order to make it a worthy temple of the Supreme. The idea of *holy flesh*, and the care to realize that idea, play an incomparably more important part in the life of Israel than of any other nation. A considerable section of Mosaic law dealing with the distinction between the pure and the impure and with the rules of purification is concerned with this. The whole religious history of the Jews may be said to have been directed towards preparing for the God of Israel not only holy souls but holy bodies as well.

If now we consider the Jews' striving for the materialization of the divine principle and their care to purify and sanctify bodily nature we shall easily understand why it was that the Jewish people presented the most suitable material environment for the incarnation of the divine Word. For both reason and piety compel us to admit that besides a holy and virginal soul, a pure and holy body was needed for God to be made man.

Clearly, this sacred materialism of the Jews does not in any way conflict with, but on the contrary serves as a direct complement to, their other two qualities — the deep religious feeling and the energy of human self-consciousness and independent activity. A believing Israelite wants the object of his faith to possess all the fulness of actuality, to be completely realized; the active human spirit cannot be content with the abstract content of ideas and ideals but demands their real embodiment; it demands that the spiritual principle should finally possess material reality through and through, and this presupposes in matter itself the capacity for being thus spiritualized — in other words, presupposes holy and spiritual corporeality. The religious materialism of the Jews springs not from disbelief but from a superabundance of faith eager for its fulfilment, not from the weakness but from the strength and energy of the human spirit which, unafraid of being defiled by matter, purifies it and uses it for its own ends.

Thus the three chief characteristics of the Jewish people in their combined effect directly corresponded to the high destiny of that people and furthered the completion of God's work in it. Firmly believing in the living God, Israel attracted to itself revelations and manifestations of the divine; believing in itself also, Israel could enter into a personal relation with Jehovah, stand face to face with Him, make a covenant with Him, serve Him not as a passive instrument but as an active ally; and striving in virtue of that same active faith for the final realization of the spiritual principle through purifying material nature, Israel prepared in its own midst a pure and holy abode for the incarnation of God the Word.

This is why the Jews are God's chosen people, this is why Christ was born in Judæa.

II

The reason why the Jewish people rejected Christ and are hostile to Christianity

All that is good in man and mankind is only preserved from distortion and perversion through union with the divine. As soon as the divinely-human bond is broken, man's inner moral balance is disturbed (though at first imperceptibly).

We have recognized three chief qualities in the Jewish character: firm faith in the living God, an intense feeling of their human and national personality, and an irresistible striving to realize and materialize their faith and their feeling, to clothe them in flesh and blood as soon as possible. Those three qualities in their rightful combination, with the due dependence of the last two upon the first, were to the greatest advantage and glory of Israel; they made it the chosen people, the friend of God, the helper in the divine incarnation. But those same three qualities, when the right relation between them is disturbed and the last two outweigh the first, become the source of great sins and disasters.

When wholehearted faith in the living God and His Providence occupies the first place, Jewish self-feeling and Jewish materialism serve the work of God and provide the foundations for true *theocracy*.

But as soon as the purely human and natural peculiarities of the Jewish character gain preponderance over the religious element, that unique and great national character manifests itself in the distorted form which accounts for the general dislike of the Jews (though it does not justify hostility towards them). In this distorted form national self-consciousness becomes national egoism and boundless self-adoration combined with contempt and hostility towards the rest of mankind; the realism of the Jewish spirit degenerates into practical utilitarianism, greediness and unscrupulousness which almost completely hide from outsiders, and especially from those who are prejudiced, the best features of the Jewish character. Many events in Jewish history, especially the chief event of Christianity, would be inexplicable apart from this profound distortion of the national character in a considerable part of the Jewish people. True, the *immediate* enemies of Jesus Christ exhibited vices and errors common to men as such and not

specifically Jewish: embittered vanity and pettiness of the
'teachers', false patriotism and imaginary wisdom of national
rulers are sufficiently well known everywhere both before and
after Christ. Personal hostility and malice aroused by Christ are
quite understandable. There is nothing enigmatic about His direct
enemies — they are the perfectly usual examples of perverted
human nature. It is understandable that those men could not be
convinced by Christ's miracles. Those miracles were acts of mercy
for the suffering and not signs for unbelievers. People who knew
of those miracles from hearsay only could easily deny their
reality and those of Christ's enemies who actually witnessed His
miraculous works did not in the least hesitate to deny their divine
character and to ascribe them to demonic powers.

But how are we to explain the fact that the common people,
carried away by the divine character of Christ's teaching and
works, suddenly denied Him and betrayed their Messiah to His
enemies? I cannot altogether agree with the usual explanation of
this fact. It is generally said that although the Jewish people were
expecting the Messiah, owing to their crudely sensuous nature
they pictured to themselves the Messiah's Kingdom *solely* as the
political triumph of Israel over all the other nations; the Gospel
teaching of the purely spiritual Kingdom of God had nothing in
common with these expectations, and that was why the Jews
could not recognize in Jesus their Messiah-King. It seems to me
that this explanation is faulty in two ways and needs double
rectifying. No doubt the Jews did expect of the Messiah, among
other things, the political victory of Judaism; there is also no
doubt that Christ preached first and foremost the kingdom of
God in spirit and in truth; but just as the Jewish expectations were
not confined to the political victory of the Messiah, so the Kingdom of God proclaimed by Christ was not limited solely to the
worship of God in spirit and in truth. As to the Jews, their
messianic expectations were primarily based upon the writings of
the prophets, and in those writings the coming kingdom of the
Messiah was pictured pre-eminently as the most complete revelation and triumph of the true religion, the spiritualization of the
Mosaic covenant, the affirmation of God's law in men's hearts,
the spreading of true knowledge of God and, finally, as the out-
pouring of God's Holy Spirit upon every creature.

Those among the Jewish people who did not recognize the

prophets (the Sadducees) did not expect *any* Messiah; and those who expected him on the strength of the prophetic writings could not exclude from their expectations the religious element which in the prophets was predominant. For the Jews who expected it, the Kingdom of the Messiah was bound to have not an exclusively political but a religiously political character; it was bound to appear to them not only in sensuous but in religiously sensuous forms. On the other hand, Christian teaching never was a doctrine of abstract spirituality. The fundamental truth of Christianity — the incarnation of the divine Word — is a spiritually *sensible* fact. When Christ said 'he that has *seen* me has *seen* the Father', He made the Deity more, and not less, accessible to man's sensuous perception.

Speaking generally, Christ's teaching did not reject the sensuous forms of religious life, but spiritualized them; nor did it deny that the Kingdom of the true God must overcome the world. If Christ's Kingdom were of this world it would have no right to possess the world; but precisely because it is not of this world and is free from worldly malice, it receives the whole world as its rightful heritage: blessed are the meek for they shall inherit the earth. The Christians, like the Jews (in the Prophets), strive not only for the renewal of the human spirit, but in accordance with this promise hope for a new heaven and a new *earth* wherein righteousness dwells. The Kingdom of God is not only inward, in the spirit, but also outward, with power: it is true *theocracy*. The Christian religion, in raising the human spirit to God, brings the Deity down to the human flesh: in this visible sacrament lies all its superiority to other religions, its fulness and perfection. Christianity differs from pagan wisdom by its very *purpose*; from Judaism it differs only by its relation to that purpose.

The final end for Christians and for Jews is the same — universal theocracy, the realization of the divine law in the human world, she incarnation of the heavenly in the earthly. This union between heaven and earth, this new covenant between God and the creature, this completed cycle and crown of universal labour is equally recognized by the Christians and the Jews. But Christianity also reveals to us the *way* to this crown, and that way is the Cross. And it was just this way of the Cross that the Jewish people of the time were unable to understand; they sought after a sign, i.e. a direct and immediate manifestation of divine *power*. The

Jews strove directly for the final conclusion, the last results; they wanted to obtain from without, by the formal way of testament, that which has to be gained through suffering, through a hard and complex process of inner division and moral struggle. Confining themselves to formal fidelity to the ancient covenant they expected to receive the Kingdom of God according to promise; they did not want to understand and accept the way of the Cross by which the Kingdom is received not directly from without, but is first acquired from within so as later to manifest itself outwardly. They did not want to understand and accept the Cross of Christ, and so for the last eighteen centuries they have against their will been bearing their own heavy cross.

The Cross of Christ through which the Kingdom of God is attained demanded of the Jewish people a twofold effort; first, to renounce their national egoism, and secondly to renounce temporarily their worldly strivings and their attachment to earthly welfare. While retaining the *positive* peculiarities of their character, the Jews ought to have widened and at the same time deepened their religion, to have given it a completely universal meaning and especially imparted to it the spirit of asceticism which it always lacked. The Jews ought to have taken up for a time the same position with regard to the world, hostile to them, as the persecuted Christian Church occupied: they ought to have risen against the pagan empire not as rebels but as martyrs; then they would have conquered and joined the Christians in a common triumph.

In order to realize the Kingdom of God on earth, it is necessary, first, to *recede* from earth; in order to manifest the spiritual idea in the material world it is necessary to be free and detached from that world. A slave of the earth cannot possess it and consequently cannot make it the foundation of God's Kingdom. In order to make the natural life an instrument and a means of the higher, spiritual life we must renounce the natural life as an end in itself. We must sever the senseless union of the spirit with matter in order to establish the true and holy combination between them.

The highest aim for Christianity is not ascetic detachment from the natural life but its hallowing and purification. But in order to purify it, one must, in the first instance, be pure from it. The purpose of Christianity is not to destroy earthly life, but to raise it towards God who comes down to meet it. And just as in the physical world a lever is needed to raise a heavy weight, i.e. the active force must be at a certain distance from the resisting body, so in the moral sphere the ideal life must be to a certain extent detached from its immediate environment so as to affect it all the more powerfully, to change and raise it up the more efficiently. Only he who is free from the world can benefit it. A captive spirit is unable to rebuild its prison into a temple of light: he must first of all free himself from it.

The purpose of Christian asceticism is not to weaken the flesh, but to strengthen the spirit for the transfiguration of the flesh. In accordance with this, Christian universalism aims not at destroying the natural peculiarities of each nation but, on the contrary, at strengthening the national spirit through purifying it from all leaven of egoism. That purpose was not foreign to the Jewish people. They cared not only about the purity and holiness of their bodily nature but also about *justifying* their national spirit. The actual method of this justification, however, was for the Jewish lawyers a matter of form rather than of substance. They sought union with God through an external conditional agreement and not through the inner deification by means of the Cross, by means of moral achievement and personal and national self-renunciation. This wonderful way, leading to the final end by receding from it, was utterly incomprehensible to the majority of the Jews, eager to reach the goal directly and as soon as possible. Their intense self-feeling rose against the Christian self-renunciation, their attachment to material life left no room for Christian asceticism; their practical mind could not reconcile the apparent contradiction between the end and the means: they were unable to understand how voluntary suffering leads to bliss, how mortification of the body results in its regeneration, and the renunciation of personal and national interests brings the fulness of personal and national life.

Since the very idea of bearing the Cross was an offence to the Jews, the Cross taken up by God Himself was a hopeless stumbling block to them, and the same Jewish nation, the best elements of which had prepared the environment and the matter for the incarnation of God the Word, proved in its mass the least receptive to the mystery of this incarnation.

The God-man, i.e. the union of the Deity with human nature in one individual person, is the *firstfruits*, the necessary ground and centre; and the end and completion is divine humanity (or, more exactly, deified humanity), i.e. the union of mankind as a whole with God, by the mediation of the God-man, and through it the union of all creation. The Jews who always seek the final practical end in everything they do, thought only of the collective union with God and failed to understand the necessity of the individual beginning and mediation for the attainment of this common end.

. . . But in denying the God-man as the one beginning of salvation, common to all, as the banner of nations, the Jews distorted the very meaning of God-manhood, making it the exclusive privilege of the people of Israel. This was wholly in keeping with the realistic character of Jewish thought. The nation, though collective, is a real, obvious entity, while humanity from the time of Babel has become an abstract idea and does not exist as a concrete self-contained whole. Therefore the Jews, who had not subordinated carnal reason to the knowledge of truth, in picturing to themselves the Kingdom of God naturally stopped at the confines of their own nation, rejecting humanity as an abstract fancy that merely robs the Kingdom of God of its real basis. Thus, on the one hand, Christianity as the proclamation of all-human brotherhood seemed to the Jews too wide, abstract and unreal; on the other, in so far as Christianity connects the work of universal salvation with the one Person of Jesus, it appeared to them narrow, arbitrary and insufficient. From both sides Christianity which aims at gathering *all* round *one* and through that *one* uniting each with all seems to the practical and realistic Jews an impossible and therefore false idea. The only way to prove to the Jews that they are mistaken is by facts — by realizing the Christian idea in practice and consistently applying it to actual life. The more fully the Christian world expresses the Christian idea of spiritual and universal theocracy, the more powerfully Christian principles affect the private life of Christians, the social life of Christian nations and the political relations within Christendom — the more clearly will the Jewish view of Christianity be refuted and the more probably and speedily will the conversion of the Jews take place. The Jewish problem, accordingly, is a Christian problem.

III

Christianity and Judaism have the same theocratical task before them — to build up a righteous society. Since the source of all truth and righteousness is in God, the righteous society is divinely-human. In it, man wholly and voluntarily submits to God, all men are unanimous with one another and enjoy complete power over material nature. According to the Jewish view such an ideal society must be embodied in the people of Israel (in the kingdom of the Messiah) and according to the Christian all nations are equally called to it. Christian universalism must not be taken to mean that all nations constitute merely impersonal material for the universal theocracy. All nations are only equal before the Gospel law in the sense in which, for instance, in a state all citizens are equal before the law of the land; this does not in the least prevent different kinds and grades of citizens having special rights arising from their special duties (thus in the most equalitarian country a doctor enjoys special rights which do not belong to a farmer, and in the most democratic republic a minister of the state has advantages over the night-watchman and so on — though they are all equal before the law which determines both the general rights of all and the special rights of each). Similarly, in the city of God (*in civitate Dei*) different nations may have different privileges, according to their special historical position and national vocation, so long as this does not conflict with mutual love and general solidarity. Thus there is no necessary contradiction between the theocratic ideas of Judaism and Christianity. If Jews have a claim to a special position and significance in the universal theocracy, we need not reject that claim beforehand, especially if we remember what St. Paul says of the Israelites 'to whom pertaineth the adoption, and the glory, and the covenants, and the giving of the law, and the service of God, and the promises; whose also are the fathers, and of whom as concerning the flesh Christ came, Who is over all, God. . . . Hath God cast away His people? God forbid! God hath not cast away His people which He foreknew. . . . I would not, brethren, that ye should be ignorant of this mystery, lest ye should be wise in your own conceits, that blindness in part is happened to Israel, until the fulness of the Gentiles be come in. And so all Israel shall be saved.'

The actions of the Jews are not worse than ours, and it is not for us to blame them. Their only fault perhaps is that they remain Jews and preserve their isolationism. Then show them visible and *tangible* Christianity so that they should have something to adhere to. They are practical people — show them Christianity in practice. Unite the Church, join it to the state by a righteous union, create a Christian state and a Christian society. The Jews are certainly not going to accept Christianity so long as it is rejected by the Christians themselves; it is not likely that they will join that which is divided in itself. Do not bring forward the argument that Christendom once upon a time enjoyed unity, and yet the Jews were not attracted by it. That was an involuntary, half-conscious unity, untried and untempted. And when trials and temptations came, the unity broke down, to the shame of the Christian world, to the triumph and justification of Judaism. And it will be right in feeling triumphant until we re-establish Christian unity freely and consciously.

. . . The union of Christians will be the great division of the Jews; but if the division of Christendom was a great calamity for it, the division of Israel will be a great blessing for the Christian world. The best elements among the Jews will enter the Christian theocracy, and the worst will remain outside, and only at the end, having suffered retribution in accordance with God's justice, shall be saved through His mercy — for St. Paul's words that 'all Israel shall be saved' are sure.

And when the Jews enter the Christian theocracy, they will bring into it that wherein they are strong.

. . . Once upon a time the flower of the Jewish race served as a receptive ground for the divine incarnation, and in the same way the Israel of the future will serve as an active medium for humanizing material life and nature and for creating the new earth wherein righteousness dwells.

III

BEAUTY
AND LOVE

1

BEAUTY IN NATURE

IT should be remembered that every philosophical theory of
art and beauty, while explaining its subject in its present
state, must open out for it wide future horizons. A theory which
merely registers and generalizes in abstract terms the actual connection between events is sterile: it is merely empirical and
scarcely rises above the wisdom of popular sayings and beliefs.
A truly philosophical theory in explaining the meaning of a fact,
i.e. its relationship to all that is akin to it, connects it thereby with
an endlessly ascending series of new facts. However bold such a
theory may appear, it will be neither arbitrary nor fantastic,
provided that its broad generalizations are based upon the true
essence of the object, discovered by the intellect in that object's
particular condition or appearance. For the essence of a thing is
necessarily greater and deeper than a particular appearance of it,
and therefore necessarily is the source of new appearances which
express or realize it more and more fully.

But in any case the essence of beauty must be grasped first of
all in its actual concrete appearances. Of the two kinds of
beautiful appearances — nature and art — we will take first that
which is wider in extent, simpler in content and prior to the other
in the order of time. The æsthetics of nature will give us the
necessary basis for a philosophy of art.

A diamond, i.e. crystallized carbon, is in its chemical composition the same as ordinary coal. Similarly, there is no doubt
that the song of a nightingale and the frantic caterwauling of a
love-sick cat are the same in their psycho-physiological nature —
namely, both are vocal expressions of an intensified instinct of
sex. But the diamond is beautiful and highly valued for its
beauty, whereas even the humblest savage is not likely to use a
piece of coal as an ornament. And while the nightingale's song
has always and everywhere been regarded as one of the manifestations of beauty in nature, cats' music, no less vividly expressive

of the same psycho-physical motive, has never given æsthetic pleasure to anyone.

These elementary instances are enough to show that beauty is something formally distinct and specific, not directly determined by its material basis of fact and not reducible to it. Being independent of the physical substratum of things and events, beauty is not conditioned, either, by the subjective valuation of practical utility or sensuous pleasure which those objects or events may have for us. It requires no proof that beautiful things are often completely useless for the satisfaction of our practical needs and that, on the contrary, the most useful things are often by no means beautiful.

Whatever its material elements may be, formal beauty as such is always completely useless. But this pure uselessness is highly valued by man, and, as we shall see later, not by man alone. And since beauty cannot be valued as a means of satisfying practical or physiological needs, it follows that it is valued as an end in itself. In beauty — even in the case of its simplest and most elementary manifestations — we come across something that is *unconditionally valuable*, that exists for its own sake and not for the sake of anything else, something that by its very presence gives joy and satisfaction to the human heart which, in beauty, finds peace and freedom from the struggles and labours of life.

Let us turn once more to the actual instances of beauty in nature. The beauty of the diamond is in no way inherent in its substance (for that substance is the same as that of a plain lump of coal) and evidently depends upon the play of light upon its crystals. This does not imply, however, that the property of beauty belongs not to the diamond itself but to the ray of light refracted in it. For the same ray reflected by some plain object produces no æsthetic impression, and if it is not reflected by or refracted in anything, produces no impression at all. Accordingly, beauty which belongs neither to the diamond's material body nor to the ray of light refracted by it is the result of interaction between the two. The play of light, retained and transformed by that body, completely conceals its crudely material appearance, and although the dark substance of carbon is present here as in coal, it is merely the bearer of the principle of light which reveals its own content in the play of colours. A ray of light falling upon a lump of coal is absorbed by its substance, and the blackness of coal is the natural symbol of the fact that in this case the power of light has not conquered the dark forces of nature.

In the union of substance and light, without division or confusion, both retain their nature but neither is visible in its separateness; all that is visible is light-bearing matter and embodied light — illuminated coal and petrified rainbow.

. . . Seeing that the beauty of the diamond wholly depends upon the transfiguration of its substance which retains and breaks up or unfolds rays of light, we must define beauty as the *transfiguration of matter through the incarnation in it of another, a super-material principle*.

. . . This conception of beauty based upon an elementary instance of beautiful visual appearances in nature is entirely confirmed by the equally elementary instance of beautiful sounds. Just as in the diamond the heavy and dark substance of carbon is clothed with radiant light, so in the song of the nightingale the physical sexual instinct is clothed in harmonious sounds. In this case the objective auditory expression of sexual passion completely hides its material basis, acquires an independent significance and may be abstracted from its direct physiological cause: one may listen to the bird's song and receive an æsthetic impression from it, completely forgetting what it is that urges it to sing; just as in admiring the diamond's brilliance we have no occasion to think of its chemical substance. But, in fact, just as it is necessary for the diamond to be a crystalized carbon, so it is for the nightingale's song to be an expression of sexual attraction partly transmuted into an objective auditory form. That song is the transfiguration of the sexual instinct, its liberation from the crude physiological fact — it is the animal sex instinct embodying in itself *the idea of love*.

. . . Thus in the case of sound, too, beauty proves to be the result of the interaction and mutual interpenetration of two factors: here, too, as in the visual instance, the ideal principle takes possession of the material fact and becomes embodied in it, while the material element receiving the ideal content into itself is illumined and transfigured thereby.

Beauty is an actual fact, the product of real natural processes taking place in the world. We have beauty in nature when ponderable matter is transformed into a luminous body, or when a fierce striving for a tangible physiological act is transformed into a

5

series of harmonious and rhythmical sounds. Beauty is absent when the material elements of the world appear as more or less *bare* — whether as crude formless bulk in the inorganic world or as unbridled animal instinct in the world of living organisms.

. . . Beauty in nature is not the expression of *any* content but only of an ideal content; in other words it is the *embodiment of an idea.*

The word 'idea' in the definition of beauty as 'an embodied idea' dispenses with the view that beauty may express *any* content; and the word 'embodied' corrects the still more prevalent view that although beauty must have an ideal content it is not an actual realization of it, but is merely an appearance or semblance (*Schein*) of the idea. On that second view the beautiful as a subjective psychological fact, i.e. as the sensation of beauty or its appearance in our mind, takes the place of beauty itself as an objective form in nature. In truth, however, beauty is an idea that is actually realized and embodied in the world prior to the human mind, and the incarnation of it is no less real and far more significant (in the cosmogonic sense) than the material elements in which it finds embodiment. The play of light in a crystalline body is in any case no less real than that body's chemical substance, and the modulations of a bird's song are as much a natural reality as is the instinct of reproduction.

Beauty or the embodied idea is the best portion of our real world, namely that portion of it which not merely exists but deserves to exist. We give the name of ideal in general to that which is in itself worthy of being.

In beauty it is essential to distinguish the general ideal essence from the specifically æsthetic form. Only the latter differentiates beauty from goodness and truth, for their ideal essence is the same — being that has value, absolute 'all-unity', freedom of particular existence in the universal unity. It is *this* that we desire as the highest good, it is *this* that we think as truth, and *this* too that we sense as beauty; but in order that we might sense an idea, it must be embodied in material reality. Beauty as such in its specific quality depends upon the completeness of such embodiment.

The criterion of worthy or ideal being in general is the greatest possible independence of parts combined with the greatest possible unity of the whole. The criterion of æsthetic worth is the most complete and many-sided embodiment of this ideal in the given material. It is obvious that in their application to particular cases those two criteria may not coincide and must be carefully distinguished. A very small degree of worthy or ideal being may be embodied with the highest degree of perfection in the given material, and the loftiest ideal motives may be expressed very poorly and imperfectly indeed. In the domain of art the distinction is obvious and only quite uncultured minds can confuse the two criteria — the generally ideal and the specifically æsthetic. The distinction is less obvious in the domain of nature, but it is undoubtedly present there too, and it is very important not to lose sight of it. Let us take two instances again — a tape-worm and a diamond. The first as an animal organism expresses to a certain extent the idea of life; the second, in its ideal content, stands for a certain degree of transfiguration of inorganic matter. The ideal of organic life, even if it be on the level of a worm, is higher than the idea of a crystallized body even though it be a diamond. In the diamond matter is illumined from outside only, while in the worm it is inwardly vitalized. In the simplest organism we find a greater number of separate parts and a greater unity among them than in the most perfect stone; every organism is more complex and at the same time more individual than a stone. Thus, according to the first criterion a tape-worm is higher than a diamond because it is richer in content. But in applying the purely æsthetic criterion we come to a different conclusion. In the diamond the elementary idea of a mineral transfused with light (a precious stone) is expressed more completely and perfectly than the higher and more complex idea of organic or, more specifically, of animal life is expressed in the tape-worm. A diamond is an object perfect of its kind, for nowhere else is such a power of resistance or impenetrability united with such luminosity, nowhere else do we find such vivid and subtle play of light upon so hard a body. The worm on the contrary is one of the most imperfect embryonic expressions of the idea of the organic life, to the realm of which it belongs.

. . . Thus, from the purely æsthetic point of view the worm, as an extremely imperfect embodiment of a comparatively high idea (of an animal organism), must be put incomparably lower than a diamond, which is a complete and perfect expression of the poorer idea of a luminous stone.

Matter is inert and impenetrable being — the direct opposite of the Idea as positive all-penetrability or all-unity. Only in *light* is matter liberated from its inertia and impenetrability, and through it the visible world is for the first time divided into two polarities. Light is the primary reality of the Idea in contradistinction to ponderable matter, and in that sense it is the first principle of beauty in nature. Further manifestations of beauty are conditioned by combinations of light with matter. Such combinations are of two kinds: mechanical or external, and organic or inward. The first result in the natural phenomena of light as such, and the second in the phenomena of life.

. . . In the inorganic world beauty belongs either to events and objects in which matter directly becomes a bearer of light or to those in which lifeless nature becomes as it were animated and manifests in its movements the character of life.

. . . Let us first say a few words about the beauty of inorganic nature *at rest*, of beauty dependent solely upon light.

The order in which the Idea incarnates, or beauty is manifested in the world, corresponds to the general cosmogonic order: at the beginning God created *heaven*. . . . Our ancestors regarded heaven as the father of gods; we, though not worshipping Svarog or Varuna, nor detecting any signs of a personal living being in the arch of heaven, admire its beauty no less than the pagans did; consequently that beauty does nót depend upon our subjective ideas, but is connected with actual properties inherent in the interstellar space visible to us. The æsthetic qualities of the sky are conditioned by light: it is beautiful only when it is illuminated. On a grey rainy day or a dark starless night the sky has no beauty whatever. In speaking of its beauty we really mean only the phenomena of light taking place in the cosmic space visible to us.

The all-embracing sky is beautiful as the image of universal unity, as the expression of serene triumph, of the eternal victory of the principle of light over chaotic confusion, of the eternal incarnation of the Idea in the whole of material existence.

We now pass from the appearances of calm, triumphant light to those of moving and seemingly free life in inorganic nature. Life in its most general sense is the free play or movement of particular forces and positions united in an individual whole. In so far as that play expresses one of the essential characteristics of worthy or ideal being, its embodiment in material phenomena — the real or the apparent life of nature — has an æsthetic significance.

This beauty of visible life in the inorganic world is notice-able first of all in flowing water in its various forms — streams, mountain-rivers, waterfalls. The æsthetic significance of this living movement is enhanced by its boundlessness, which seems as it were to express the insatiable longing of finite beings separated from the absolute all-inclusive unity.

And the boundless sea itself acquires a new beauty in its stormy motion as the symbol of rebellious life, of the gigantic struggle of elementary forces which cannot break the universal intercon-nectedness of the cosmos or destroy its unity, and only fill it with movement, brilliance and thunder.

. . . Chaos, i.e. utter formlessness, is the necessary background of all earthly beauty, and the æsthetic value of such things as the stormy sea depends precisely on the fact that chaos is stirring underneath them.

Outbursts of elemental forces or strivings of elemental im-potence, having no beauty in themselves, become willy-nilly the material for the more or less clear and complete expression in nature of the universal Idea or the positive all-embracing unity.

The architectonic principle of the universe, the Logos, reflected by matter from without as light and kindling the flame of life in matter from within, builds up in animal and plant organisms definite and stable forms of life which, gradually ascending to greater and greater perfection, may at last serve as the material and the soil for the true embodiment of the all-embracing and indivisible Idea.

The actual substratum of the organic forms, the material of the biological process, is *entirely* taken from the inorganic world: that is the booty won by the creative mind from chaotic matter. In other words, organic bodies are merely transformations of in-organic substance — in the same sense in which St. Isaac's Cathedral is a transformation of granite, or Venus of Milo is a transformation of marble.

. . . On the formal side we have in the structure of living or-ganisms a new and comparatively higher degree of the expression of the same architectonic principle which has been at work in the inorganic world — a new and comparatively more perfect way of embodying the same Idea which was already finding expression in inanimate nature, though more superficially and less definitely. The same image of the all-embracing unity which the cosmic artist has sketched in bold and simple strokes in the starry heaven or in the many-coloured rainbow is painted by him in subtle detail in plant and animal organisms.

... The general picture of the organic world presents two fundamental characteristics both of which must be equally recognized if we are to understand cosmic life and have a philosophy of nature and an æsthetic theory of it. In the first place, there is no doubt that the organic world is not the product of a so-called direct creation, or that it cannot be *directly deduced* from one absolute creative principle, for, if it were, it would have to be unconditionally perfect, serene and harmonious not only as a whole but also in every one of its parts. But reality by no means corresponds to such an optimistic conception. In this respect certain facts and discoveries of positive science are of decisive significance. In considering organic life on earth, especially in the palæontological age, sufficiently well known in our day, we find a clear picture of a complex and difficult process, determined by the struggle between different principles, which only after long efforts reaches a certain stable equilibrium. This is utterly unlike absolutely perfect creation proceeding directly from the creative will of the divine artist alone. Our biological history is a slow and painful process of birth. We see in it clear signs of inner opposition, blind groping, jerks and spasmodic shocks, unfinished sketches of failures — and what a number of monstrous creatures and abortions! All those palæozoa, those antediluvian monsters: megatheria, plesiosauri, ichthyosauri, pterodactyls — can they be direct and perfect creations of God? If they fulfilled their end and deserved the Creator's approbation, how could it have happened that they finally disappeared from our earth, making room for more balanced and harmonious forms?

The second fundamental characteristic of organic nature is that, although the life-giving agent of the cosmic process throws over his unsuccessful attempts without regret, he values not only the final end of the process, but also each of its innumerable stages, provided they embody the idea of life as well and as fully as they can. Winning step by step from chaotic elements the material for its organic creations, the cosmic mind treasures every one of its gains, abandoning only those which proved to be apparent only and on which boundless chaos had set its indelible mark.

At every new stage of cosmic development, with every new increase in the depth and complexity of natural existence there opens out a possibility of new and more perfect embodiments of the all-inclusive Idea in beautiful forms — but only a possibility. We know that increase in the power of natural life is not as such a guarantee of beauty, that the cosmogonic criterion does not coincide with the æsthetic and indeed is, in part, directly opposed to it. That is understandable. The elemental basis of the world, blind natural will, when raised to a higher level of being and thus inwardly intensified, is enabled thereby to submit more fully to the ideal principle of the cosmos — which then embodies in it a new and more perfect form of beauty; but at the same time its power of resistance to the ideal principle is also intensified, and at this higher stage it is able to carry out such resistance by more complex and significant means. The beauty of living (organic) beings is higher, but at the same time rarer than the beauty of inorganic nature; we know, too, that positive hideousness begins only where life begins. Passive plant-life offers but little resistance to the ideal principle which embodies in it the beauty of pure and clear forms that have not much content. The chaotic element, petrified in the mineral and slumbering in the vegetable kingdom, first awakes to active self-assertion in the animal life and mind, opposing its inner insatiableness to the objective idea of a perfect organism.

. . . The general palæontological history of the animal kingdom as a whole and the individual embryological history of each animal organism bear the clear stamp of the obstinate resistance of the vivified chaos to the higher organic forms designed from all eternity in the mind of the cosmic artist; in order to win lasting victories, he has to narrow down the battlefield more and more. And each new victory opens up possibilities of a new defeat: each time that a higher stage of beauty and organization is reached, there appear greater deviations, worse ugliness, as a more vivid manifestation of the primary formlessness that lies at the basis of life and of all cosmic being.

The cosmic artist had to work long and hard to embody ideal beauty in the domain of animal life, the basic matter of which is formless protoplasm and the typical representative — a worm.

The cosmic artist knows that the basis of the animal body is ugly and tries in every way to cover it up and adorn it. His purpose is not to destroy or thrust aside the ugliness, but to make it, first, clothe itself in beauty and, finally, transform itself into beauty. Therefore by means of secret suggestions which we call instinct he incites the creatures to make out of their own flesh and blood all kinds of beautiful coverings; he causes the snail to get into a fancifully coloured shell of its own making, which, for the purposes of utility (if it had any), did not in the least need to be ornamental; it impels the disgusting caterpillar to put on multicoloured wings which it had itself grown, and induces fishes, birds and beasts to cover themselves completely with sparkling scales, bright feathers, smooth and fluffy fur.

The higher animals — birds and still more certain mammals (those of the feline family and also deer, gazelles, etc.) — in addition to their handsome outer covering are in their whole appearance a beautiful embodiment of the idea of life — of graceful strength, harmonious co-ordination between the parts and free mobility of the whole. This ideal definition includes all the multifarious types and varieties of animal beauty, the description and enumeration of which does not form part of my task. It is the business of descriptive zoology. We also must leave aside the question of how, in what ways, the constructive power of the cosmic artist leads nature to create beautiful animal forms: that question can only be dealt with by metaphysical cosmogony. The present argument about beauty in nature may be concluded by pointing out facts which, as mentioned above, empirically confirm the objective character of that beauty.

The facts of sexual selection observed by Darwin and other naturalists are quite insufficient for explaining the beauty of all animal forms: they refer almost exclusively to outer ornamental beauty of various animals. What matters, however, in this connection is not the actual importance of the facts, but the unquestionable proof they provide of the independent objective significance of the æsthetic motive even in its most superficial expressions.

While many unbending minds were attempting in the interests of scientific positivism to reduce human æsthetics to a utilitarian basis, the greatest modern representative of that same school of thought showed that the æsthetic motive is independent of utilitarian purposes even in the animal kingdom and thus for the first time provided a positive basis for a truly idealistic æsthetic. This indisputable merit would alone be sufficient to immortalize Darwin's name even if he had not created the theory of the origin of species through natural selection in the struggle for existence — a theory that clearly defined and carefully traced one of the most important material factors of the cosmic process.

An animal's life is determined by two main interests: to support itself by means of nutrition and to perpetuate its species by means of reproduction. That latter aim is not, of course, consciously present to the animal, but is achieved by nature indirectly through exciting sexual attraction in individual entities of the opposite sex. The cosmic artist, however, makes use of sexual attraction in order not merely to perpetuate, but also to adorn the particular animal forms. Creatures belonging to the active sex, the males, pursue the female and struggle with one another on her account; and it appears, says Darwin, that contrary to all expectations, the power *to please* the female is in certain cases of more importance than that of beating other males in open battle.

The meaning of these facts is both simple and significant. Man finds certain things in nature beautiful, they give him æsthetic pleasure; most philosophers and scientists are convinced that this is merely a subjective peculiarity of the human mind and that in nature as such there is no beauty, any more than there is truth or goodness in it. But it appears that those very combinations of forms, colours and sounds which in nature please man, please also the creatures of nature themselves — the animals of all types and classes. They please them so much, have so great an importance for them, that the upkeep and development of those useless peculiarities, sometimes actually harmful from the utilitarian point of view, lies at the basis of their existence as a species. Accordingly, we cannot possibly say that the wings of a tropical butterfly or a peacock's tail are beautiful only on our subjective view, for their beauty is valued just as much by the female butter-flies and pea-hens. But in that case we are bound to go further. Once it has been admitted that a peacock's tail is objectively beautiful, it would be the height of absurdity to insist that the beauty of the rainbow or of the diamond is merely a subjective appearance in the human mind. Of course, if in a particular given case there is no sentient subject at all, there is no sensation of beauty; what matters, however, is not the sensation but the quality of the *object* capable of producing similar sensations in the most different subjects. But if, in general, beauty in nature is objective, it must have a certain general ontological basis — it must be, on different levels and in different ways, a sensuous embodiment of one absolutely objective all-inclusive Idea.

The cosmic mind, in obvious opposition to the primeval chaos and in secret agreement with the world-soul or nature — rent by that chaos and more and more amenable to the mental suggestions of the architectonic principle — creates in it and through it the complex and magnificent body of our universe. This creation is a *process* having two closely interconnected purposes, the general and the particular. The general purpose is the embodiment of the real Idea, i.e. of light and life, in different forms of natural beauty; the particular purpose is the creation of man, i.e. of the form which together with the greatest bodily beauty presents the highest inner concentration of light and life, called self-consciousness. Even in the animal world, as has just been shown, the general cosmic purpose is attained with the help and co-operation of the creatures themselves, through exciting in them certain inner feelings and strivings. Nature does not build up or adorn animals as some external material, but makes them build up and adorn themselves. Finally, man not merely participates in the activity of cosmic principles, but is capable of *knowing the purpose* of that activity and consequently of striving to achieve it freely and consciously. The same relation that obtains between human self-consciousness and animals' inner feeling, holds between beauty in art and beauty in nature.

2

THE MEANING OF ART

A TREE growing beautifully in the open and the same tree beautifully painted on canvas produce the same kind of æsthetic impression, are subject to the same æsthetic valuation — it is not for nothing that in both instances the same word is used to express it. But if it were merely a case of such visible, super-ficial similarity, the question might well be asked — and indeed it has been asked — why this reduplication of beauty? Is it not a childish amusement to repeat in a picture what already has a beautiful existence in nature? The usual answer to this is (for instance, given by Taine in his *Philosophie de l'art*) that art repro-duces not the actual objects and events as such but only as seen by the artist, and a true artist sees in them merely their typical, characteristic features; the æsthetic element of natural events, after passing through the artist's consciousness and imagination, is cleansed from all material accidents and thus is intensified and seen more clearly; beauty, disseminated in nature in forms and colours, appears concentrated, condensed, emphasized in a pic-ture. This explanation is not completely satisfactory, if only be-cause it is quite inapplicable to vast and important domains of art. What natural events are emphasized, for instance, in Beethoven's sonatas? The æsthetic connection between art and nature is ob-viously much deeper and more significant. In truth it consists not in the repetition, but in the continuation of the artistic work begun by nature — in a further and more complete solution of the same æsthetic task.

The result of the natural process is man — to begin with, as the most beautiful,[1] and, secondly, as the most conscious of natural beings. In this second capacity man is not simply the result of the cosmic process but an *agent* in it, thus answering more perfectly its

[1] I am speaking in this connection of beauty in a general and objective sense, and mean that man's exterior is capable of expressing a more perfect (a more ideal) inner content than can be expressed by other animals.

ideal purpose — the complete mutual interpenetration and free solidarity of the spiritual and the material, the ideal and the real, the subjective and the objective factors and elements of the universe. But why, then, it may be asked, do we consider the cosmic process begun by nature, and continued by man, from the æsthetic point of view, as the solution of some artistic problem? Would it not be better to regard its purpose as the realization of truth and goodness, the triumph of the supreme reason and will? If, in answer to this, we recall that beauty is simply an embodiment in sensuous forms of that very ideal content which, prior to such embodiment, is called truth and goodness, that will call forth a fresh objection. A strict moralist will say that goodness and truth need no æsthetic embodiment. To do good and to know truth is all that is needed.

In answer to this objection let us suppose that the good is realized not merely in someone's personal life, but in the life of the whole society, that an ideal social order is established, that there is complete solidarity and universal brotherhood. The impenetrability of egoism is done away with: all find themselves in each, and each in all. But if this universal mutual interpenetrability which is the essence of the moral good stops short of material nature, if the spiritual principle (having conquered the impenetrability of human psychological egoism) cannot overcome the impenetrability of matter, the physical egoism, that means that the power of goodness or love is not strong enough, that the moral principle cannot be realized to the end and fully justified. The question then arises: if the dark force of material being finally triumphs, if it is unconquerable by the principle of the good, is it not then the ultimate truth of all that is, and is not the good, as we call it, merely a subjective mirage? And, indeed, how can one speak of the triumph of the good when a society organized on the most ideal moral principles may perish any moment because of some geological or astronomical cataclysm? Absolute alienation of the moral principle from material being is fatal for the former, but certainly not for the latter. The very existence of the moral order in the world presupposes its connection with the material order, a certain co-ordination between the two. It might be imagined that this co-ordination should be sought for, apart from any æsthetics, in the direct power of human reason over the blind forces of nature and in the absolute mastery of the spirit over blind matter. Apparently, several important steps have been already taken in this direction; when the end is reached, and when, owing to the achievements of applied science, we conquer, as some optimists believe, not only space and time but death itself, the existence of moral life in the world, on the basis of the material, will be finally safeguarded; this will have no relation to the æsthetic motive, so that even then the contention that the good does not need beauty will remain in force. And yet, will in that case the good itself be *complete*? It consists not in the triumph of one over another, but in the solidarity of all. But can the beings and agents of the natural world be excluded from that *all*? They too cannot be regarded as merely the means or instruments of human existence, they too must enter as a positive element into the ideal structure of life. To be *secure* the moral order must rest upon material nature as the medium and the means of its existence, but to be *complete* and perfect it must include the material basis of existence as an independent part of moral activity which at this point becomes æsthetic; for material being can enter into the moral order only through spiritualization and enlightenment, i.e. only in the form of beauty. Beauty, then, is needed for the fulfilment of the good in the material world, for it is beauty alone that enlightens and subdues the evil darkness of this world.

But has not this work of bringing light to the universe been already done apart from us? Natural beauty has already clothed the world with its radiant veil; formless chaos stirs uneasily under the harmonious form of the cosmos, but cannot throw it off either in the limitless expanse of heavenly bodies or in the narrow range of earthly organisms. Should not art strive merely to clothe in beauty human relations alone and embody in sensible images the true meaning of human life? But in nature dark forces are merely subdued, and not won over by the universal reason; the victory is superficial and incomplete, and the beauty of nature is merely a veil thrown over the evil life and not the transfiguration of that life. That is why man with his rational mind must be not only the final end of the natural process but, also in his turn, a means for a more profound and complete action of the ideal principle upon nature. We know that in nature the realization of that principle differs in degree and that every increase in depth on the positive side is accompanied by a corresponding increase or inner intensification on the negative. In inorganic matter the evil principle acts merely as heaviness and inertia; in the organic world it manifests itself as death and dissolution (and here, too,

hideousness is less obviously triumphant in the destruction of
plants than in the death and decomposition of animals, and in the
case of higher animals more so than in that of the lower); in man,
in addition to showing itself more completely and intensely on the
physical side, it also expresses its deepest essence as moral evil.
But, on the other hand, it is possible for man to triumph over it
finally and to embody that triumph in eternal and incorruptible
beauty. According to the old conception, now widely prevalent
again, moral evil is identical with the dark, unconscious physical
life, and moral goodness with the rational light of consciousness
that develops in man. That the light of reason is in itself good is
unquestionable; but physical light cannot be called evil either.
Both the one and the other have the same significance in their
respective spheres. In physical light [1] the universal idea (positive
all-unity, the life of all for one another in the one) is realized in a
reflected form only: all events and objects are able to exist for one
another or are revealed to one another in their mutual reflections
by means of a common imponderable medium. In a similar way
all that exists is reflected in reason by means of general abstract
notions which do not express the inner being of things but only
their superficial logical schemata. Hence, in rational knowledge we
find only a reflection of the universal idea and not its real presence
in the knower and the known. For their true realization goodness
and truth must become a creative power in the subject, transforming reality and not merely reflecting it. In the physical world
light is transformed into life and becomes the organizing principle
of plants and animals, so that it is not merely reflected by bodies,
but is incarnate in them; in the same way, the light of reason
cannot be confined to knowledge alone, but must artistically embody the apprehended meaning of life in a new setting that is more
in keeping with it. Of course, before creating in beauty or transforming the not-ideal reality into an ideal one, the difference
between the two must be known — and known not merely in

[1] I am speaking here, of course, not of the visual sensations of light in man
and in animals, but of light as the movement of an imponderable medium
which interconnects material bodies and thus conditions their objective being
for one another independently of our subjective sensations. 'Light' alone is
mentioned for shortness, but the same thing may be said of other dynamic
phenomena: heat, electricity, etc. We are not concerned here with any
hypotheses of physical science, but only with the fact that there is an unquestionable difference between the nature of those phenomena and ponderable
matter.

the abstract, but first of all through immediate feeling inherent in the artist.

The difference between ideal, i.e. valuable or worthy being, and unworthy or wrong being depends, generally speaking, upon the particular relation of the given elements to one another and to the whole. When, to begin with, particular elements do not exclude one another but on the contrary mutually posit themselves in one another and are at one; when, secondly, they do not exclude the whole but build up their particular being upon one universal basis; when, thirdly, that universal basis or absolute principle does not suppress or engulf the particular elements but, manifesting itself in them, gives them complete freedom within itself — such being is ideal or valuable, that which ought to be. Indeed, in itself it *is* already, though to us it appears not as a given reality, but as an ideal only partly and gradually realized; in that sense it becomes the final end and absolute norm of our vital activities. The will strives towards it as the highest good, thought is determined by it as the absolute truth, and it is partly sensed and partly divined by our feelings and imagination as beauty. These positive ideal determinations of valuable being are essentially identical, just as are the corresponding negative principles. Every kind of evil consists at bottom in the violation of the mutual solidarity and balance between parts and whole; and all falsehood and ugliness can be reduced to that too. When a particular or single element asserts itself in its separateness, striving to exclude or to suppress other beings; when particular or single elements together or separately strive to put themselves in the place of the whole, to exclude or deny its independent unity and consequently the common bond between themselves; or when, on the contrary, the freedom of particular being is diminished or taken away in the name of unity — all this, exclusive self-assertion (egoism), anarchic separatism and tyrannical uniformity, must be pronounced *evil*. The same thing transferred from the practical sphere to the theoretical is *falsehood*. An idea is false when it is solely concerned with some one particular aspect of reality to the exclusion of all the others; an intellectual outlook is false when it admits only an indefinite collocation of particular empirical events and denies the general meaning or the rational unity of the cosmos; equally false is abstract monism or pantheism that denies all particular existence in the name of absolute unity. The same essential characteristics that determine evil in the moral sphere and falsity in the intellectual determine ugliness in the æsthetic sphere. Everything in which one part grows out of all proportion and predominates over others, all that is lacking in wholeness and unity and, finally, all that is deficient in free multiplicity is ugly. Anarchic multiplicity is as much opposed to goodness, truth and beauty as is dead, crushing unity: the attempt to realize such a unity in a sensuous form results in the idea of infinite emptiness, devoid of all special and definite forms of being — i.e. in mere formlessness.

Worthy or ideal being requires equal freedom for the whole as for the parts; consequently it does not mean freedom from particular determinations but only from their exclusiveness. The fulness of such freedom requires that all particular elements should find themselves in one another and in the whole, that each should posit itself in the other and the other in itself, that each should be aware of its own particularity in the unity of the whole, and of the unity of the whole in its own particularity — in short, that there should be absolute solidarity between all that is, and God should be all in all.

Complete sensuous realization of that universal solidarity or positive all-unity — perfect beauty not merely as an idea reflected from, but as actually present in matter — presupposes in the first instance the closest and deepest interaction between the inner or spiritual and the outer or material being. This is the fundamental æsthetic requirement, the specific difference between beauty and the two other aspects of the absolute idea. An ideal content which remains merely an inner property of the spirit, of its will and thought, is devoid of beauty, and absence of beauty means that the idea is impotent. Indeed, so long as the spirit is incapable of giving direct external expression to its inner content and of incarnating itself in material phenomena, and, on the other hand, so long as matter is incapable of receiving the ideal action of the spirit and of being penetrated by or transmuted into spirit, there is no true unity between these two main realms of being. That means that the idea which is the perfect harmony of all that is has not as yet, in this particular manifestation of it, sufficient power fully to realize or fulfil itself. Neither abstract spirit incapable of creative incarnation nor soulless matter incapable of spiritualization corresponds to ideal or worthy being, and both bear a clear stamp of their unworthiness inasmuch as neither can be beautiful. The fulness of beauty requires, first, direct material embodiment of the spiritual essence and, secondly, complete spiritualization of the material appearance as the inherent and inseparable form of the ideal content. To this twofold condition there is necessarily added a third — or, rather, it follows from it of necessity. When the spiritual content is immediately and indissolubly united in beauty to its sensuous expression and there is complete mutual interpenetration between them, the material appearance that has really become beautiful, i.e. has actually embodied the idea, must become as permanent and immortal as the idea itself. In Hegelian æsthetics beauty is the incarnation of the eternal universal idea in particular and transitory events, which still remain transient and disappear like separate waves in the stream of the material process, reflecting but for a moment the radiance of the eternal idea. But this can only be if the relation between the spiritual principle and the material event is one of impassive indifference. True and perfect beauty, however, expressing as it does complete oneness and mutual interpenetration between these two elements, must of necessity make the material one actually participate in the other's eternity.

The beautiful appearances of the physical world are far from conforming to those demands or conditions of perfect beauty. To begin with, in natural beauty the ideal content is not sufficiently transparent; it does not reveal itself in all its mysterious depth, but only manifests its general outline, illustrating, so to speak, through concrete particular facts the simplest characteristics of the absolute idea. Thus light in its sensuous qualities expresses the all-pervading and imponderable character of the ideal principle; plants show in their visible form the expansiveness of the idea of life and the general striving of the earthly soul towards the higher forms of being; beautiful animals express the intensity of vital motives united in a complex whole and sufficiently balanced to admit free play of the forces of life, and so on. The idea undoubtedly is embodied in all this but only externally, in a general and superficial way. The superficial materialization of the ideal principle in natural beauty is in keeping with the equally superficial spiritualization of matter, and that leads to the possibility of apparent contradictions between form and content: a typically ferocious beast may be very beautiful. The contradiction is only apparent because, being superficial, natural beauty expresses the idea of life not in its inner moral quality, but merely in its external physical characteristics such as swiftness, force, freedom of movement, etc. The third essential imperfection of natural beauty is connected with the same fact: since it does not wholly and inwardly pervade the chaotic nature of material being, but merely throws an external covering over it, that beauty remains eternal and unchangeable *in general* only, in the genera and species — while each particular beautiful appearance and entity remains in the power of the material process which first damages its beautiful form and subsequently destroys it altogether. From the naturalistic point of view this instability of all individual appearances of beauty is a fatal and unalterable law. But in order to be even theoretically reconciled to this triumph of the all-destroying material process it is necessary to admit — as consistent adherents of naturalism do — that beauty and all other ideal contents of the world are a subjective illusion of human imagination. We know, however, that beauty has an objective significance, that it acts outside the human world, and that nature herself is not indifferent to beauty. And if nature has not succeeded in realizing perfect beauty in the domain of physical life, it is with good reason that through great labours and efforts, terrible catastrophes and monstrous creations — necessary, however, for the final end — she rises from that lower realm into the sphere of conscious human life. The task that cannot be fulfilled by means of physical life must be fulfilled through human creativeness.

Hence the threefold task of art in general is: (1) to give a direct objective expression to the deepest inner qualities and determinations of the living Idea which nature is incapable of expressing, (2) to spiritualize natural beauty and through this (3) to perpetuate its individual appearances. That means transforming physical life into spiritual, i.e. into a life which, in the first place, has its own word or revelation in itself and is capable of direct outward expression; which, in the second place, is capable of inwardly transforming and spiritualizing matter or of being truly incarnate in it; and which, thirdly, is free from the power of the material process and therefore abides forever. Completely to embody this spiritual fulness in our actual world, to realize absolute beauty in it or to create a universal spiritual organism is the highest task of art. Clearly the fulfilment of this task must coincide with the end of the cosmic process as a whole. While history still continues there can be only partial and fragmentary anticipations of perfect beauty. In their highest achievements the arts that exist at present catch glimpses of eternal beauty in our transitory existence and, extending them further, anticipate and give us a foretaste of the reality beyond, which is to come. They are thus a transition stage or a connecting link between the beauty of nature and the beauty of the life to come. Interpreted in this way art ceases to be empty play and becomes important and instructive work, not, of course, in the sense of a didactic sermon but of an inspired *prophecy*. The indissoluble connection that once existed between art and religion proves that this exalted significance of art is not an arbitrary demand. The original inseparability between the religious and the artistic work is certainly not to be regarded as an ideal. True and complete beauty demands greater scope for the human element and presupposes a higher and more complex development of social life than could be attained in primitive culture. The present alienation between art and religion is a transition from the ancient fusion to a future free synthesis. The perfect life, anticipations of which true art gives us, will also be based, not upon the submergence of the human element by the divine, but upon their free interaction.

We can now formulate a general definition of real art as such: every sensuous expression of any object or event from the point of view of its final state or in the light of the world to come is a work of art.

The anticipations of perfect beauty in human art are of three kinds: (1) direct or *magic*, when the deepest inner states connecting us with the true essence of things and the transcendental world (or, if preferred, with the *an-sich-Sein* of all that is) break through all conventions and material limitations, and find direct and complete expression in beautiful sounds and words (music and, partly, pure lyrics); (2) indirect, through the intensification of the given beauty. The inner, essential and eternal meaning of life concealed in the particular and accidental appearances of the natural and the human world is but vaguely and insufficiently expressed by their natural beauty; it is revealed and clarified by the artist who reproduces those appearances in a concentrated, purified and idealized form. Thus, architecture reproduces in an idealized form certain regular shapes of natural bodies, expressing in this way the victory of those ideal forms over the fundamental anti-ideal property of matter — gravity; classic sculpture, in idealizing the beauty of the human form and strictly observing the fine but definite line that distinguishes bodily beauty from the carnal, anticipates in its achievement the spiritual corporeality which shall one day be revealed to us in actual fact; landscape painting (and, partly, lyrical poetry) reproduce in a concentrated form the ideal aspect of the complex phenomena of physical nature, cleansing them from all material accidents (and even from three-dimensional extendedness); religious painting and poetry are an idealized reproduction of such facts of human history as had revealed in advance the higher meaning of our existence. (3) The third kind of æsthetic anticipation of the perfect reality of the future is also indirect, and consists in reflecting the ideal from an environment alien to it, and intensified by the artist to make the reflection more vivid. The disharmony between the given reality and the ideal or the higher meaning of life may be of different varieties. To begin with, a certain human reality, perfect and beautiful after its own kind (namely, after the kind of the *natural* man), falls short of the absolute ideal intended for the *spiritual* man and humanity. Achilles and Hector, Priam and Agamemnon, Krishna, Arjuna and Rahma are unquestionably beautiful, but the more artistically they and their deeds are depicted the clearer *in the last resort* it is that they are not what true men should be, and that true human achievement is different from their exploits. Homer probably — and the authors of the Indian poems certainly — had no such idea in mind, and we must regard heroic epic poetry as a vague and unconscious reflection of the absolute ideal from a beautiful but inadequate human reality.

. . . A deeper attitude towards the unrealized ideal is to be found in tragedy, where the characters themselves are imbued with the sense of an inner contradiction between their given reality and that which ought to be. Comedy, on the other hand, intensifies and deepens the feeling for the ideal, first by emphasizing that aspect of reality which cannot in any sense be called beautiful, and secondly by representing men who live in that reality as perfectly content with it — thus making them still more at variance with the ideal. It is this *complacence* and not the outer setting of the plot that constitutes the essential nature of the comical as distinct from the tragical element.

In order to see that even the greatest poetical works express the meaning of spiritual life merely by *reflecting* it from the non-ideal human reality, let us take Goethe's *Faust*. The positive meaning of this lyrico-epic tragedy is directly revealed only in the last scene of the second part and is abstractly summed up in the final chorus,

Alles Vergängliche ist nur ein Gleichnis, and so on. But what is the direct organic bond between this apotheosis and the rest of the tragedy? The heavenly powers and *das ewig Weibliche* appear from above, and therefore, after all, from outside, and are not revealed from within the subject. The idea of the last scene is present in *Faust* throughout, but it is merely reflected from the partly real, partly fantastic plot of the tragedy itself. Just as a ray of light plays on a diamond to the delight of the spectator, but without producing any change in the material composition of the stone, so the spiritual light of the absolute ideal refracted in the artist's imagination illumines the dark human reality without in the least altering its essence. Let us suppose that a poet mightier than Goethe or Shakespeare did present in a complex poetic work an artistic, i.e. a true and concrete, picture of truly spiritual life — of the life which ought to be and which realizes the absolute ideal to perfection — even that miracle of art, not achieved so far by any poet, [1] would in our present world be merely a magnificent mirage in an arid desert, heightening but not satisfying our spiritual thirst. The final task of perfect art is to realize the absolute ideal not in imagination only but in very deed — to spiritualize and transfigure our actual life. If it be said that such a task transcends the limits of art, the question may well be asked, who has laid down those limits? We do not find them in history; we see there a changing art, art in the process of development. Separate branches of it attain their perfection and develop no more; to make up for this, other branches come into being. All are probably agreed that sculpture was brought to its final perfection by the ancient Greeks; nor is it likely that further progress will be made in heroic epic poetry and pure tragedy. I venture to go further and do not think it too bold to assert that just as the ancients had perfected those forms of art, so the modern European nations have exhausted all other species of art known to us; if art has a future, it lies in quite a new sphere of activity. Of course, this future development of æsthetic creativeness depends upon the general course of history; for art in general is the sphere of the embodiment of ideas and not of their original inception and growth.

[1] In the third part of the *Divine Comedy* Dante describes paradise in a way which may be true, but is certainly not sufficiently vivid and concrete — a fundamental defect which cannot be redeemed by the most musical verses.

3

THE MEANING OF
LOVE

THE meaning of sexual love is generally supposed to consist in subserving the propagation of the species. I consider this view to be mistaken — not on the ground of any ideal considerations as such, but first and foremost on grounds of natural history. That the reproduction of living creatures does not need sexual love is clear if only from the fact that it does not even need the division into sexes. A considerable part both of vegetable and animal organisms multiply sexlessly: by division, budding, spores, grafting. True, the higher forms in both the organic kingdoms reproduce themselves sexually. But to begin with, the organisms that do so *may* also multiply sexlessly (grafting in the plant world, parthenogenesis among the higher insects), and secondly, admitting that as a general rule higher organisms multiply by means of sexual union, the conclusion to be drawn is that the sex factor is connected not with reproduction as such (which may take place without it) but with the reproduction of *higher* organisms. Hence, the meaning of sexual differentiation (and, consequently, of sexual love) must be sought for not in the idea of generic life and its reproduction, but only in the idea of a higher organism.

A striking confirmation of this is provided by the following great fact. Among animals that reproduce themselves solely in the sexual way (the vertebrates), the higher we go in the organic scale, the less is the power of reproduction and the greater the force of sex attraction. In the lowest class of this section — the fishes — the rate of reproduction is enormous: the spawn yearly produced by every female are counted in millions; they are fertilized by the male outside the body of the female, and the way in which it is done does not suggest strong sexual attraction. Of all vertebrate creatures this cold-blooded class undoubtedly multiplies most and

150

shows least trace of love-passion. At the next stage — among the amphibians and the reptiles — the rate of reproduction is much lower than among the fishes, though some of the species of that class justify the Bible description of them as 'swarming'; but, with a lower rate of reproduction, we find in those animals closer sexual relations. In birds the power of reproduction is much smaller than, for instance, in frogs, to say nothing of fishes, while sexual attraction and mutual affection between the male and the female are developed to a degree unexampled in the two lower classes. Among mammals (or the viviparous) reproduction is much slower than among the birds, and sexual attraction is much more intense, though for the most part less constant. Finally, in man the rate of reproduction is lower than in the rest of the animal kingdom, but sexual love attains the greatest force and significance, uniting in the highest degree the permanence of relations (as with birds) with the intensity of passion (as with the viviparous).

Thus sexual love and reproduction of the species are in *inverse ratio* to each other: the stronger the one, the weaker the other. Altogether, the animal kingdom as a whole develops in this respect in the following order: at the lowest level there is an enormous power of reproduction and a complete absence of anything like sexual love (since there is no division into sexes); further, in more perfect organisms there appear sexual differentiation and, corresponding to it, a certain sexual attraction, very weak at first; at the further stages of organic development it increases, while the power of reproduction diminishes (i.e. it increases in direct ratio to the perfection of the organism and in inverse ratio to the power of reproduction), until at last, at the top of the scale, in man, there may be intense sexual love without any reproduction whatever. If, then, at the two opposite poles of animal life we find, on the one hand, reproduction without any sexual love, and on the other, sexual love without any reproduction, it is perfectly clear that these two facts cannot be indissolubly interconnected; it is clear that each of them has an independent significance of its own, and that the meaning of one cannot consist in serving as a means for the other. The same conclusion follows if we consider sexual love exclusively in the human world, where it acquires, incomparably more clearly than in the animal kingdom, an individual character, in virtue of which *precisely this* person of the opposite sex has an absolute significance for the lover as unique and irreplaceable, as an end in itself.

At this point we meet with a popular theory which, while admitting that sexual love as such serves the generic instinct and is a means of reproduction, attempts to explain the individualization of love in the case of man as a certain trick or deception practised by nature or the cosmic will for its own ends. In the human world, where individual peculiarities have far more significance than in the animal or the vegetable kingdom, nature aims not merely at preserving the species, but also at realizing within the limits of it a number of possible specific types and individual characters. Apart from this general purpose of manifesting the greatest possible variety of forms, the life of mankind as a historical process has for its purpose to raise and improve human nature. This requires not merely as many different specimens of humanity as possible, but also its *best* specimens, valuable both in themselves as individual types and for their uplifting and improving influence upon others. Thus the moving power of the cosmic and the historical process — whatever we may call it — is concerned not only with the continual reproduction of human individuals after their own kind, but also in certain particular and so far as possible significant specimens being born. For this purpose simple reproduction through promiscuous and fortuitous union of the sexes is insufficient: to produce individually determined offspring, the union of individually determined parents is required, and consequently the general sexual attraction that serves the purposes of reproduction among animals is not enough. With human beings it is not producing offspring as such that matters, but producing a particular kind of offspring, most suitable for world-purposes; and since this given individual can produce such offspring, not with any individual of the opposite sex, but only with one particular person, that person alone must have for him or her a special power of attraction and appear exceptional, irreplaceable, unique and capable of bestowing the highest bliss. It is this individualization and exaltation of the sexual instinct that distinguishes human love from animal, but it too is aroused in us by an alien, though perhaps a higher, power for its own ends, foreign to our personal consciousness; it is aroused as an irrational, fatal passion that takes possession of us and disappears like a mirage as soon as the need for it is over.

If this theory were correct, if the individual and exalted nature of the love-feeling had its whole meaning, reason and purpose in something external to itself, namely, in the quality of the offspring required for world-purposes, it would logically follow that the degree of the individualization and intensity of love was in direct ratio to the character and significance of the offspring to which it gave rise: the more valuable the offspring, the greater the love between the parents, and, *vice versa*, the stronger the love between two particular persons, the more remarkable their offspring should be. If, speaking generally, the love feeling is aroused by the cosmic will for the sake of the required offspring and is merely *a means* for producing it, in each given case the strength of the means used by the cosmic mover must be proportionate to the importance of the end to be achieved. The more the cosmic will is interested in the offspring-to-be, the more strongly it must attract to each other and bind together the two necessary progenitors. Suppose a world-genius of enormous importance for the historical process has to be born; in so far as a genius is more rare than ordinary mortals, the higher power controlling the historical process would obviously be proportionately more interested in his birth than in others; and consequently the sexual attraction, by means of which the cosmic will (according to this theory) secures the end so important to it, should be proportionately more intense than usual. The champions of the theory may, of course, deny the presence of an exact quantitative ratio between the importance of a given individual and the intensity of his parents' passion, since such things admit of no exact measurement; but it is absolutely indubitable (from the standpoint of the theory in question) that if the cosmic will is *extremely interested* in the birth of some person, it must take *extreme measures* to secure the desired result, i.e. it must arouse in the parents a passion of extreme intensity, capable of overcoming all obstacles to their union.

In reality, however, we find nothing of the kind. There is no correlation whatever between the intensity of the love-passion and the importance of the progeny. To begin with, there is the fact, utterly inexplicable for the theory we are considering, that the most intense love often remains unrequited and produces no offspring whatever, let alone valuable offspring. If as a result of such love people take monastic vows or commit suicide, why should the cosmic will concerned with posterity have troubled about them? But even if the ardent Werther [1] had not committed

---

[1] I illustrate my arguments by instances taken chiefly from great literary works. They are better than instances from real life, for they represent types and not particular cases.

suicide, his unhappy passion would remain an inexplicable riddle for the theory of qualified offspring. From the point of view of that theory Werther's intense and highly individualized love for Charlotte showed that it was only with Charlotte he could produce the offspring of special value and importance for humanity, for the sake of which the cosmic will aroused in him this extraordinary passion. But how was it, then, that this omniscient and omnipotent will proved incapable, or did not think of similarly affecting Charlotte, without whose reciprocity Werther's passion was quite unnecessary and served no purpose? For a teleologically acting substance *love's labour lost* is an utter absurdity.

Exceptionally intense love is generally unhappy, and unhappy love very often leads to suicide in one form or another, and each of these suicides through unhappy love disproves the theory that intense love is aroused solely for the purpose of producing descendants whose importance is indicated by the intensity of the love. But in all such cases it is the very intensity of love that rules out the possibility of any descendants at all.

As a general rule from which there are hardly any exceptions, particular intensity of sexual love either altogether excludes reproduction or results in offspring the importance of which in no way corresponds to the power of the love feeling and to the exceptional character of the relations arising from it.

To find the meaning of sexual love in successful childbearing is the same as to find meaning where there is no love, and where there is love, to deprive it of all meaning and justification. This fictitious theory of love when put to the test of facts proves to be not an explanation but, rather, a refusal to explain anything.

Both with animals and with man sexual love is the finest flowering of the individual life. But since in animals the life of the genus is of far more importance than that of the individual, the highest pitch of intensity achieved by the latter merely profits the generic process. Although sexual attraction is not simply a means for the propagation or the reproduction of organisms, it serves to produce *more perfect* organisms through sexual rivalry and selection. An attempt has been made to ascribe the same significance to love in the human world, but, as we have seen, quite in vain. For in the human world individuality has an independent significance and in its strongest expression cannot be merely a means for the ends of the historical process external to it. Or, to put it better, the true end of the historical process does not admit of the human personality being merely a passive and transitory means to it.

The conviction that man has absolute worth is based neither upon self-conceit nor upon the empirical fact that we know of no other more perfect being in the order of nature. Man's unconditional worth consists in the absolute form (or image) of *rational* consciousness undoubtedly inherent in him. Being aware, as animals are, of his experiences, detecting certain connections between them and, on the basis of those, anticipating future experiences, man also has the faculty of passing judgments of value on his own states and actions, and on facts in general, in their relation not only to other particular facts but to universal ideal norms; man's consciousness is determined not only by empirical facts but by the *knowledge of truth*. Conforming his actions to this higher consciousness man can infinitely perfect his life and nature *without transcending the human form*. This is why he is the highest being in the natural world and the true end of the process of world-creation; for, next to the Being which is Itself the absolute and eternal truth, comes the being which is capable of knowing and realizing truth in itself; it is highest not relatively but unconditionally. What rational ground can be adduced for creating new and essentially more perfect forms when there already exists a form capable of infinite self-perfectibility and of receiving the whole fulness of the absolute content? Once such a form has appeared, further progress can only consist in new degrees of its own development and not in replacing it by some other creatures, some hitherto non-existent forms of being. This is the essential difference between the cosmogonic and the historical process. The first (before the appearance of man) creates a succession of new kinds of beings: the old are partly destroyed, as unsuccessful experiments, and partly coexist with the new in a purely external way, accidentally coming together, but forming no *real* unity because they have no common consciousness to connect them with one another and with the cosmic past. Such common consciousness appears in man. In the animal world the succession of the higher forms upon the lower, however regular and purposive, is a fact utterly external and foreign to the animals themselves and indeed non-existent for them: an elephant or a monkey can know nothing about the complex process of geological and biological transformations that conditioned their actual appearance upon the earth; the comparatively high level of intelligence reached by this or that animal or by a particular species does not mean any progress in the *general* consciousness in which those intelligent animals are as completely lacking as a stupid oyster. The complex brain of a higher mammal is as little use for throwing light upon nature as a whole as the rudimentary nerve-ganglia of a worm. In humanity, on the contrary, general consciousness progresses through the achievements of the individual consciousness in the realms of religion or science. The individual intelligence is in the case of man not only an organ of personal life, but also an organ of memory and anticipation for all mankind and even for the whole of nature.

. . . *The whole truth* — the positive unity of all — is latent from the first in man's living consciousness and is gradually realized in the life of humanity, being consciously handed down. This successive consciousness can be expanded indefinitely and is continuous, and therefore man can, while remaining himself, understand and realize all the infinite fulness of being, so that he need not and cannot be replaced by any higher kinds of entities. Within the limits of his given reality man is only a part of nature; but he is constantly and consistently transcending those limits. In his spiritual progeny — religion and science, morality and art — he manifests himself as the centre of the universal consciousness of nature, as the soul of the world, as the self-realizing potency of the absolute all-unity; consequently only that absolute itself in its perfect actuality or its eternal being, that is, God, can be higher than man.

Man's privilege over other natural beings — his power of understanding and realizing the truth — is both generic and individual: *every* man is capable of knowing and realizing the truth, everyone can become a living reflection of the absolute whole, a conscious and independent organ of universal life. The rest of nature also contains truth (or the image of God), but only in its objective universality, unknown to particular beings; this truth forms them and acts in and through them as the power of fate, as the unknown-to-them law of their being to which they involuntarily and unconsciously submit; in themselves, in their inner feeling and consciousness, they cannot rise above their given, partial existence; they find themselves only in their separateness, in isolation from *all* — consequently outside of truth; therefore,

truth or the universal unity can only triumph in the animal kingdom through the change of generations, the permanence of the
species and the destruction of the individual life incapable of
comprehending the truth. The human individuality, however,
just because it is capable of comprehending the truth, is not cancelled by it, but is preserved and strengthened through its
triumph.

But in order that an individual being should find in Truth
— in the all-unity — its own affirmation and justification, it
must be not only conscious of truth but be *in* it. Primarily and
immediately, however, an individual man is not in Truth, any
more than an animal is: he finds himself as an isolated particle of
the cosmic whole and in his egoism affirms this partial existence
as a whole for himself; he wants to be all in his separation from
the whole, outside of Truth. Egoism as the real basic principle of
individual life penetrates it right through, directing and concretely determining everything in it, and therefore a merely
theoretical consciousness of truth cannot possibly outweigh and
abolish it. Until the living force of egoism meets in man with
another living force opposed to it, consciousness of truth is only
an external illumination, a reflection of another light. If man
could only in this sense accept the truth, his connection with it
would not be inward and indissoluble; his own being remaining,
like that of animals, outside Truth, would be, like theirs, doomed
to disappear in its subjectivity and would only be preserved as an
idea in the absolute mind.

Truth as a living power taking possession of man's inner being
and really saving him from false self-affirmation is called love.
Love as the actual abolition of egoism is the real justification and
salvation of individuality. Love is higher than rational consciousness, but without it it could not act as an inner saving power which
sublimates and does not destroy individuality. Only thanks to
rational consciousness (or, what is the same thing, to the consciousness of truth) man can distinguish himself, i.e. his true individuality, from his egoism, and therefore in sacrificing this egoism and
surrendering himself to love, he finds in it both a living and a
life-giving power; he does not lose, together with his egoism, his
individual being, but on the contrary preserves it forever.

... The meaning of human love in general is *the justification and
salvation of individuality through the sacrifice of egoism*. Starting with
this general position, we can deal with our specific task and

explain the meaning of sexual love. It is highly significant that sexual relations are not only called love, but are generally recognized as pre-eminently representative of love, being the type and the ideal of all other kinds of love (see The Song of Songs and the Revelation of St. John).

The evil and falsity of egoism certainly do not consist in the fact that man prizes himself too highly or ascribes absolute significance and infinite dignity to himself: he is right in this, for every human subject as an independent centre of living powers, as the potency of infinite perfection, as a being capable of embracing in his life and consciousness the absolute truth, has unconditional significance and dignity, is something absolutely irreplaceable and cannot prize himself too highly (in the words of the Gospel, what shall a man give in exchange for his soul?). Not to recognize one's absolute significance in this sense is tantamount to renouncing one's human dignity. The fundamental evil and falsity of egoism lie not in the recognition of the subject's own absolute significance and value, but in the fact that while he justly ascribes such significance to himself, he unjustly denies it to others; in recognizing himself as a centre of life, which he is in reality, he refers others to the circumference of his being, setting upon them only an external and relative value.

Of course, theoretically and in the abstract every man who is in his right mind always admits that other people have exactly the same rights as he; but in his vital consciousness, in his inner feeling and in practice, he makes an infinite, incommensurable difference between himself and others: he, as such, is all, they, as such, are nothing. But it is precisely this exclusive self-affirmation that prevents man from being in fact what he claims to be. The unconditional significance and absoluteness which, speaking generally, he rightly recognizes in himself, but wrongly denies to others, is in itself merely potential — it is only a possibility demanding realization. God *is* all, i.e. possesses in one absolute act all the positive content, all the fulness of being. Man (in general, and every individual man in particular), being in fact only *this* and not *another*, may become all only by abolishing in his consciousness and his life the inner limits which separate him from others. 'This' man may be 'all' only *together with others*; only together with others can he realize his absolute significance and become an inseparable and irreplaceable part of the universal whole, an independent, unique and living organ of the absolute life. True individuality is a certain definite form of universal unity, a certain definite way of apprehending and assimilating the whole. In affirming himself outside of all else, man robs his own existence of its meaning, deprives himself of the true content of life and reduces his individuality to an empty form. Thus egoism is certainly not the self-affirmation and self-consciousness of individuality, but, on the contrary, its self-negation and destruction.

Physical and metaphysical, social and historical conditions of human existence modify and soften our egoism in all kinds of ways, putting various formidable obstacles to the undisguised manifestations of it in all its terrible consequences. But all this complex system of correctives and obstacles, predetermined by Providence and realized by nature and history, does not affect the actual basis of egoism which constantly peeps out from under the cover of personal and public morality and at times manifests itself in its full force. There is only one power which may and actually does undermine egoism at the root, from within, and that is love, and chiefly sexual love. The evil and falsity of egoism consist in ascribing absolute significance exclusively to oneself and denying it to others; reason shows that it is unwarranted and unjust, and love abolishes this unjust relation in fact, compelling us to recognize not in abstract thought, but in inner feeling and vital will the absolute significance of another person for us. Through love we come to know the truth of another not in abstraction but in reality, and actually transfer the centre of our life beyond the confines of our empirical separateness; and in doing so we manifest and realize our own truth, our own absolute significance, which consists precisely in the power of transcending our actual phenomenal existence and of living not in ourselves only but also in another.

All love is a manifestation of this power, but not every kind of love realizes it to the same extent or undermines egoism with the same thoroughness. Egoism is a real and fundamental force rooted in the deepest centre of our being and spreading from there to the whole of our reality — a force that continually acts in every department and every detail of our existence. If egoism is to be undermined right through, it must be counteracted by a love as concretely determined as it itself is, penetrating and possessing the whole of our being. The 'other' which is to liberate our individuality from the fetters of egoism must be correlated with the whole of that individuality. It must be as real, concrete and objectivized as we are, and at the same time must differ from us in every way, so as to be really 'other'. In other words, while having the same essential content as we, it must have it in another way, in a different form, so that our every manifestation, our every vital act should meet in that 'other' a corresponding but not an identical manifestation. The relation of the one to the other must thus be a complete and continual exchange, a complete and continual affirmation of oneself in another, a perfect interaction and communion. Only then will egoism be undermined and abolished, not in principle only, but in all its concrete actuality. Only this, so to speak, chemical fusion of two beings of the same kind and significance, but throughout different in form, can render possible (both in the natural and the spiritual order) the creation of a new man, the actual realization of the true human individuality. Such fusion, or at any rate the nearest approximation to it, is to be found in sexual love, and that is the reason why it has an exceptional significance as a necessary and irreplaceable basis of all further growth in perfection, as the inevitable and constant condition which alone makes it possible for man to be actually in Truth.

Fully admitting the great importance and the high dignity of other kinds of love by which false spiritualism and impotent moralism would like to replace sexual love, we find nevertheless that only the latter satisfies the two fundamental conditions without which there can be no final abolition of selfhood through complete vital communion with another. In all other kinds of love there is absent either the homogeneity, equality and interaction between the lover and the beloved, or the all-inclusive difference of complementary qualities.

Thus in mystical love the object of love is reduced in the last resort to absolute indifference that engulfs human individuality; egoism is here abolished only in the very insufficient sense in which it is abolished in deep sleep (with which the union of the individual soul with the universal spirit is compared and sometimes actually identified in the Upanishads and the Vedanta). A living man and the mystic 'Abyss' of absolute indifference are so heterogeneous and incommensurable that the two cannot coexist, to say nothing of being in any vital communion: if the object of love is there, there is no lover — he has disappeared, lost himself, sunk as it were into a deep dreamless sleep, and when he returns to himself, the object of love disappears, and absolute indifference is replaced by the variegated multiplicity of actual life against the background of one's own egoism adorned by spiritual pride. There certainly were in history mystics and whole schools of mysticism that interpreted the object of love not as absolute indifference, but as able to assume concrete forms allowing vital relations with it; very significantly, however, those relations acquired a perfectly clear and consistent character of sexual love.

Parental, and especially maternal, love approximates to sexual love both in respect of the intensity of feeling and the concreteness of its object, but on other grounds it cannot have the same significance for the human personality. It is conditioned by the fact of reproduction and the law that successive generations replace one another — a law that dominates life in the animal world but has not, or at any rate ought not to have, the same significance in human life. With animals the succeeding generation directly and rapidly cancels its predecessors and shows their existence to be meaningless, and then is in its turn convicted of the same meaningless existence by its own progeny. Maternal love, which in human beings attains at times heights of self-sacrifice not to be found in a hen's love, is a relic, no doubt still necessary, of that order of things. In any case it is unquestionable that in maternal love there can be no complete reciprocity and life-long communion, if only because the lover and the beloved belong to different generations and that for the latter, life is in the future, with new independent problems and interests among which representatives of the past appear only as pale shadows. It is sufficient to say that the parents cannot be the object of the children's life in the same sense in which the children can be the object of life for the parents.

A mother who puts her whole soul into her children certainly sacrifices her egoism, but she also loses her individuality, and though her love may strengthen the children's individuality, it preserves and even intensifies their egoism. Besides, in maternal love there is really no recognition of the beloved's absolute significance and true individuality, for although a child is precious to its mother above all, this is precisely because it is *her* child, just as with animals, i.e. the apparent recognition of another person's absolute significance is really conditioned by an external physiological bond.

Other varieties of sympathetic feeling have even less claim to

6

replace sexual love. Friendship between persons of the same sex lacks the all-round formal distinction between the mutually complementary qualities, and when, in spite of this, such friendship attains particular intensity, it becomes an unnatural substitute for sexual love. As to patriotism and love for humanity, however important those feelings are, they cannot in themselves concretely and actually eradicate egoism, for the lover and the object of love are incommensurable: neither humanity nor the nation can be for the individual man as concrete an entity as he himself is. It is possible, of course, to sacrifice one's life for the nation or for humanity, but to make oneself into a new creature, to manifest and realize true human individuality on the basis of this extensive love, is impossible. The old egoistic self still remains the real centre, while the nation and humanity are relegated to the periphery of consciousness as ideal objects. The same thing must be said about love of science, art, etc.

. . . The meaning and value of love as a feeling consists in the fact that it makes us actually, with our whole being, recognize in *another* the absolute central significance which owing to egoism we feel in ourselves only. Love is important, not as one of our feelings, but as the transference of our whole vital interest from ourselves to another, as the transposition of the very centre of our personal life. This is characteristic of every kind of love, but of sexual love [1] pre-eminently; it differs from other kinds of love by greater intensity, greater absorption and the possibility of a more complete and comprehensive reciprocity; that love alone can lead to the actual and indissoluble union of two lives made one, and only of it does the word of God say that the two shall be one flesh, i.e. shall become one real being.

The love-feeling demands such fulness of inner and final union, but as a rule things go no further than this subjective striving and demand, and that too proves to be transitory. Instead of the poetry of the eternal and central union we have a more or less continuous, but in any case temporal, a more or less intimate, but in any case external and superficial nearness between two limited beings within the narrow framework of every-day prose. The object of love does not preserve in fact the absolute significance ascribed to

[1] For lack of a better term I give the name of 'sexual love' to an exclusive attachment (both reciprocal and one-sided) between persons of the opposite sex capable of being in the relation of husband and wife, but I do not in the least prejudge the significance of the physiological side of the matter.

it by the dream of love. To an outsider this is obvious from the first, and the involuntary tinge of irony that inevitably colours other people's attitude to lovers proves to be merely an anticipation of their own disillusionment. Sooner or later the ecstatic element of love disappears.

. . . And so if we consider only that which generally happens and look only at love's actual outcome, love must be recognized to be a dream possessing us for a time and then disappearing without any practical result (since child-bearing is not the work of love as such). But if evidence compels us to admit that the ideal meaning of love is not realized in fact, must we admit that it is *unrealizable*?

. . . It would be quite unjust to deny that love is realizable simply because it has never yet been realized: the same was true in the past of many other things — all arts and sciences, civic society, control of the forces of nature, and so on. Rational consciousness itself before it became a fact in man was only a vague and fruitless striving in the animal world. A number of geological and biological epochs passed in unsuccessful attempts to create a brain capable of becoming an organ for the embodiment of rational thought. So far love is for man what reason was for the animal world: it exists in its rudiments or tokens, but not as yet in fact. And if stupendous cosmic periods — witnesses of unrealized reason — have not prevented it from manifesting itself at last, the fact that love has not been realized in the course of the comparatively few thousands of years lived by historical humanity gives us no right to conclude that it cannot be realized in the future. Only it must be remembered that while the reality of rational consciousness appeared *in* man but not through man, the realization of love as the highest step in humanity's own life must take place both in him and *through* him.

The task of love is to *justify in fact* the meaning of love which is at first given only as a feeling — to create such a union of two given limited beings as would make of them one absolute ideal personality. Far from containing any inner contradiction, or being at variance with the meaning of the world as a whole, this task is directly set to us by our spiritual nature, the distinguishing characteristic of which is that man can, while remaining himself, comprehend the absolute content and become an absolute personality. But in order to be filled with absolute content (which in religious language is called eternal life or the Kingdom of God) the human form itself must be reinstated in its wholeness. In empirical reality there is no man *as such* — he exists only in a one-sided and limited form as a masculine or a feminine individual (all other differences develop upon this basis). The true human being in the fulness of its ideal personality obviously cannot be merely a man or merely a woman, but must be the higher unity of the two. To realize this unity or to create the true human being as the free unity of the masculine and the femine elements, which preserve their formal separateness but overcome their essential disparity and disruption, is the direct *task* of love. If we consider the conditions required for carrying it out, we shall see that it is only because those conditions are not observed that love invariably comes to grief and has to be pronounced an illusion.

The first step towards successfully solving any problem is to state it consciously and correctly; but the problem of love has never been consciously formulated and therefore has never been properly solved. People have always regarded love solely as a given fact or as a state (normal for some and painful for others) experienced by man, but not imposing any obligations upon him. True, two concerns are bound up with it — physiological possession of the object of love and permanent alliance with it — which do impose certain duties, but in these two respects the matter is subject to the laws of animal nature on the one hand, and to the laws of civic community on the other; and love, left to itself from beginning to end, disappears like a mirage. Of course, love is in the first place a fact of nature (or a gift of God), a natural process arising independently of us; but this does not imply that we cannot and must not stand in a conscious relation to it and of our own will direct this natural process to higher ends.

Everyone knows that in love there always is a special *idealization* of the object of love which appears to the lover in quite a different light than it does to other people. I am speaking of light not in a metaphorical sense only, not only of a particular moral and intellectual valuation, but of special sensuous perception as well: the lover actually *sees*, visually apprehends, something different from what others do. True, for him too this light of love soon disappears, but does that imply that it was false, that it was merely a subjective illusion?

The true being of man in general and of every man in particular is not confined to his given empirical expressions; no rational grounds to the contrary can be adduced from any point of view.

... We know that in addition to his material animal nature man has an ideal nature connecting him with the absolute truth or God. Besides the material or empirical content of his life every man contains the image of God, i.e. a special form of the absolute content. That image of God is known to us in the abstract and in theory through reason, and concretely and actually through love. The revelation of the ideal being, generally concealed by the material appearance, is not confined in love to an inner feeling, but sometimes becomes apprehensible by the outer senses; and this imparts all the greater significance to love as the beginning of the visible reinstatement of the image of God in the material world, of the incarnation of true ideal humanity. The power of love transforming itself into light, transfiguring and spiritualizing the form of external appearances, reveals to us its objective force, but it is for us to do the rest: we must understand this revelation and make use of it so that it should not remain an enigmatic and fleeting glimpse of some mystery.

The spiritually-physical process of the reinstatement of the image of God in material humanity cannot possibly happen of itself, apart from us. Like all that is best in this world it begins in the dark realm of unconscious processes and relations; the germ and the roots of the tree of life are hidden there, but we must tend its growth by our own conscious action. The passive receptivity of feeling is enough to begin with, but it must be followed by active faith, moral endeavour and effort in order to preserve, strengthen and develop the gift of radiant and creative love and by means of it embody in oneself and in the other the image of God, forming out of two limited and mortal beings one absolute and immortal personality. Idealization, inevitably and involun-tarily present in love, shows to us through the material appearance the far-off ideal image of the loved one — not in order that we should merely admire it, but that by the power of true faith, active imagination and real creativeness we should transform in accordance with that true image the reality that falls short of it, and embody the ideal in actual fact.

But who has ever thought anything of the kind apropos of love? Mediæval minstrels and knights, strong in faith but weak in intellect, were content simply to identify the ideal of love with a given person, refusing to see the obvious discrepancy between them.

... In addition to the faith which merely made them piously

contemplate and ecstatically sing the praises of the fictitiously embodied ideal, mediæval love was, of course, also connected with a longing for heroic deeds. But those military and destructive deeds, being in no way related to the ideal that inspired them, could not lead to its realization.

... The whole of mediæval chivalry suffered from the severance between the celestial visions of Christianity and the 'wild and furious' forces of actual life, until finally the last and most famous of knights, Don Quixote de la Mancha, having killed many sheep and broken down many windmills, but not brought the Toboso dairymaid the least bit nearer to the ideal of Dulcinea, arrived at the just but purely negative conviction of his error.

... Don Quixote's disappointment was the legacy of chivalry to the new Europe. We are still feeling its effects. The idealization of love, having ceased to be the source of absurd heroic deeds, does not inspire any deeds at all. It proves to be merely a bait causing us to desire physical and practical possession, and disappears as soon as this far from ideal purpose is attained. The light of love serves to no one as the guiding ray to the lost paradise; it is regarded as a fantastic illumination of a short 'love prologue in heaven', extinguished by nature at the proper time as utterly unnecessary for the subsequent earthly performance. But in truth the light is extinguished by the weak and unconscious character of our love which distorts the true order of sequence.

External union, practical and especially physiological, has no definite relation to love. It may exist without love, and there may be love without it. It is necessary for love not as its essential condition and independent goal, but only as its final realization. If this realization is made an end in itself, prior to the ideal work of love, it ruins love.

... The actual feeling of love is merely a stimulus suggesting to us that we can and must recreate the wholeness of the human being. Every time that this sacred spark is lit in the human heart, all the groaning and travailing creation waits for the first manifestation of the glory of the sons of God. But without the action of the conscious human spirit, the divine spark dies down, and disappointed nature creates new generations of the sons of men for new hopes.

These hopes will not be fulfilled until we decide fully to recognize and realize to the end all that true love demands, all that is contained in the idea of it. Given a conscious attitude to love and real determination to accomplish the task it sets us, we are first of all hindered by two facts which apparently doom us to impotence and justify those who regard love as an illusion. In the feeling of love, in accordance with its essential meaning, we affirm the absolute significance of another personality and, through it, of our own. But an absolute personality cannot be *transitory* and it cannot be *empty*. The inevitability of death and the emptiness of our life are incompatible with the emphatic affirmation of one's own and another's personality contained in the feeling of love. That feeling, if it is strong and fully conscious, cannot resign itself to the certainty that decrepit old age and death are in store both for the beloved and the lover. And yet, the indubitable fact that all men have always died and go on dying is taken by everyone, or almost everyone, to be an absolutely unalterable law of nature. True, many believe in the immortality of the soul; but it is precisely the feeling of love that shows best the insufficiency of that abstract faith. A discarnate spirit is an angel and not a man; but if we love a human being, a complete human personality, and if love is the beginning of that being's spiritualization and enlightenment, it necessarily demands the preservation, the eternal youth and immortality of this particular person, this living spirit incarnate in a bodily organism.

. . . But if the inevitability of death is incompatible with true love, immortality is utterly incompatible with the emptiness of our life. For the majority of mankind life is merely an alternation of hard mechanical labour and crudely sensuous pleasures that deaden consciousness. And the minority that has a chance of actively concerning itself not only with the means but also with the ends of life uses its freedom from mechanical labour chiefly for following meaningless and immoral pursuits.

. . . It is obvious at first glance that such an existence is incompatible with immortality. But closer inspection will show that even apparently fuller lives are equally incompatible with it. If instead of a society lady or a gambler we take, at the opposite pole, great men, geniuses who have bestowed on mankind immortal works of art or changed the destiny of nations, we shall see that the content of their life and its historical fruits have significance only as given once and for all, but would lose all meaning if those geniuses continued their earthly life forever. The immortality of works obviously does not require and, indeed, excludes the infinitely continued existence of the persons who produced them. It is impossible to imagine Shakespeare endlessly writing his plays, or Newton endlessly studying the heavenly mechanics, to say nothing of the absurdity of continuing forever the kind of activity for which Alexander the Great or Napoleon are famed. Art, science and politics, while providing the content of certain particular strivings of the human spirit and satisfying the temporary, historical needs of humanity, obviously do not impart an absolute, self-sufficient content to the human *personality* and therefore do not require that it should be immortal. Love alone needs this, and it alone can achieve it. True love not only affirms in subjective feeling the absolute significance of human personality in another and in oneself, but also justifies this significance in reality, actually delivers us from the inevitability of death and fills our life with absolute content.

'Dionysos and Hades are one and the same', said the most profound thinker of the ancient world. Dionysos, the young and blooming god of material life in the full intensity of its seething forces, the god of turbulent and fruitful nature, is the same as Hades, the pale lord of the silent and tenebrous realm of departed shades; the god of life and the god of death are one and the same god. This is an indisputable truth for the natural organic world. The fulness of vital forces seething in an individual creature is not its own life but an alien life of the genus, indifferent and pitiless to it, which for it is death. On the lower levels of the animal world this is perfectly clear: there individual entities exist solely in order to procreate themselves, and then die. In many species they do not survive the act of reproduction and die on the spot, in others they survive it for a short time only. But although this connection between birth and death, between the preservation of the species and the destruction of the particular entity is a law of nature, nature herself in her progressive development limits and relaxes this law more and more; it still remains necessary for the particular entity to serve as a means for carrying on the genus and then to die, but the necessity manifests itself less and less directly and exclusively as the organic forms increase in perfection and individual entities grow more conscious and independent. Thus the law of identity between Dionysos and Hades, generic life and individual death — or, what is the same thing, the law of conflict and opposition between the genus and the individual entity — is most pronounced at the lower stages of the organic world and becomes less and less stringent as the higher forms develop. If that be the case, does not the appearance of the un-conditionally highest organic form embodying a self-conscious and self-active being which separates itself from nature, regards it as an object and is consequently capable of inwardly liberating himself from the demands of the genus — does not the appearance of such a being suggest an end to this tyranny of the genus over the individual? If in the course of the biological process nature strives to limit the law of death more and more, ought not man in the historical process to abolish this law altogether?

It is self-evident that so long as man reproduces himself like an animal, he also dies like an animal. But it is equally evident that mere abstention from the act of procreation does not in any way save one from death: persons who have preserved their virginity die, and so do eunuchs, and neither enjoy even particular lon-gevity. This is quite understandable. Speaking generally, death is the disintegration, the falling apart of a creature's constituent elements. But division into sexes, not remedied by their external and transitory union in the act of reproduction, the division between the masculine and the feminine elements of the human being, is in itself a state of disintegration and the beginning of death. To remain in sexual dividedness means to remain on the path of death, and those who cannot or will not leave that path must from natural necessity tread it to the end. He who supports the root of death must necessarily taste its fruit. Only the whole man can be immortal, and if physiological union cannot reinstate the wholeness of the human being, it means that this false union must be replaced by a true union and certainly not by abstention from all union, i.e. not by a striving to retain *in statu quo* the divided, disintegrated and consequently mortal human nature.

In what, then, does the true union of the sexes consist and how is it realized? Our life is in this respect so far from the truth that we regard as a norm what is in reality only the less extreme and outrageous abnormality.

Numerous perversions of the sexual instinct studied by psychiatry are merely curious varieties of the general and all-pervading perversion of sexual relations in mankind — the per-version which supports and perpetuates the kingdom of sin and death. The three relations or bonds between the sexes, normal for the human being in its wholeness, do actually exist in the human world — the bond in the animal life according to the lower nature, the morally-civic bond under the law, and the bond in the spiritual life or union in God — but they are realized unnaturally, that is, separately from one another, in an order of sequence contrary to their true meaning and interdependence, and to an unequal degree.

The animal physiological bond is given the first place in our reality, while in truth it ought to have the last. It is regarded as the basis of the whole thing, while it ought to be only its final culmination. For many the basis in this case coincides with the culmination: they do not go beyond the animal relations; others build upon this broad foundation the socially moral superstructure of the legal family union. Then the medium level of everyday existence is taken for the culminating point, and that which ought to be a free and conscious expression in the temporal process of the eternal unity becomes an involuntary channel of meaningless material life. As a rare exception there is left for the few elect the pure spiritual love, robbed beforehand by the other lower bonds of all actual content, so that it has to be satisfied with dreamy and sterile sentimentality without any real task or vital purpose. This unfortunate spiritual love resembles the little angels in old paintings who have nothing but head and wings. Those angels cannot do anything, for they have no hands and cannot move forward, for their wings are only strong enough to hold them up at a certain height. Spiritual love finds itself in the same exalted but extremely unsatisfactory position. Physical passion has a certain task before it, though a shameful one; legal family union also fulfils a task, necessary at present, though of middling value. But spiritual love as it has so far appeared has no task whatever to accomplish, and therefore it is not surprising that the majority of practical people *glaubt an keine Liebe, oder nimmt's für Poësie.*[1]

This exclusively spiritual love is obviously as much of an anomaly as exclusive physical passion or a loveless legal union. The absolute norm is the reinstatement of the wholeness of the human being, and in whatever direction that norm is violated, the result always is abnormal and unnatural. Pseudo-spiritual love is not merely abnormal but also utterly purposeless, for the separation of the spiritual from the sensuous for which it strives is in any case performed in the best possible way by death. But true spiritual love is not a feeble imitation and anticipation of

[1] Does not believe in love, or takes it for poetry.

death, but triumph over death, not the separation of the immortal from the mortal, of the eternal from the temporal, but the transformation of the mortal into the immortal, the reception of the temporal into eternity. False spirituality is the negation of the flesh, true spirituality is its regeneration, salvation and resurrection.

... 'So God created man in His own image, in the image of God created He him; male and female created He them.'

'This is a great mystery, but I speak concerning Christ and the Church.' The mysterious image of God in which man was created refers originally not to one separate part of the human being, but to the true unity of its two essential aspects, the male and the female. The relation that God has to His creation and that Christ has to His Church, must be the relation of the husband to the wife. Those words are generally known, but their meaning is little understood. As God creates the universe, as Christ builds the Church, so must man create and build his feminine complement. It is, of course, an elementary truth that man stands for the active and woman for the passive principle and that he ought to have a formative influence upon her mind and character; we are concerned, however, not with this superficial relation, but with the 'great mystery' of which St. Paul speaks. That great mystery is essentially analogous to, though not identical with, the relation between the human and the divine.

... God's relation to the creature is that of everything to nothing, i.e. of the absolute fulness of being to the pure potency of being; Christ's relation to the Church is that of actual to potential perfection, which is being raised into actuality; but the relation between husband and wife is that between two differently acting but equally imperfect potencies which attain perfection only through a process of interaction. Or, to put it differently, God receives nothing, i.e. gains no increase from the creature, but gives everything to it; Christ receives no increase from the Church in perfection, and gives all perfection to it, but He does receive from the Church increase in the fulness of His collective body; finally, man and his feminine *alter ego* complete each other both really and ideally, attaining perfection through interaction only. Man can creatively reinstate God's image in the living object of his love only by reinstating that image in himself as well; but he has no power of his own to do it, for if he had, he would not need any reinstatement; and not having the power, he must receive it from God. Hence man (husband) is the creative and formative principle in relation to his feminine complement not in himself, but as a mediator of the divine power.

. . . The work of true love is based first of all upon *faith*. The basic meaning of love, as already shown, consists in recognizing the absolute significance of another personality. But in its actual, sensuously apprehended existence that personality has no unconditional significance: it is imperfect and transitory. Consequently, we can only ascribe absolute significance to it through faith which is 'the substance of things hoped for, the evidence of things not seen'. But what is the object of faith in this case? What exactly does it mean to believe in the unconditional and therefore infinite significance of this individual person? To affirm that it as such, as separate and particular, has absolute significance would be both absurd and blasphemous.

. . . By faith in the object of our love we must mean the affirmation of that object as existing in God and in that sense possessing infinite significance.

. . . Since for the eternal and indivisible God everything is together and at once, to affirm an individual being in God means to affirm it not in its separateness but in all, or, more exactly, in the unity of all. Since, however, this individual being in its given actuality does not enter into the unity of all, but exists separately, as a materially isolated fact, the object of our believing love necessarily differs from the empirical object of our instinctive love, though it is indissolubly bound up with it. It is one and the same person in two different aspects or two different spheres of being — the ideal and the real. The first is so far only an idea. But in true, believing and clear-sighted love we know that this idea is not our arbitrary invention: it expresses the *truth* of the object, unrealized as yet in the sphere of outward existence.

Although this true idea of the beloved shines through its material embodiment at moments of love's ecstasy, it appears more clearly at first as an object of imagination. The concrete form of it, the ideal image with which I clothe the beloved at the moment, is, of course, created by myself, but it is not created out of nothing; the subjectivity of that image as such, the fact, that is, that it appears here and now before my mental vision, in no way proves that the imagined object itself is subjective, i.e. exists for me alone. If for me, standing on this side of the transcendental world, a certain ideal object appears as a product of my imagination, this does not prevent it from being fully real in another, higher realm of being. And although our actual life lies outside that higher realm, our mind is not quite a stranger to it, and we can have some speculative knowledge of its laws. And this is its first and fundamental law: while in this world separate and isolated existence is an actual fact, and unity is only a concept or idea, there, on the contrary, it is the unity, or, more exactly, the all-unity, that is real, and isolation and separateness have only potential and subjective existence.

It follows that the being of *this* person in the transcendental sphere is not individual in our sense of the term. There, i.e. in truth, an individual person is only a ray, living and actual, but an inseparable ray of one ideal light — of the one universal substance. This ideal person or personified idea is merely an individualization of the all-unity which is indivisibly present in each one of its individual expressions. And so when we imagine the ideal form of the beloved, the all-embracing unity itself is given us in that form. How, then, is it to be conceived?

God as one, in distinguishing from Himself His 'other', i.e. all that is not He, unites that other to Himself, positing it before Him together and all at once, in an absolutely perfect form and consequently as a unity. This *other* unity distinct, though inseparable, from God's primary unity, is in relation to God a passive, feminine unity, for in it eternal emptiness (pure potency) receives the fulness of the divine life. But though *at the basis* of this eternal femininity lies pure nothing, for God this nothing is eternally concealed by the image of absolute perfection which He bestows upon it. This perfection, which for us is still in the process of being realized, for God, i.e. in truth, actually *is* already. The ideal unity towards which our world is striving and which is the goal of the cosmic and historical process cannot be merely a subjective idea (for whose idea could it be?), but truly is the eternal object of divine love, as God's eternal 'other'.

This living ideal of the divine love, prior to our love, contains the secret of its idealization. The idealization of the lower being is the beginning of the realization of the higher, and herein lies the truth of love's exaltation. The complete realization, the transformation of an individual feminine being into a ray of the divine eternal feminine, inseparable from its radiant source, will be the real, both the subjective and the objective, reunion of the individual human being with the Deity, the reinstatement of the living and immortal image of God in man.

The object of true love is not simple but twofold: we love, first, the ideal entity (ideal not in an abstract sense, but in the sense of belonging to a higher realm of being) which we must bring into our real world, and secondly, we love the natural human entity which provides the real personal material for such realization; it is idealized through love, not in our subjective imagination, but in the sense of being actually and objectively regenerated. Thus, true love is indivisibly both *ascending* and *descending* (*amor ascendens* and *amor descendens*, or the two Aphrodites whom Plato rightly distinguished but wrongly separated — Ἀφροδίτη Οὐρανία and Ἀφροδίτη Πάνδημος). For God His *other* (i.e. the universe) has from all eternity the image of perfect femininity, and He wills that this image should exist not for Him only, but that it should be realized and embodied for every individual being capable of uniting with it. The eternal feminine itself strives for such realization and embodiment, for it is not a mere passive image in the divine mind but a living spiritual being possessing the fulness of powers and activities. The whole cosmic and historical process is the process of its realization and incarnation in an endless multiplicity of forms and degrees.

In sexual love rightly understood and truly realized this divine essence finds a means for its complete and final embodiment in the individual life of man, for the deepest and at the same time most outwardly sensible and real union with him. Hence those glimpses of unearthly bliss, that breath of heavenly joy, which accompany even imperfect love and make it the highest felicity for men and gods — *hominum divumque voluptas*. And hence, too, the deepest suffering of love that is incapable of holding its true object and recedes from it further and further.

A legitimate place is thus provided for the element of adoration and infinite devotion which is so characteristic of love, but so meaningless if it refers solely to its earthly object apart from the heavenly.

Immediate and instinctive feeling reveals to us the meaning of love as the highest expression of the individual life which, in union with another being, finds its own infinity. But is this momentary revelation enough?

... A *momentary* infinity is a contradiction intolerable for the intellect; a bliss that is only in the past is pain for the will.

... If that infinity and that bliss are merely a deception, the very memory of them brings with it the shame and bitterness of disillusionment; but if they were not an illusion, if they did reveal to us a reality which afterwards was hidden from us and disappeared, why should we resign ourselves to its disappearance? If that which was lost was real, the task for our mind and will is to understand and remove the cause of the loss, and not to accept it as irretrievable.

The immediate cause, as already pointed out, is the distortion of the love-relation itself. That begins very early: no sooner has the first exaltation of love shown us a glimpse of another and a better reality with a different principle and law of life, than we immediately try to utilize the access of energy brought about by this revelation, not in order to go where it calls us, but to settle more firmly and securely in the bad old reality above which love had just raised us. We take the good news from the lost paradise — the news of being able to return to it — for an invitation to be finally *naturalized* in the land of exile, and hasten to enter into full hereditary possession of our little plot with all its thorns and thistles. The breakdown of the limits of selfhood, which is the sign and the essential meaning of the love passion, leads in practice merely to egoism *à deux*, then *à trois* and so on. It is, of course, better than solitary egoism, but the dawn of love opened up quite different horizons.

As soon as the vital sphere of the love-union is transferred to the material reality in its present state, the order of union is at once distorted accordingly. Its 'unearthly' mystical basis which made itself so strongly felt in early passion is forgotten as a fleeting exaltation, and that which ought to be merely the last and conditional expression of love is recognized as its first condition, its final and most desirable purpose. When this last thing — the physical union — is put in the first place, thus being deprived of its *human* meaning and restored to the animal, it not only makes love powerless against death, but itself inevitably becomes the moral grave of love long before the physical grave receives the lovers.

Direct personal counteraction to this order of things is more difficult to carry out than to understand: it can be indicated in a few words. To abolish this bad order we must first of all recognize it as abnormal, affirming thereby that there is another, normal order in which everything external and accidental is subordinated to the inner meaning of life. Such affirmation should not be merely verbal; the experience of the outer senses must be countered not with an abstract principle, but with another kind of experience — *the experience of faith.*

. . . But if faith is not to remain a dead faith, it must constantly defend itself against the environment in which meaningless chance builds its rule on the play of animal passions and still worse human passions. Against those hostile forces the believing love has but one weapon — endurance unto the end. To deserve its bliss, it must take up its cross. In our material environment it is impossible to preserve true love except through understanding and accepting it as a moral task. It is not for nothing that in the marriage service the Orthodox Church remembers holy *martyrs* and compares the bridal crowns to theirs.

Religious faith and moral endeavour preserve the individual man and his love from being engulfed by the material environment while he lives, but they do not give him triumph over death. The inner regeneration of the love-feeling, the correction of the perverted love-relation, do not correct or cancel the bad law of the physical life either in the external world or even in man himself. *In fact* he remains limited as before and subject to material nature. His inner, mystical and moral union with the personality that completes his own cannot overcome either their mutual separateness and impenetrability or their common dependence upon the material world. The last word belongs not to the moral achievement but to the merciless law of organic life and death; and people who have to the end championed the eternal ideal die with human dignity but with animal helplessness.

. . . It is only together with all other beings that the individual man can be really saved, i.e. can regenerate and preserve forever his individual life in true love. It is his right and his duty to defend his individuality from the bad law of the general life, but not to separate his own good from the true good of all that lives. The fact that the deepest and strongest manifestation of love is to be found in the relation between two beings complementary to each other by no means implies that this relation should be isolated and separated from all else as something self-sufficient; on the contrary, such isolation is the ruin of love, for the sexual relation as such, in spite of all its subjective importance, proves (objectively) to be only a transitory empirical event. Nor does the fact that the perfect union of two particular beings will always be the basis and the true form of individual life by any means imply that this form must remain empty and isolated in its individual perfection; on the contrary, owing to the very nature of man, it is capable of being filled with universal content and is destined for it. Finally, if the moral meaning of love requires the reunion of that which has been wrongly separated and demands the identification of one's own self with the other, it would be contrary to this moral meaning to separate the attainment of our individual perfection from the process of universal unification, even if it were physically possible to do so.

If the root of false existence is impenetrability, i.e. mutual exclusion of one another's being, true life means living in another as in oneself or finding in another positive and absolute completion of one's own being. The foundation and pattern of this true life is and always shall be sexual or conjugal love. But as we have seen, that love cannot be realized without a corresponding transformation of the whole external environment; the integration of the individual life necessarily requires the same integration in the domains of social and of cosmic life.

The definite distinction between the different spheres of life, both individual and collective, never will and never should be abolished, for if it were, the universal mergence would lead to uniformity and emptiness and not to the fulness of being. True union presupposes true difference between its terms, in virtue of which they do not exclude but mutually affirm each other, each finding in the other the fulness of his own life. In individual love two different beings, equal in rights and value, are not a negative limit, but a positive complement to each other, and it must be the same in every sphere of the collective life. Every social organism must be for every one of its members not an external limit to their activities, but their positive support and completion: just as in sexual love (in the domain of personal life) the individual 'other' is at the same time 'all', so the social *all*, in virtue of the solidarity of all its elements, must appear to each of them as a real unity, as, so to speak, another living being completing him (in a new and wider sphere of life).

The relations between the individual members of society must be brotherly (and filial with respect to past generations and their social representatives), and their connection with different social wholes — local, national and, finally, universal — must be still more inward, many-sided and significant. The bond between the active personal human principle and the all-embracing idea embodied in the social spiritual-bodily organism must be a living *syzygic* relation.[1] Not to submit to one's social environment and not to dominate it, but to be in loving interaction with it, serve for it as an active fertilizing principle of movement, and to find in it the fulness of vital conditions and possibilities — that is the relation of the true human personality, not only to its immediate social environment and to its nation, but to humanity as a whole. In the Bible, cities, countries, the people of Israel and then the entire regenerated humanity or the universal Church are represented in the form of feminine beings, and this is not a mere metaphor. The image of unity of social bodies is not perceptible to our outer senses, but this by no means implies that it does not exist: why, our own bodily image is utterly imperceptible and unknown to a particular brain-cell or blood-corpuscle. If we, as personalities capable of attaining fulness of being, differ from those elementary entities both by greater clarity and breadth of rational consciousness and by a greater power of creative imagination, I do not see why we should renounce this privilege. But in any case, whether with or without images, what is needed in the first instance is that we should treat our social and cosmic environment as an actual living being with which we are in the closest and most complete interaction, without ever being merged in it. This extension of the syzygic relation to the domains of collective and universal existence perfects our individuality, imparting to it unity and fulness of vital content, and thereby uplifts and perpetuates the fundamental individual form of love.

... As the all-embracing idea becomes actually realized through the strengthening and greater perfection of its individually human elements, the forms of false separation or impenetrability of beings in space and time inevitably grow less pronounced. But in order that they should be abolished altogether and all individuals, both past and present, should finally become eternal, the process of integration must transcend the limits of social or strictly human life and include the cosmic sphere from which it started. In ordering the physical world the divine

[1] From the Greek *syzygia* — conjunction. I have to introduce this new term, for I cannot find another better one in the existing terminology.

idea threw the veil of natural beauty over the kingdom of matter and death; through man, through the activity of his universally rational consciousness, it must enter that kingdom *from within* in order to give life to nature and make its beauty eternal. In this sense it is essential to change man's relation to nature. He must enter with it too into the same relation of syzygic unity which determines his true life in the personal and social sphere.

Nature has so far been either an omnipotent despotic mother of the child man, or a slave, a thing foreign to him. In that second epoch poets alone preserved and kept up a timid and unconscious love for nature as a being possessing full rights and having, or capable of having, *life in itself.*

... To establish a truly loving or syzygic relation between man and his natural and cosmic, as well as his social, environment is a purpose that is quite clear in itself. But the same thing cannot be said about the ways in which an individual man can attain it. Without going into premature and therefore dubious and unsuitable details, one can confidently say one thing on the basis of well-established analogies from cosmic and historical experience. Every conscious human activity, determined by the idea of universal syzygy and having for its purpose the embodiment of the all-embracing ideal in some particular sphere, actually produces or liberates spiritually-material currents which gradually gain possession of the material environment, spiritualize it and embody in it certain images of the all-embracing unity — the living and eternal likenesses of absolute humanity. And the power of this spiritually-material creativeness in man is merely the transformation or the *turning inwards* of the creative power which in nature, being turned outwards, produces the bad infinity of the physical reproduction of organisms.

Having connected in the idea of universal syzygy individual sexual love with the true essence of universal life I have fulfilled my task and defined the meaning of love.

IV

MORALITY, LEGAL JUSTICE, POLITICS

1

THE IDEA OF THE
CHRISTIAN STATE

CHRISTIANITY appeared not at the end but in the middle of
... the historical process; the Kingdom of God proclaimed
by it was not and could not be for mankind a ready-made, perfect
order of things which it had simply to accept: it was given to men
as a morally-historical task, to be accomplished by their own free
efforts, for it is the kingdom of the sons of God and not of slaves.
If humanity were merely the arithmetical sum of separate individuals, the obstacles to the complete realization of God's Kingdom would consist solely in personal evil will. God's activity in
mankind would in that case be directed solely and immediately
upon each separate soul, which would either be receptive of it
and enter into God's Kingdom, or reject it. The solution of that
problem, absolutely separate for each soul, might be attained
outside space and time; world history would be utterly unnecessary and life meaningless. Fortunately humanity is not a
heap of psychical dust, but a living, animate body, which is being
formed and transformed, is developing regularly and gradually,
richly and variously differentiated and united, and connected in
many different ways with the rest of the world. In its every aspect
it receives the spirit of God — peripherally and centrally, in
units and in groups, in parts and as a whole. This social body
essentially differs from biological bodies (animal and vegetable)
by the fact that its final elements are moral units, free personal
beings (free in principle), having as such absolute inner value.
But every one of them can have that value precisely because it is
unseverably connected with all, and the purpose of universal
history is that this bond should become wholly conscious and
free, that cosmic oneness should not weigh on the individual
in a purely mechanical way, nor merely organically determine his
place and destination within the whole, but should also be morally

affirmed by him himself as his own purpose — that he should desire and feel it as his own true good.

Solidarity existed and developed among mankind in the pre-Christian world, not only among the Jews, but also among pagans. There was the family union based not upon physiological and economic necessity alone, but upon inner spiritual attraction as well; there existed civic communities inspired by patriotism, there existed great monarchies in which the unity of the nation was embodied in its deified ruler; finally, there existed *pax Romana* achieved through the *imperium Romanum*, and that unity was not merely a result of crude violence and injustice. Unsightly and sometimes monstrous facts represented an idea, and while Roman emperors were uniting historical humanity by the force of arms and laws, Roman philosophers such as Seneca affirmed, on the strength of the unity of human reason and nature, the natural solidarity of all men and the insignificance of any artificial and accidental barriers between them.

But solidarity that developed in the pre-Christian world in a natural, historical way was only relative: it was a unity on the one hand more or less limited and external (in the state) and on the other more or less abstract (in philosophical ideas). At the time of Augustus the external unity of the Roman Empire embraced almost the whole of historical humanity, and the abstract idea of the unity of mankind was formulated with perfect clearness — but neither satisfied the human soul that demands absolute and complete perfection. Such perfection was revealed both in Christ as the individual incarnation of the Deity, and in the idea proclaimed by Him of the Kingdom of God, i.e. of the perfect and absolute oneness of mankind (see Christ's high-priestly prayer, 'That they all may be one; as thou, Father, art in me, and I in thee, that they also may be one in us' — John xvii. 21).

. . . Christianity has directly put before mankind an absolute ideal, has set it a final task to work out.

But precisely because Christianity has given its fulness to mankind as an ideal and a task, and not as a ready-made, completed reality, the natural course of historical development does not stop with the New Testament revelation, but merely assumes a more conscious and definite character, becomes more clear-sighted. And just as a lame and blind man does not throw away his crutches on recovering his sight, but uses them better than before and walks with them more securely until his lameness is healed, so mankind, having opened its eyes, thanks to the Christian revelation, but being still infirm and weak in body, could not and ought not to throw away all that had upheld and improved its imperfect life. If Christ said to the Jews that He had come not to destroy but to fulfil the law and the prophets, Christianity had to take up the same position towards the pagan world: pagans had their own law and prophets — justice and the state, brought to their relative perfection by Rome; philosophy, poetry and art, left to the world by the Greeks.[1] And, indeed, Christianity does not reject either Roman justice or Hellenic wisdom, but uses them as human forms and instruments of God's work and God's truth. Nevertheless the long and fierce struggle of Christianity against political and philosophical paganism — against Romanism and Hellenism — was perfectly natural and necessary, not because Christianity wanted to destroy those chief elements of human culture, but because it put them in their proper place corresponding to their relative character. Before the coming of Christianity they were the highest achievements of history; accordingly, they claimed absolute significance and would not surrender their primacy to Christianity without a struggle. The Roman Empire with its deification of the Cæsars considered itself the absolute form of human unity, the final embodiment of objective reason in the world, and regarded its laws and its conception of justice as the unconditional norm of human life; it was not likely that this huge self-sufficient whole would without desperate resistance submit to a higher principle and give up its false absoluteness in order to acquire the true one through freely serving God's cause and taking part in the building up of God's Kingdom.

. . . Christian apologists in their petitions to the Roman emperors and their protests against persecution referred to the principles of justice which had been developed by Rome itself through its jurists and philosophers. To do violence to people solely because of their religious beliefs was undoubtedly contrary to simple human justice; in entering this path the Roman Empire ceased to be an embodiment of justice on earth, i.e. lost its deepest inner *raison d'être*. In their cruel persecutions the Roman authorities, abandoning their highest principle — justice — could only

---

[1] For the benefit of ignorant zealots who might be offended by this analogy I hasten to remind them that it was actually used by the Fathers (Clement of Alexandria and Justin the Philosopher) and I have merely generalized it to some extent.

appeal to the so-called political necessity, to the interests of state unity, which seemed incompatible with the existence of the Christian Church as an independent society, a *status in statu*. The Christian striving to unite all men in the true faith and a perfect ideal of life might seem merely a dangerous pretension, destructive of the actual, already existing unity of the state. Indeed, at its beginning the Roman Empire might have appeared not merely as one self-contained whole, but as the *only* social bond embracing the whole of the historical humanity. Had its unity remained an expression of reason and justice — of the principle that implies and brings about unity — it could not have been disrupted; but in that case it could not have rejected Christianity, since reason which gives us mastery over the lower forces of nature and of the natural humanity demands submission to a higher, divinely-human power. Rome, which by the force of reason subjugated other peoples, ought in virtue of that same reason to have submitted itself to Christians as to the people of God. In not doing this it was losing its human image, was replacing reason by brute force, and instead of being one universal state was becoming one of those beast-like kingdoms which rose and fell in the East from the time of Nebuchadnezzar till Antioch.

Constantine the *Great* has, of course, many claims to this appellation. He was a first-class general who always won victories, both over barbarians and over his political rivals; he re-established the greatness and unity of the Empire, having gathered together all its disjointed parts under his own power after a number of brilliant victories; impartial historians admit that he had the mind of a great statesman and praise the laws he issued. . . . But the outstanding thing about Constantine, unique in its way, is that his reign heralds a new idea in history — the idea of the Christian state; and if that idea remains hitherto a paradox and a stumbling block for politicians and philosophers, that merely testifies to its profound significance, and the difficulty of realizing it. It is rooted in Christianity itself, and is a deduction from the central idea of the Gospel — the idea of the Kingdom of God.

Christ revealed the truth to humanity and set it the task of transforming its life in accordance with that truth. In truth all are one, and God — the absolute unity — is all in all. But the actual life of mankind is not in truth, and the divine all-embracing unity is concealed from us as a kind of mystery by the obvious disruption of the world-whole into spatial parts and temporal events, and, still more, by the egoistic isolation of our own minds. Humanity itself, which in its higher nature is the image and likeness of God and should be the unifying and governing reason of the material world, is in fact divided and scattered over the earth. After long efforts and much hard work it achieved through a complex historical process merely a formal and external union in the universal monarchy of Rome. Incomplete even outwardly, that Roman unity was quite insufficient inwardly. The real principle of cosmic dis-union — human egoism with all the passions and vices that follow from it — is an actual, real fact: it could not be undermined by the mere formal principles of law and justice. The complete impotence of state justice as an external good over the inner evil of the human heart was clearly expressed in the fact that the most striking instances of every kind of evil and madness were provided by the representatives of this outward universal good — the Roman emperors.

In order that universal unity should be not an empty form, not a whited sepulchre, but a living form filled with appropriate content, it was necessary first of all to provide a new unifying basis for human life itself, to re-establish the bond connecting it with the absolute principle of true unity. If that bond was to counteract actual evil, it had to be something more than an abstract idea or a vague feeling — it had to be an objective reality. Thus the first thing that was needed was a *divinely-human fact*. Such a fact was and is given in the historical revelation of the incarnate Son of God, and in all that directly follows from His incarnation — the grace of the sacraments, the Church as holy and sanctifying, as the real and mystical body of Christ. But the true bond between man and God, worthy of God's perfect goodness, is a free or mutual bond; it requires, not the abolition of the human reality, but its conformity to the divine truth. True unity is not posited from outside, but is reached by free effort, by persistent and many-sided activity of mankind itself, which thus becomes connected with the Deity not only in its mysterious essence but in its manifest actuality, not only at the source but in the centre of its life. Christ came not to destroy the world, but to save it; and the socially-political organism of humanity — the world in the narrow sense — must be not destroyed by the holiness of Christianity, but saved by it, i.e. converted, transformed, spiritualized.

The divinely-human bond must find expression not only in what is given to men — the dogmas of faith, the continuity of grace in sacraments and apostolic succession — but also in what is done by men themselves. This is the second, *actual* unity apart from which our current reality and the historical process would remain outside Christianity, and then the purpose of Christianity itself would not be realized. That purpose is the third and final aspect of the divinely-human unity, conditioned by the first two — the complete correspondence of the whole of external reality to the inner principle of the true life. In so far as we, in coming into this world, are actually separated from the divine unity by hereditary evil, that unity must first be given as a real object independent of us — as the Kingdom of God which comes down to us, the objective and external Church. But having once accepted this given union with God, mankind must assimilate it through its own efforts, introducing it into the whole of its actual life as the principle which transforms it. That is the Kingdom of God 'which is taken by violence', and only after it has been actively taken, can the Kingdom of God, eternally existing within us as a hidden potency, be finally revealed as a manifested reality. First given to us as a sacred fact, then realized through our activity as a living reality, it can at last manifest itself in us and in everything as the perfect state of invincible love, peace and joy in the Holy Spirit.

And so, corresponding to Christ's three forms of service and of power, the Christian world (or the universal Church in the broad sense of the term) develops as a threefold divinely-human union. There is the sacred union in which the divine element predominates in a traditional, unchangeable form, constituting the Church in the narrow sense — the temple of God. There is the royal union in which the human element (relatively) predominates, forming the Christian state (by means of which the Church must realize itself in the living body of humanity). Finally, there is the prophetic union, not attained as yet, in which the divine and the human elements must fully interpenetrate each other, forming in their free and mutual combination the perfect human society (the Church as the bride of God).

The Christian Church, the Christian state and the Christian society as the three inseparable modifications of the Kingdom of God (in its earthly form) have one and the same essence — God's truth and righteousness. The Church believes in it and serves it as the absolute truth; the state in its relative sphere realizes it in practice as justice; and Christian society must develop it in itself as the fulness of freedom and love.

. . . In so far as the Church in the sense of a sacred institution is an accomplished fact, and the free brotherhood of all through love is as yet only a prophetic ideal, the most vital and practical significance attaches to the middle term, the state, whose attitude to Christianity directly determines the historical destinies of mankind.

Speaking generally, the purpose of the state is to defend human society from the most concrete and clearly manifested forms of evil or injustice — from obvious or public evil. Since the true social good is the solidarity of all, social evil is nothing other than the violation of this solidarity. The actual life of mankind exemplifies three kinds of real and obvious violation of universal solidarity: first, it is violated when one nation deprives another of existence or of national independence; secondly, when some social class or institution oppresses another; and thirdly, when an individual openly rebels against the general order by committing a crime. To prevent such violations from happening and to counteract them after they have taken place is the direct task of the state. But in fulfilling it the state itself, represented by sinful men, may violate justice in respect of the violators, not only because of possible ill will on its part, but also because of the crudely mechanical interpretation of justice or of universal solidarity as the good of the majority. Such misinterpretation, natural in a pagan state, ought not to be allowed in a Christian state.

True solidarity is not the good of the majority, but the good of all and each without exception. It presupposes that every element (collective or individual) of the great whole, besides having a right to exist, has an inherent value of its own which does not permit of its being made a mere tool or means of general welfare. It was through not knowing this true justice that the state of antiquity defended itself and preserved social order by exterminating its enemies, enslaving the working classes, and tormenting and killing criminals. Christianity, in recognizing the infinite value of every human being, ought to have completely altered the behaviour of the state. Social evil in its threefold expression — international, civil and criminal — remained the same; the state had, as before, to struggle against it, but the final end and the means of the struggle could not remain the same. Having accepted Christianity, i.e. having recognized the truth of the absolute solidarity of all, the state had to be true to that truth, and in carrying out its immediate task, i.e. in counteracting the violations of social justice, it had to be just towards the violators themselves and not violate their human rights. The pagan state had to do with enemies, slaves, criminals. An enemy, a slave, a criminal had no rights whatever. The Christian state, inseparable from the Church, has to do with members of the body of Christ — suffering, humiliated, vicious; it must quench national hatred, rectify social injustice, correct individual vice. In a Christian state the foreigner does not lose his civic rights, the slave acquires the right to be free, the criminal has the right to be morally healed and re-educated.

It clearly follows from this that for a Christian state the following things are absolutely inadmissible: first, wars inspired by national egoism, and conquests that raise one nation upon the ruins of another; secondly, civic and economic slavery, making one social class a passive means for the enrichment of another; and, finally, legal punishments which do not finally aim at the reformation of the criminal, but deal with him simply from the point of view of social security.

2

MORALITY, POLITICS AND THE MEANING OF NATIONALITY

COMPLETE separation between morality and politics is one of the prevalent errors of the present age. From the Christian point of view and within Christendom, those two realms—the moral and the political — ought to be most intimately connected, though they cannot *coincide*.

Just as Christian morality has in view the realization of the Kingdom of God within the individual, so Christian politics should be preparing the coming of God's Kingdom for humanity as a whole consisting of large parts — nations, races and states.

Past and present politics of historical nations have very little in common with such a purpose and for the most part are in direct contradiction to it — this is an indisputable fact. The politics of Christian peoples are still ruled by godless hostility and strife, and the Kingdom of God is left out altogether. Most people are content to leave it at that: so it is, and so it must be. But such an attitude of bowing down to facts cannot be consistently kept up, for then we should have to bow down to plague and cholera which also are facts. Man's whole dignity consists in consciously struggling against a bad reality for the sake of a better one. Prevalence of disease is a fact, but health is the end to be aimed at; the means of transition from the bad fact to a better end is the science of medicine. In the general life of humanity the predominance of evil and strife is a fact, but the end to be sought is the Kingdom of God, and the means of transition from the bad reality to that final end is called Christian politics.[1]

It is commonly believed that every nation ought to have a

---

[1] Such politics are not *utopian* in the derogatory sense of that term, i.e. blind to the bad reality and building up its ideals in the void; on the contrary, Christian politics are primarily concerned with facts, and first and foremost are intended as a remedy against actual evil.

policy of its own aimed solely at observing the interests of that particular nation or state.

... This view may involve a misunderstanding due to the indefinite meaning of the word 'interests': the whole point is *what* interests are meant. If, as is generally the case, the interests of a nation are supposed to be wealth and external power, it is obvious that however important those interests are, they *ought not* to be the supreme and final end of politics, or else they may be used to justify every kind of crime, as indeed is the case.

... If this were the only possible kind of patriotism, it would be better to give up patriotism altogether. But there need be no such alternative. We venture to think that true patriotism is compatible with Christian conscience, that there may be other politics than those of self-interest, or rather, that Christian people have other interests, which do not require and indeed rule out international *cannibalism*. That international cannibalism is not anything commendable is felt even by those who indulge in it most. The policy of material gain is seldom advocated in its unadulterated form.

... The crude striving for one's own advantage becomes a lofty idea of one's cultural mission.

... And yet the principle of a cultural mission is a false and cruel principle. Its cruelty is visibly attested by the melancholy shadows of peoples that have been spiritually enslaved and lost their vital forces; and its falsity and inherent untenability are plainly demonstrated by the fact that it cannot be applied consistently. The conceptions of a higher culture and of a cultural mission are so indefinite that every historical nation has at one time or another laid a claim to such a mission and considered itself justified in doing violence to other nations in the name of its higher calling.

... But one nation's claim to a privileged position in humanity is incompatible with a similar claim made by another nation. Consequently, either all those claims are mere bragging, useful only as a cloak for the oppression of weaker neighbours, or there must arise a deadly struggle between the great nations for the right to use cultural violence. The issue of such a struggle, however, will in no way prove the real superiority of the victor's mission, for superior military power is not evidence of cultural excellence. The hordes of Tamerlane and Batu had that military preponderance, and some day the Chinese may gain it because of their numbers, but that would not make anyone pay homage to the cultural superiority of the Mongolian race.

The idea of a cultural mission may only be sound and fruitful when such a mission is regarded not as an assumed privilege, but as an actual duty — not as domination, but as service.

Every individual has material interests, but he also has duties, or, what is the same thing, *moral interests*, and a person who neglects them and acts only from motives of gain or vanity deserves the utmost censure. The same thing must be recognized in the case of nations.

. . . A nation has a moral duty towards other nations and mankind as a whole. To regard this common duty as a mere metaphor and at the same time to defend the common national interest as something real is an obvious contradiction. If a nation is only an abstract notion, it certainly can have no duties, but neither can it have any interests or any mission. But that is an obvious error. A nation has interests, and it also has a conscience. And if that conscience manifests itself but feebly in politics and does little to restrain the expressions of national egoism, this is unhealthy and abnormal, and everyone must admit that it is not right.

There is another incongruity in the theory of national self-interest fatal to it. Once the priority of one's own interests, as such, is recognized as legitimate in politics, it becomes quite impossible to determine what are the limits of 'one's own'. A patriot regards the interests of his nation as his own in virtue of national solidarity, and this, of course, is much better than personal egoism, but it is not clear why national solidarity must have precedence over the solidarity of any other social group, not coinciding with the limits of the nation. During the French Revolution, for instance, the legitimist *emigrés* found they had far more in common with foreign rulers and aristocrats than with the French Jacobins; German socialists felt that the Paris *communards* were much closer to them than Pomeranian landowners. It may have been very wrong on the part of the emigrants and the socialists, but from the point of view of political self-interest no reasons can be adduced for condemning them.

To raise one's own interest, one's self-conceit, to the rank of a supreme principle means, both for the individual and the nation, to sanction and perpetuate the dissensions and strife that tear humanity asunder. The general fact of struggle for existence present everywhere in nature is to be found in natural humanity too. But all historical progress, all human achievements, consist in limiting that struggle and gradually raising humanity to a

7

higher ideal of love and righteousness. That ideal, that new man, was revealed to us in the living reality of Christ. And it befits us not, after putting on the new man, to turn again to the weak and beggarly elements; to the strife, abolished on the Cross, between the Greek and the barbarian, the Jew and the Gentile. We are required in the name of patriotism to put the interests and the significance of our own nation above all else. From *such* patriotism we have been delivered by the blood of Christ shed by the Jewish patriots in the name of their national interest!

What shall we say then? Does the Christian religion abolish nationality? No, it preserves it. It abolishes, not *nationality*, but *nationalism*. The bitter persecution and crucifixion of Christ was not the work of the Jewish race of which (as concerns His humanity) Christ was the finest flower, but the work of the narrow and blind nationalism of such patriots as Caiaphas.

. . . We distinguish nationality from nationalism by their fruits. The fruits of the English nation are Shakespeare and Byron, Berkeley and Newton; the fruits of English nationalism are world-wide pillage, the exploits of Warren Hastings and Lord Seymour, destruction and killing. The fruits of the great German nation are Lessing and Goethe, Kant and Schelling, and the fruit of German nationalism is the compulsory germanization of their neighbours from the times of Teutonic knights to our own day. Nationality is a positive force, and every nation in accordance with its particular character is destined for a special mission. Different nations are different organs in the body of humanity — for a Christian this is an obvious truth. The organs of the physical body quarrel with one another only in Menenius Agrippa's fable, but the organs of humanity — nations, consisting not only of elemental but also of conscious and voluntary components — may and actually do oppose themselves to the whole, strive to single themselves out and to separate from it. In such striving the positive force of nationality is transformed into the negative effort of nationalism. It is nationality in abstraction from its vital powers, sharpened to conscious exclusiveness and directing that sharp point against all else. Nationalism in its extreme form ruins the nation that succumbs to it, making it an enemy of mankind, which will always prove stronger than any particular nation. By abolishing nationalism Christianity saves nations, for the supernational is not the nationless. The word of God is applicable here too: he that findeth his life shall lose it, and he that loseth his life shall find it. The nation intent at all costs to find its life in exclusive and self-contained nationalism shall lose it, and only in giving its whole soul to the super-national, universal cause of Christ shall a nation preserve it. Personal self-renunciation, victory over egoism, is not the annihilation of self, of personality as such, but, on the contrary, the raising of it to a higher level of being. The same thing is true of a nation: in renouncing exclusive nationalism it does not lose its independent life, but discovers its true vital task. That task reveals itself not as a venturesome pursuit of base interests, not as carrying out a fictitious and arbitrary mission, but in fulfilling a historical duty that unites it with all other nations in the common universal cause. Patriotism raised to this level does not conflict with personal morality, but imparts fulness to it. The highest aspirations of the human heart, the loftiest commands of Christian conscience, are then *applied* to political problems and tasks instead of being opposed to them. We must not deceive ourselves: inhumanity in international and social relations, the politics of cannibalism, will finally ruin both personal and family morality — as indeed can be seen to some extent already throughout Christendom. After all, man is a logical creature and cannot endure for long the monstrous duality between the rules of personal and of political activity. And so, if only for the sake of saving personal morality, we must beware of making that duality into a principle and demanding that a man who behaves in a Christian way to his friends, and remains at any rate within the bounds of law with regard to his fellow citizens, should as a representative of state and national interests be guided by a code natural to highwaymen and African savages. It ought to be recognized, if only in theory to begin with, that the true guiding principle of *all* politics is not self-interest and not self-conceit, but moral obligation.

The Christian principle of obligation or moral service is the only definite and complete or perfect principle of political activity. It is the only consistent one — for, taking self-sacrifice as its starting point, it carries it right through: it requires not only that the individual should sacrifice his exclusiveness for the sake of the nation, but that the nation and mankind as a whole should renounce all exclusiveness, for all are equally called to the work of *universal salvation*. That is from its very nature the highest and unconditional good and consequently provides a sufficient reason for self-sacrifice; but from the standpoint of self-interest it is not by any means evident why I must sacrifice my personal interests to those of my nation. Nor is it evident why I must bow down to the collective conceit of my fellow countrymen, while my personal conceit is considered by everyone as merely a weakness of my moral character and certainly not as a normal principle of action. Further, the Christian idea of obligation is the only *definite* principle of politics, for, on the one hand, self-interest and gain are as such something utterly boundless and insatiable, and, on the other, the belief in one's higher and exclusive calling gives, as such, no positive guidance in every particular case and situation, while Christian duty always tells us how we ought to act in each given case. Besides, it demands of us only that which we undoubtedly are able to do, that which lies within our power (*ad impossibilia nemo obligatur*), while the striving after material gain in no way guarantees the possibility of attaining it, and the belief in our exclusive vocation usually lures us on to heights we cannot reach. We are therefore justified in saying that the motives of self-interest and self-conceit are *fantastic* motives, and the principle of Christian duty is something perfectly stable and real. Finally, it is the only *complete* principle containing all the positive content of the other principles which find their solution in it. Self-interest and self-conceit in their exclusiveness confirm rivalry and strife between nations and do not admit in politics of the higher principle of moral obligation — but that principle does not in the least deny either the legitimate interests, nor the true vocation of every nation; on the contrary, it presupposes both. For if only we admit that a nation has a moral duty, there can be no doubt that its real interests and its true vocation are bound up with carrying out that duty. It is not required that a nation should neglect its material interests and give no thought to its special calling; all that is required is that it should not devote its heart and soul to it and make it its final end. Then, subordinate to the higher considerations of Christian duty, both material welfare and national self-consciousness themselves become positive forces and actual means or instruments of the moral purpose, for then the gains of that nation are actually of benefit to all the others and its greatness really magnifies the whole of humanity. Thus the principle of moral obligation in politics, embracing the other two, is the most complete, just as it is the most definite and self-consistent. And our co-believers should remember that it alone is a Christian principle. The politics of self-interest, the striving for wealth and power, proper to the natural man, are a pagan concern, and in adopting that ground, Christian nations revert to paganism. The assertion of one's exclusive mission, the deification of one's nation, is the point of view of ancient Judaism, and in taking it up Christian nations succumb to Old Testament Judaism.

To stifle and swallow others for one's own gratification is the work of animal instinct, inhuman and godless both for the individual and for a nation. To pride oneself on one's higher calling, to assume special rights and privileges over others, is, both for the nation and for the individual, the work of pride and self-assertion — human, but un-Christian. To admit one's duty, to recognize one's obligation, is a Christian work of humility and self-knowledge, the necessary beginning of moral achievement and of the true divinely-human life — for the nation as for the individual. Everything is then decided, not by one's opinions, but by conscience which is the same for all, and therefore in this case there can be no false claims.

. . . At the present stage of humanity the satisfaction of material needs and requirements of self-defence cannot in every instance directly follow from the dictates of moral duty, either for the individual or for the nation. For nations too there is such a thing as the concern of the moment, the evil of the historical day apart from its direct connection with the higher moral ends. We are not called upon to speak of those momentary concerns. But there are great vital questions in dealing with which a nation must be guided first and foremost by the voice of conscience, putting aside all other considerations. In those great questions the salvation of the national soul is at stake, and then every nation must think of its duty only, not looking round at other nations, not asking or expecting anything from them. It is not in our power to make others fulfil their duty, but we can and must fulfil our own, and by fulfilling it we shall be serving the common universal cause; for in that cause every historical nation has its own special service according to its special character and place in history. It may be said that this service is *forced upon* a people by its history in the form of great vital problems which it cannot by-pass. A nation may be tempted, however, to solve those problems not according to its conscience, but to considerations of pride and self-interest. This is the great danger, and to give warning of it is the duty of true patriotism.

3

MORALITY AND
LEGAL JUSTICE

THE demands of morality and those of legal justice only partly coincide. Murder, theft, violence are contrary both to the moral and to the juridical law — they are both sins and crimes. A lawsuit with one's neighbour about property or on account of a personal offence is contrary to morality, but is quite in accordance with law and is sanctioned by it. Anger, envy, malicious gossip, inordinate sensuous pleasures are tacitly allowed by law, but are condemned by morality as sins. What is the principle of differentiation?

It can be reduced to three main points:

(1) A purely moral demand such as that of love for one's enemies is essentially unlimited or all-embracing. It presupposes an unconditional striving for moral perfection. All limitation admitted as a *matter of principle* is contrary to the nature of the moral commandment and undermines its dignity and significance. Those who renounce the absolute ideal in principle renounce morality itself and leave the moral ground. The law of the state, on the contrary, is essentially limited, as can be clearly seen in all cases of its application; instead of perfection, it is content with the lowest, minimal degree of morality and merely demands that certain extreme expressions of evil will should be inhibited. But this obvious and general distinction is not a contradiction leading to real conflict. From the moral point of view it cannot be denied that the demands of the law conscientiously to fulfil one's financial obligations, to abstain from murder, robbery and so on, are demands for what is, in any case, not evil but good, though elementary, and that if we ought to love our enemies, it goes without saying that we ought to respect the life and property of our neighbours. There is no contradiction between moral and

juridical law, and indeed the first presupposes the second: there is no fulfilling the greater without fulfilling the lesser; those who cannot rise to the first stage are not capable of reaching the highest. There would be a crude and obvious contradiction if this natural connection were broken — if, for instance, a man who was breaking criminal law considered himself to have attained moral perfection. On the other hand, though the law of the state does not demand moral perfection, it does not deny it; in forbidding everyone to commit murder and fraud, it cannot, and indeed need not, prevent anyone from loving his enemies; so there is no contradiction here whatever. With regard, then, to the first point, the relation between the two fundamental principles of practical life may be expressed as follows: *law* (the demands of legal justice) *is the lowest limit or the minimum of morality, equally binding upon all.*

(2) The unlimited nature of the purely moral demands accounts for another difference between them and legal norms. The higher moral commandments do not prescribe any definite external actions, but let the spiritual disposition express itself in actions appropriate in the given circumstances; the actions as such have no moral value, and by no means exhaust the demands of the moral law which remain infinite. The law of the state, on the contrary, has for its object concretely determined external actions, by the performance of or abstention from which it is perfectly satisfied. But in this distinction, again, there is no contradiction whatever: a spiritual disposition by no means excludes external actions in which it finds a natural though not a complete expression; a legal command or prohibition of certain actions presupposes a corresponding spiritual approval or censure. Both the moral law and the law of the state refer to man's inner being, to his will, but the first is concerned with that will in its integral universality, and the second merely with its partial realization with regard to certain external facts that are the special province of legal justice — the inviolability of life and property, and so on. The important thing from the juridical point of view is the practical attitude of the moral will to those objects, expressing itself in performing certain actions or in refraining from them. This is the second essential characteristic of legal justice, defined in the first instance as a certain minimum of morality: completing this definition we may now say that legal justice is the demand for the practical fulfilment of this minimal moral content. In other words,

the essential purpose of legal justice is *to secure the practical realization of a definite minimum of good*, or, what is the same thing, to do away with a certain amount of evil, while morality in the strict sense is directly concerned not with the external realization of the good, but with its inner existence in the human heart. Since, generally speaking, a small but actually realized good is preferable to the great and most perfect but non-existent, there is nothing derogatory or humiliating to legal justice in the fact that it secures the practical realization of the minimum good.

(3) This second distinction leads to the third. The demand for moral perfection as an inner state presupposes free or voluntary fulfilment; any compulsion, whether physical or even psychological, is here from the nature of the case both undesirable and impossible. On the other hand, external realization of law and order, or of definite conditions of a certain relative good, naturally admits of direct or indirect *compulsion*. In so far as the direct or immediate purpose of legal justice is precisely the objective existence of a certain good — e.g. of public safety — the compulsory character of law becomes a necessity, for it is obvious that all murders, frauds, etc., cannot be stopped forthwith by verbal persuasion alone.

Combining those three characteristics we obtain the following definition of law in its objective relation to morality: *legal justice is a compulsory demand to realize a definite minimal good or a social order which does not allow of certain extreme forms of evil.*

The question may now be asked, what is the ground for such a demand, and how is this compulsory order compatible with the purely moral, which by its very nature seems to exclude all compulsion? If the perfect good is recognized by the mind as the absolute ideal, should not everyone be left freely to realize it as far as he is able? Why make the compulsory minimum of morality into a law, when conscience demands that we should freely fulfil the maximum? Why command under penalty 'do not kill', when we ought mildly to exhort men not to be angry?

... The good as such must be absolutely free — that is indisputable. What is in dispute is the freedom of evil; it too should be free, but only with certain limitations which are demanded by reason.

There can be no human dignity and no high moral development without personal freedom. But man cannot exist and consequently cannot develop his freedom and morality apart from society. So that the same moral interest that demands personal freedom demands at the same time that personal freedom should not conflict with the conditions of society's existence. The absolute ideal of moral perfection taken in the abstract as the goal of free individual efforts cannot harmonize personal freedom with public self-preservation: it saves and perfects those who recognize it, but has no practical significance for those who do not. In its name the most is required of them — love for their enemies — but not even the least is in fact given them, such as making them refrain at any rate from killing and plunder. A strict moralist might say 'we do not want people to refrain from crime unless they do it voluntarily', but that would be simply a proof of extreme selfishness: a high-flown demand for free virtue addressed to a murderer would not bring his victim back to life, nor help the murderer himself to become, at least, a decent man.

... The complete idea of the moral good inevitably includes altruism and a demand for its practical application, i.e. compassion for the troubles of others, prompting us actively to save them from evil; therefore moral duty can certainly not be confined to merely recognizing and proclaiming the moral ideal, while the practical conditions of attaining it are denied. In the natural course of events, which cannot be changed by good words, whilst some would be freely striving for the highest ideal and growing perfect in dispassionateness, others would practise, unhindered, every kind of villainy and would certainly exterminate the first before they could really attain moral perfection. And besides, even if men of good will were by some miracle preserved from extermination by the evil men, obviously those good men themselves would be *insufficiently* good if they had nothing but good words to offer to their bad fellow-creatures tormenting one another.

The purpose of moral law is that man should live thereby, and man can live only in society. And the existence of society depends not upon the perfection of some, but upon the security of all. This security is not ensured by the moral law, to which men with predominantly anti-social instincts are deaf, but is safeguarded by the compulsory law perceptible even to them. To reject it, appealing to the gracious power of Providence to restrain and instil reason into criminals and lunatics, is sheer blasphemy: it is impious to lay upon the Deity the tasks that can be carried out by an efficient police.

And so the moral principle demands that men should freely

seek perfection; to this end the existence of society is necessary; but society cannot exist if everyone who wishes to do so may without let or hindrance kill or do bodily harm to his neighbours; hence the compulsory law which actually prevents those extreme expressions of the evil will, destructive of society, is a *necessary* condition of moral progress and as such is required by the moral law itself, though it is not a direct expression of it.

Let it be granted that the highest morality (in its ascetic aspect) makes us indifferent to the prospect of being killed, maimed or robbed; but that same morality (on its altruistic side) does not allow us to be indifferent to letting our neighbours become robbers and murderers or being robbed and murdered, or to the danger of destruction to society apart from which an individual cannot live and strive after perfection. Such indifference would be a clear sign of moral death.

The demand for personal freedom presupposes, for the sake of its own realization, restraint upon freedom in so far as, at the present stage of human development, it is incompatible with the existence of society or with the common good. The interests of individual freedom and general welfare, opposed to each other in abstract thought but equally binding morally, coincide in fact. Legal justice is born of their union.

. . . Legal justice is the historically changing form of the enforced balance between two moral interests: the formally moral interest of personal liberty and the materially moral interest of the common good.

A person is directly interested in his freedom, society is directly interested in its security and welfare, but the direct interest of legal justice and of a state founded upon law is the rational *balance* between those two empirically opposed interests. Balance is the specific characteristic of law. . . . Moral law is concerned only with the rightful relation between the two main theoretical delimitations of the human life: the freedom of the individual and the good of society. If law confines itself to this and does not introduce its compulsory element into the more complex and intimate sphere of private relations which do not infringe upon either limit, it best accords with morality. Man must reach moral heights freely, and for this he must have freedom down below, he must have a certain amount of *freedom to be immoral.* Legal justice secures him this freedom in a measure, without in the least encouraging him to use it.

... The harmony between the two moral interests is particularly clear in the domain of penal law. Every man's freedom, or natural right to live, act and strive for perfection, would obviously be an empty sound if it depended upon the whim of every other man who might like to kill or maim him or deprive him of the means of subsistence. And if it is my natural right to defend by compulsory measures my freedom and safety from the attacks of other people's evil will, it is my direct moral duty to defend others from it by the same means. This common duty is carried out by public justice provided with all necessary sanctions.

In safeguarding the freedom of peaceful citizens law leaves sufficient room for the exercise of the evil will and does not compel anyone to be virtuous. Only when the evil will attacks the objective, generally recognized norms of human relations and threatens the safety of society itself, is it necessary in the interests of the common good, which coincides with the interests of peaceful citizens, compulsorily to limit the criminal's freedom. In the interests of freedom, legal justice allows men to be bad and does not interfere with their free choice between good and evil, but in the interests of the common good it prevents the evil man from remaining a triumphant *evil-doer* dangerous to the very existence of society. The task of legal justice is certainly not to transform the world which lies in wickedness into the Kingdom of God, but merely to prevent it from becoming hell before its time.

Penal Law. The Retributive and Deterrent Theories of Punishment

In the primitive and simplest form of society — the kinship-group — social norms follow from the blood-tie between the members of the group and are safeguarded by the law of blood-vengeance. The roots of law are at this stage deeply hidden in the soil of natural instinctive relations which are still very close to the facts of the animal kingdom. An animal attacked by another intending to devour it defends itself out of the instinct of self-preservation with teeth, horns and claws to the best of its ability. No one will seek for moral motives in this, any more than in the physical self-defence on the part of man whose poor natural means of attack and defence are supplemented or replaced by artificial weapons. But like many lower animals, a savage does not live by himself; he belongs to some social group — a group of kinsfolk, a clan, a band. Therefore, in case of encounter with an enemy, the result of single combat does not end the matter. Damage to life or limb or any other wrong suffered by one member of a group is felt by the group as a whole and calls forth general resentment. In so far as it includes compassion for the victim, it involves a moral element, but, of course, the predominant feature of this reaction against the injury is the instinct of collective self-preservation, as with bees and other social creatures: in defending its member, a clan or a class defends itself; in avenging its member, it avenges itself. But the aggressor's kin or clan defends him for the same reason. Individual conflicts thus become wars between societies.

... The place which later on is occupied by legal justice is at this stage entirely taken up by the generally recognized and unconditionally binding custom of blood-vengeance.

... With the formation of the state there arises the distinction, which did not exist before, between public and private right, especially with regard to criminal offences. At the kinship-group stage the interests of the collective whole and the individual with regard to blood-vengeance and other important matters were identical. This was all the more natural as in a small social group such as the clan or the tribe all or at any rate most of its members could know one another personally and thus each was for all, and all for each, a concrete unit. But in the state the social group embraced hundreds of thousands and even millions of people, and the concrete personal relation between the parts and the whole became impossible. There thus appeared a more or less clear distinction between private and public interests and corresponding rights. In opposition to our modern legal notions at that stage murder, robbery, bodily injuries, etc., were treated as violations of private rights. Formerly, at the kinship-group stage, all such crimes were regarded as directly affecting the interests of the community, and the whole clan retaliated upon the culprit and his kinsmen. When a wider political union was formed, this right and duty of blood-vengeance as leading to endless wars was taken away from the clan, but did not pass, unchanged, to the state.

... We find that with regard to the defence of private persons and property the state is, at first, content with very little. For bodily injury or other violence to a free man, and even for the murder of a free man, the culprit or his relatives pay to the family of the victim compensation in money.

. . . At this stage of social development all offences against the life and property of private persons are regarded as private quarrels rather than crimes, and the business of public authority is to see that they are properly settled. Strictly speaking, the only 'crimes' are direct attacks upon the foundations of social order, i.e. such violations of the law as are to this day referred to a special class of 'political' crimes. This distinction is preserved throughout history and only its concrete application alters in accordance with the historical setting. In the Middle Ages the importance of personal safety for normal society, the interest that the community has in counteracting homicide, and therefore the criminal nature of that act, were not yet fully clear to the legal consciousness. Killing a man seemed to the state far less important than a violation of fiscal interests, and while the majority of homicides went scot-free, false coining was punished by painful death. It was regarded as a crime harmful to the society as a whole, infringing upon the privileges of the central authority and therefore political.

Elementary distinction between public and private rights prevalent at the stage of the so-called 'composition' for offences could not be stable.

. . . At the new and higher stage the solidarity of the central power with its individual subjects becomes more clear. The distinction between crimes directed against the government (political crimes) and those infringing upon private interests only is still retained, but it is now merely a distinction of degree. Every citizen becomes a member of the state, which undertakes to protect his safety; every violation of it is regarded by the state as an attack upon its own rights, as a hostile action against the social whole. All attacks against person and property are regarded as violations of the law of the state and no longer as private offences, and are therefore, like political crimes, for the state itself *to avenge*.

Thus, in spite of all the changes brought about by the formation of the state and its growing strength and expansion, the prevalent view of crime and punishment remained essentially the same from primitive times down to the middle of the eighteenth or the beginning of the nineteenth centuries, and partly down to our own day. Crime was regarded as an offence or a hostile action requiring retaliation; the criminal was an enemy, and punishment was blood-vengeance. At first the true subject of offence and consequently the avenger was the family or clan, and then after a temporary and unstable transitional period of money 'compositions', it was replaced by the state.

. . . Our mental attitude to crime has remained morally and practically the same, but it has undergone one important theoretical change. The criminal is still regarded as an *enemy* — the enemy of the given society; but in the old days this attitude was wholly and finally determined by the objective aspect of his action: he had done it, and so he must be exterminated. The question as to his own personal relation to what had happened was not raised. It made no difference whether the thing was done accidentally or in a fit of madness or through feeblemindedness; it was the objective fact that mattered and its actual connection with this particular person. The personal, subjective side had so little importance that it might be altogether absent — the criminal need not have been a person, i.e. a human being, at all: as late as the Middle Ages legal charges were brought against animals.

This purely external point of view which I propose to call *savage* was widely prevalent at the early stages of society. But gradually, with the development of insight, another and in some respects opposite point of view was worked out theoretically, though the practical attitude to the matter remained the same. . . . Crime is now chiefly considered as the manifestation of a person's evil will, hostile to the laws of normal social life. The criminal is no longer an integral part of an evil fact but is its cause, the guilty party; punishment is not the actual redemption by blood of the iniquity that has been done, but retribution for guilt, for the manifested evil will. This evil will is recognized as the full and only cause of the crime, which presupposes absolute freedom of choice, *liberum arbitrium indifferentiae*; accordingly, punishment has the same formally unconditional character of equivalent retribution: you have killed — you must be killed.

This 'absolute' theory of crime and punishment — which I call *barbaric* — if it be regarded in accordance with its own claims as final and absolute, is one of the most extraordinary specimens in the rich collection of human aberrations.

. . . 'Crime is a violation of right; right must be re-established; punishment, i.e. equal violation of the criminal's right, performed in accordance with a definite law by public authority, balances the first violation and thus right is re-established.' The idea of re-establishing violated right is just and clear when it is a case of violations which may be either directly expressed as so much material loss or can be more or less adequately assessed quantitatively. Thus if someone appropriates without sufficient reason a sum of money belonging to another person and is made to pay it back, this undoubtedly is a restitution of the violated right. But when this idea is transferred from the realm of offences against property to that of crimes of violence, the result is mere play with words which might be called childish if human lives were not at stake.

Indeed, right is always *somebody's* right (there must be a concrete subject of rights). Whose right, then, is meant in case of crimes of violence? At first it seems to mean the right of the person injured. Let us put this concrete content in the place of the abstract term. Peaceful shepherd Abel has a right to exist and enjoy all the good things of life; but a wicked man, Cain, comes and deprives him of this right by murdering him. The violated right must be re-established; to do so public authority comes on the scene and, against the direct warning of Holy Writ (Genesis iv. 15) hangs the murderer. Well, does this re-establish Abel's right to live? Since it has never happened that the execution of the murderer raised his victim from the dead, the word 'right' must mean in this connection not the right of the injured person but of somebody else. The other subject of right violated by the crime may be society itself organized as a state. All private rights are guaranteed by the state; it vouches for their inviolability in placing them under the defence of its laws. . . . But this merely implies that crimes in general are punishable; the question as to the actual nature of punishments remains open.

There is no doubt that once a certain normal order expressed by existing laws has been recognized its violation cannot be overlooked, and that it is the business of the state to see to it. But in this respect, that is, as violations of the law, all crimes are identical. If a law is sacred in itself as proceeding from the state, this is true of all laws in an equal degree. They all equally express the right of the state; and the violation of any law whatever is the violation of this supreme right. Material differences between crimes have to do with the particular interests that are infringed; but on its formal side, in relation to what is universal, that is, to the state *as such* and to its law and power, every crime, if, of course, it is committed by a responsible agent, presupposes a will opposed to the law, a will that sets it at nought and is therefore criminal. On the strength of the formal principle that every crime is equally a violation of law, all crimes ought logically to require the same punishment.

. . . To avoid such an absurdity it is necessary to presuppose, in addition to the general principle of punishability, a certain other specific principle which determines the particular connection between *this* crime and *this* punishment. The doctrine of retribution discovers this connection in the fact that the right violated by a particular criminal action is re-established by a corresponding or *equal* action — for instance, a murderer must be killed. It has already been pointed out that no *real* re-establishment is thus brought about, and this is indisputable. But is there any kind of correspondence or equality in it at all? The most famous champions of the doctrine conceive of the matter as follows: Right is something positive, say a + (plus); the violation of it is something negative − (a minus). If the negation in the form of crime has taken place (e.g. a man has been deprived of life), it must call forth equal negation in the form of punishment (taking the murderer's life). Then such double negation, or the negation of the negative, will once more bring about a positive state, i.e. re-establish the right: *minus multiplied by minus makes plus.* Let us make a conscientious effort to take seriously this 'play of mind' and observe that the idea of the negation of the negative logically expresses a direct inner relation between two opposed acts. Thus, for instance, if an impulse of ill-will in man is 'negative', is, namely, a negation of the moral norm, the opposite act of will, suppressing that impulse, will indeed be a 'negation of the negative' and the result will be a positive one — man's affirmation of himself as normal. Similarly, if crime as an active expression of ill-will is negative, the criminal's active repentance will be a negation of the negative (i.e. not of the fact, of course, but of the inner cause that produced it), and the result will again be positive — his moral regeneration. But what is the real, fruitful connection of one negation with another in the execution of a criminal? Here the second negation is directed, not upon the first, but upon something positive — upon human life. It cannot be maintained that the execution of the criminal negates his crime, for that crime is an irrevocably accomplished fact, and, according to the remark of the Fathers of the Church, God Himself cannot undo what has been done. Nor does it negate the criminal's evil will, for he has either repented of his crime — and in that case there is no longer any evil will — or he remains obdurate to the end, and then his will is inaccessible to the treatment he is receiving— and in any case external violence cannot change the inner state of will. If, however, what is really negated by the execution of the criminal is not his crime and not his evil will, but only the positive good of life, this is once more merely a simple negation and not a 'negation of the negative'.

But a simple succession of two negatives cannot lead to any- thing positive. The misuse of the algebraic formula makes the argument really absurd. In order that two minuses, that is, two negative quantities, should make a plus, it is not sufficient to place them one after another, but it is necessary to multiply one by the other. But there is no intelligible meaning in *multiplying crime by punishment*. Clearly we cannot in this case go beyond the addition of the material results: the corpse of the victim may be added to the corpse of the hanged murderer and then there will be two lifeless bodies — that is, two negative quantities, two minuses.

The inherent absurdity of the doctrine of retribution or 'avenging justice' is clearly emphasized by the fact that, with the exception of a few and merely apparent instances, it bears no relation whatever to the existing penal laws, i.e. it has no real application. If legal practice conformed to this doctrine, a thief ought to be punished by being robbed. . . . And with regard to other crimes it is simply impossible to invent an equivalent retribution. By what equal action can one retaliate upon a false coiner, a perjurer, a bigamist, a forger? In modern penal codes the only instance of equal retribution — and that an apparent and a gradually disappearing one — is death penalty for murder. This is why the pseudo-philosophical arguments in defence of the doctrine of retribution refer precisely to this single instance — a bad omen for a principle which lays claim to universal significance. . . . The best argument against the doctrine is the circumstance that it finds its fullest application in the penal codes of some half- savage peoples, or in laws prevalent at the epoch of barbarism, when, for example, for inflicting a certain injury the culprit underwent a similar injury, for speaking insolent words a person had his tongue cut out, and so on. A principle the application of which proves to be incompatible with a certain degree of culture is condemned by the verdict of history.

The legal doctrine of retribution, utterly devoid, as we have seen, both of logical and of moral sense, is merely a survival of savagery; and in so far as punishments are still intended to cause the criminal physical suffering or privations as a penalty for his crime, they are merely a historical modification of the primitive law of blood-vengeance. Originally the victim was avenged by a small social unit called the kinship-group or clan, and later by a larger and more complex union called the state. In the old days the aggressor lost all human rights in the eyes of the injured clan, now he has become a rightless subject of punishment in the eyes of the state which revenges itself upon him for violating its laws.

But what conclusion can be drawn from the unquestionable fact that penal justice is a historical transformation of blood-vengeance? Does this historical basis justify us in determining the state's reaction against crime and our attitude towards the criminal by the idea of vengeance, i.e. of paying evil for evil, pain for pain? Speaking generally, logic does not allow us to make such deductions from the genetic connection between two events. Not a single Darwinist, so far as I know, has drawn the conclusion that because man is descended from the lower animals he ought to be a brute.

. . . Legal justice *starts* from blood-vengeance, but for that very reason it draws further and further away from it. 'Absolute' theories of retribution are a desperate attempt to support by abstract arguments that which is falling to pieces for living thought. The weakness of those *a priori* arguments about satisfying justice by killing and torture is so obvious that the adherents of the conservative tendency in criminal law have to find empirical support in the principle of *intimidation*. That principle, indeed, has always formed part of the doctrine of retribution. The popular aphorism 'to the dog a dog's death' has generally been accompanied by the addition 'as a warning to others'.

This principle can hardly be said to be valid even from the utilitarian and empirical point of view. No doubt fear is an important motive of action and of refraining from action both for animals and for men at the lower stages of development. But that motive, or at any rate the fear of death, has no decisive significance, as can be seen from the ever-increasing number of suicides on the part of most ordinary people. Prolonged solitary confinement or penal servitude may in fact be worse than death for the person concerned, but the idea of it does not produce an immediate terrifying effect upon a coarse mind. I will not dwell upon these and other well-known arguments against the theory of intimidation, such as the fact that the criminal always hopes to avoid detection or escape punishment. More weight attaches to the following consideration. All crimes may be divided into two categories, those committed under the influence of passion and those committed by habitual criminals. The very existence of crimes that have become a regular occupation or profession clearly shows that intimidation is insufficient as a deterrent. As to crimes of the first category, the essential characteristic of strong passion is precisely that it drowns the voice of reason and suppresses the very basis of all practical good sense — the instinct of self-preservation.

Untenable for practical reasons, the theory of intimidation is finally refuted on moral grounds, first, as a matter of principle, because it directly contradicts the fundamental moral law, and secondly, in practice, because that contradiction compels the champions of intimidation to be inconsistent: on the strength of moral considerations they are obliged to give up the most clear and direct demands of their theory.

. . . The moral principle, recognized in its essence by all normal people, though on different grounds and with different degrees of clearness, asserts that human dignity must be respected in every person, and that therefore no one may be made merely a means or an instrument for the advantage of others. According to the deterrent theory, however, the criminal who is being punished is regarded as merely a means for intimidating others and safeguarding public safety. The penal law may intend to benefit the criminal himself by deterring him, through fear of punishment, from committing the crime. But once the crime has been committed, this motive obviously disappears, and the criminal in being punished becomes solely a means of intimidating others, i.e. a means to an end external to him; and this is in direct contradiction to the unconditional law of morality. From the moral point of view a punishment inspiring fear would only be permissible as a threat; but a threat which is never fulfilled loses its meaning. Thus the principle of intimidation can be moral only on condition of being useless, and can be materially useful only on condition of being applied immorally.

In point of fact the theory of intimidation finally lost its sting from the time when all civilized and half-civilized countries abolished cruel corporal punishments and capital punishment accompanied by torture. It is clear that if the object of punishment is to intimidate both the criminal and others, the most cruel means are certainly the most effective and rational. Why, then, do the champions of intimidation renounce that which from their point of view ought to be recognized as the best? Probably because they recognize that those measures, excellent from the point of view of intimidation, are not permissible as immoral and contrary to the demands of pity and humanity. In that case, however, intimidation ceases to be the *determining* factor in punishment. It must be one or the other: either the meaning of punishment is intimidation — and in that case execution accompanied by torture must be admitted as pre-eminently intimidating; or the nature of punishment must be determined not only by considerations of practical utility but by its conformity with the moral principle which decides what is and what is not permissible — and then intimidation must be given up altogether, as a motive essentially immoral or inadmissible from the moral point of view.

The Death Penalty

Capital punishment is the last stronghold still defended by *barbaric* justice (the direct descendent of *savage* custom) in the modern world. The issue of the battle may be regarded as settled. The once dense crowd of defenders is gradually thinning round the decrepit and half-decayed idol unsteady on its two damaged feet of clay: the theory of retribution and the theory of intimidation.

In considering the retributive theory of punishment, we have taken account only of the two extreme points of it: the *terminus a quo*, the primitive crude custom of blood-vengeance, and the *terminus ad quem*, the scholastically abstract 'absolute' theory of equitable retribution. The development of legal justice includes, however, a third element which lost long ago direct practical significance in this domain, but still exercises a hidden influence upon conservative minds, precisely in the question of capital punishment.

There is not any doubt that the separation of legal and political norms and institutions from the religious took place comparatively late, and that originally these two domains were merged together. This involved facts and ideas utterly unexpected from our point of view. If a modern man who knew Latin but was not a classical scholar read in the law of Twelve Tables the short formula of punishment for some crime, such as stealing fruit at night, *sacer esto*, he would not guess at once that this really meant, let the man be killed or devoted to the deity for destruction. In any case such a homonym would seem to him very strange. But as a matter of fact it was not a case of using a homonym at all, i.e. of using one word for two different ideas: the word expressed one idea only, for at a certain epoch *consecrating* a living creature simply meant putting it to death. Generally speaking, to consecrate meant to put apart some objects of a group (of men, of animals, fruits and so on) in order to devote them to the deity. The original, primary method of doing this was sacrifice, that is, solemn destruction of the chosen objects which was their final sanctification. There were many grounds on which some objects rather than others were singled out for sanctification or destruction. For the most part those grounds were either natural such as primogeniture (the first-born of men and animals, the first-fruits, etc.) or social, in virtue of which criminals, prisoners of war and foreigners were sacrificed (which was particularly gratifying to the native deity). Since social norms were intimately associated with divine worship as direct expressions of the supreme will, all violation of those norms was regarded as an offence against the deity to whom the offender was bodily surrendered: *sacer esto*!

In the realm of Biblical ideas there may be detected a mystical connection between the two grounds of 'sanctification' — primogeniture and crime, in so far as the first man Adam and his first-born Cain were both first criminals, one directly against God, and the other against man. Without going into the theological aspect of the matter, it should be observed, however, that the Bible taken as a whole raises human consciousness far above the dark and bloody ground of savage religion and religious savagery, above which pagan nations rose to some extent in their upper classes thanks to the development of Greek philosophy and Roman jurisprudence.

In the Bible three chief moments emerge with reference to the subject under discussion: (1) After the first murder, the proclamation of the norm: a criminal, even if he be a fratricide, is not to suffer death at the hands of men: 'And the Lord set a mark upon Cain, lest any finding him should kill him'. (2) After the flood, brought about by the extreme manifestations of evil in man, *the adaptation of the norm* to 'the hardness of men's hearts': 'whoever sheds man's blood, by man shall his blood be shed'; this adaptation is worked out in detail and made more complicated in Mosaic law. (3) *Return to the norm* in the prophets and in the Gospel. 'Vengeance is mine; I will repay, saith the Lord.' How will He repay? 'I will have mercy and not sacrifice.' 'I am come to seek and to save that which was lost.'

The Bible is a complex spiritual organism that has taken a thousand years to grow; it is completely devoid of external uniformity and exactitude, but remarkable for the inner unity and harmony of the whole. Arbitrarily to snatch out of this whole intermediary parts without beginning or end is a false and meaningless procedure; and to quote the *Bible in general* in support of capital punishment is a sign either of hopeless lack of understanding or of boundless insolence. Those who, like Josèphe de Maistre, bring together the ideas of the death penalty and of redeeming sacrifice forget that the redeeming sacrifice for all has already been made by Christ; it has abolished all other bloody sacrifices and itself continues only in the unbloody Eucharist. It is extraordinary that people who profess to be Christians should forget this. To admit any other redeeming sacrifices means to deny the work of Christ and is a betrayal of Christianity.

The bad pseudo-religious putty cannot mend the cracked clay of the 'absolute' theory of punishment requiring the retention of the death penalty as a due retribution for crime. Let us see whether there is more strength in the hideous idol's other foot of clay — in the utilitarian view that capital punishment is the most efficient way of defending society against the worst criminals.

Very few criminologists who take the utilitarian point of view interpret the usefulness of capital punishment in the direct sense, as the simplest and cheapest way of getting rid of the criminal. Most of the writers on the subject are ashamed of that simplicity. And yet from the exclusively utilitarian point of view there is no gainsaying the security and cheapness of the gallows as compared with prison. It is also clear that if hanging is profitable in the case of ten or twenty criminals, it is even more profitable in the case of ten thousand, and that the most advantageous thing for society is to hang all criminals and all men who are a burden to it. But if people are ashamed of such a conclusion, that means they are also ashamed of the principle from which this conclusion follows with logical necessity. But what value can a theory have, if its champions must recognize its very principle as shameful?

. . . If those who defend the death penalty as a necessary means of intimidation, deterring people from crime, were consistent and in earnest, they ought to ponder over the following *reductio ad absurdum* of their view. If the fear of the death penalty is a *necessary* deterrent, it follows that in so far as capital punishment drops out of use, the number of crimes must proportionately increase; apart from this, it increases, of course, owing to the natural increase and greater density of the population. Let us look at the facts. In England under Henry VIII 5,000 criminals were annually put to death; since then[1] the population has increased by twelve times; consequently, if 'the necessary' means of intimidation were applied as before, 60,000 criminals per year ought to be executed now; but as a matter of fact at present only an average of 15 people are hanged in the year, i.e. 4,000 times less than there ought to be. Such a reduction of the 'necessary' means of intimidation ought proportionately to have increased the number of crimes: if in the reign of Henry VIII (on the generous reckoning) there were as many crimes as there were executions, i.e. 5,000 a year, at the present time those crimes, no longer punishable by death, ought to reach the figure of at least 20 millions per year.

The champions of the intimidation theory can make only one answer to this absurd conclusion — an answer which really means abandoning their main position. They may say that the large number of executions is only a conditional necessity, and a matter of time: under Henry VIII it was necessary to execute 5,000 a year because of the general social instability and the coarse and savage customs and morals, but now fifteen executions are sufficient for intimidating the most dangerous criminals. But if social progress and favourable change in the conditions of life have done so much to reduce criminal tendencies, the struggle against crime must be carried on by those positive measures to the end, and executions abandoned as a useless cruelty.

. . . The last blow to the theory of intimidation has been dealt in our own day by the abolition of public executions. It is clear that an execution performed shyly and secretly is not intended for outward effect. The fact of such secrecy speaks for itself, but the

[1] Written in 1897.—*Ed.*

reason given for it is perhaps even more significant: it was found that public executions had a demoralizing effect on the spectators and led to an increase of crime in the neighbourhood.

Compare this timid, blushing legal murder made as far as possible comfortable for the victim and done within the prison walls, in the morning twilight — compare it with the splendours of the old times: for days together, in crowded market places, to the ringing of bells, hundreds of people were solemnly flayed, disembowelled, burnt on slow fire, broken on the rack, had hot lead poured down their throats, were boiled in water, in hot oil and wine! All this had to be abandoned; and if hell itself could not withstand the awakened conscience, can its pale and trembling shadow do so?

... Materially useless for society, capital punishment is spiritually harmful to it, as an immoral action of the society itself. It is an impious, inhuman and shameful action. In the first place, capital punishment is impious, for, being unconditional and final, it implies that human justice has an absolute character which, in truth, can belong to God's judgment alone as the expression of divine omniscience. Deliberately and consciously deleting this person from among the living, society declares: I *know* that this man is absolutely guilty in the past, absolutely worthless in the present, and absolutely incorrigible in the future. But since in truth society knows nothing for certain either about the man's incorrigibility in the future or even about his guilt in the past — as is sufficiently shown by many miscarriages of justice — this is an obviously impious intrusion into the precincts of eternity. In its blind madness human pride puts its relative knowledge and conditional justice in the place of God's all-seeing righteousness. Either the death penalty has no meaning whatever, or its meaning is impious.

Secondly, capital punishment is *inhuman* — not from the point of view of feeling, but of moral principle. It is entirely a question of principle: *ought* we to recognize in the human personality something sacred and inviolable, some limit to the external action upon it? The horror inspired by homicide clearly shows that there is such a limit, and that it is connected with man's life.

... But suppose the horrible thing has happened: a man has turned his fellow-man into a soulless thing. Let us admit that it could not have been helped and that society is not to blame so far. It is revolted and indignant, and that is a good thing: it would be very sad indeed if it remained indifferent. But justly horrified by murder, how does it express its feeling? — By taking another life. No logic can prove that a repetition of evil is good. Homicide is revolting not because a good man has been killed — the victim may have been a villain. What is revolting is the action of the will that oversteps the moral limit, revolting is the man who says to another 'you are nothing to me, you have no significance in my eyes, no rights, not even the right to exist' and confirms his words by his deed. But this is precisely how society acts towards the criminal, and does so without any extenuating circumstances, without passion, or vicious propensities, or mental breakdown. A crowd which under the influence of instinctive indignation lynches a criminal on the spot is guilty, but there is something to be said for it; society which does it slowly, carefully and in cold blood has no excuse whatever.

The peculiar horror and evil of murder lie, of course, not in the actual taking of life but in the inner rejection of the basic moral law, in the decision finally to break, on one's own initiative and by one's own action, the bond of universal human solidarity with regard to this concrete fellow-man who, like me, bears the image and likeness of God. This decision to do away with a man is far more clearly and fully expressed in capital punishment than in ordinary murder, for indeed it consists of nothing but the decision and the putting it into effect. The attitude of society to the con-demned criminal is *animus interficiendi* in absolutely pure form, perfectly free from all those psychological and physiological con-ditions and motives which obscured and concealed the essence of the matter from the criminal himself, whether he committed the murder for the sake of gain, or under the influence of some less shameful passion. In the case of capital punishment there can be no such complicating motives: the only purpose of it is to do away with this man, to put him out of existence. Capital punish-ment is murder as such, absolute murder, that is, the rejection in principle of the basic moral relation to a human being.

This indeed is admitted by the champions of the death penalty, who sometimes give themselves away in a most unexpected manner. One of them answered the demand for the abolition of capital punishment by the famous phrase 'let messieurs the murderers begin first!' It definitely puts capital punishment on a level with murder, and the society that is practising it on a par with 'messieurs the murderers', i.e. with individual criminals who are given the privilege of serving as a pattern and guide for the rest of society on the way to reform.

. . . Impious and inhuman, capital punishment has also a shameful character which general feeling has attached to it for ages, as can be seen from the universal contempt for the *hangman*. War, duelling, open murder may be inhuman, horrible and from a certain point of view senseless, but there is no specific element of shamefulness about them. Whatever the pacifists may say, a military man fighting against armed opponents with danger to his own life cannot in any case inspire contempt. Though duelling cannot be compared to war, and a duellist justly arouses public indignation and is prosecuted by law, yet no one can genuinely despise a man simply because he fights a duel, and for the same reason: the man at any rate rises above the instinctive fear of death and shows that his own physical life as such, apart from certain moral conditions (even if wrongly understood), has no value for him. The same thing may be said in a sense about certain cases of murder. But all these aspects of self-sacrifice or of risk to one's own life and liberty which justify war, excuse duelling and sometimes even mitigate the horror of direct murder are completely absent in capital punishment. There a disarmed and defenceless person is put to death by a man who is provided with a weapon, who runs no risk whatever and acts solely from motives of low gain. Hence the specifically shameful character of the whole thing and boundless general contempt for the hangman.

Being contrary to the basic principles of morality, capital punishment is at the same time a negation of justice as such. We have seen that the essence of legal justice is the balance between two moral interests — personal freedom and general good. It directly follows from this that the second interest (general good) may only *limit* the first (the individual freedom of each), but cannot possibly aim at doing away with it altogether, for in that case the balance would obviously be destroyed. Accordingly, any measures inspired by the concern for general welfare against an individual may never go so far as to eliminate that individual as such by taking his life or imprisoning him forever. Consequently, laws that allow capital punishment, life-long penal servitude or life-long imprisonment cannot be justified from the juridical point of view, for they abolish the relation essential to legal justice by abolishing one of the members of that relation.

. . . The general good must by its very definition be the good of *this man* also; when it deprives him of life or of the possibility of free action, and consequently of the possibility of any good at all, this pseudo-general good thereby ceases to be good for him and therefore loses its general character. It itself becomes merely a private interest and accordingly has no right to limit personal freedom.

At this point we see that the moral ideal is in perfect agreement with the true nature of legal justice. Although, speaking generally, in so far as legal justice enforces the minimal good, it differs from morality in the strict sense, it serves by its use of compulsion the real interests of morality and cannot in any case be opposed to it. Therefore, if some law of the state contradicts in principle the moral consciousness of the good, we may be sure that it also contradicts the essential demands of justice. The interests of justice demand certainly not the preservation of such laws but their *lawful* abolition.

Normal Penal Justice

. . . A criminal, like every immoral man in general, receives his real punishment from the judgment of God in accordance with moral laws. Human justice must simply be an efficient reaction of the society against criminal actions for purposes of necessary self-defence, of the actual protection of those who are menaced by them and of the possible reformation of the criminal himself. Since no action of the criminal can abolish his unconditional rights as a man, true legal justice must, while protecting society from crimes, have in view the criminal's own interests; otherwise it would be simply an instance of violence, like the crime itself.

This general idea of true, dispassionate and impartial justice, free from malice and vindictiveness, directly implies certain definite rules of judicial procedure and of the penal system.

The first step in the right and reasonable treatment of a criminal is temporarily to deprive him of liberty. This is necessary not only for the protection of others from him, but for himself as well. In the interests of his relatives and his own, a spendthrift is rightly deprived of freedom in the administration of his property; it is all the more just and necessary that a murderer or a ravisher should be first of all deprived of freedom in misusing his body, both for other people's and his own good. It is especially important for the criminal himself as a *pause* in the development of the evil will, as an opportunity to come to his senses, bethink himself and change his mood. For this it is necessary that the short preliminary confinement should be solitary. Even if the prisoner proves to be innocent, no harm will have been done, since solitude and change of surroundings are good for everyone. But to put the accused, who may be innocent, into the company of condemned criminals, and into the same conditions with them, is in any case senseless and barbarous.

. . . The criminal's further fate is at present finally decided by the court, which both determines his guilt and decrees his punishment. If, however, the motives of revenge and intimidation are consistently banished from penal law, the conception of punishment as of a measure *determined beforehand* — and, at bottom, *arbitrarily* — must disappear also. There is, of course, even now no absolute predeterminateness: a certain amount of freedom is given both to the jury in determining the guilt, and to the judges in deciding upon the punishment, and afterwards the sentence may be reduced by the central power which has the prerogative of mercy. But all this is merely a concession to moral feeling, and not a consistent intellectual recognition of the truth that a just and reasonable punishment has to do with the criminal *in concreto*, i.e. with this particular individual and not with an accidental sample of this or that genus, species or subspecies of criminality. To subsume the given criminal under these formal definitions is the preliminary task of penal justice and is the business of law, whose representatives have the formal legal education necessary for the purpose. But the final and real action of society upon the criminal, desirable for the good of both, is obviously concerned, not with the general conceptions of justice and with certain articles of law, but with the actual mental condition of the criminal himself, the changes in which cannot be determined beforehand. The law court can therefore only establish the facts concerning the legal side of the matter, determine the nature of guilt, the degree of the criminal's responsibility and of his further danger to society; the right of the state to continue compulsory measures against him depends on whether he goes on being dangerous. But those measures, if they are to serve a good purpose, cannot be fixed beforehand. The law court can and must make a general diagnosis and prognosis of the particular disease, but it is contrary to reason to prescribe unconditionally the means and the length of the period of treatment. The course and the methods of treatment must, obviously, differ according to the changes in the course of the illness, and the court of law, which after pronouncing the sentence has nothing more to do with the criminal, should leave this entirely to penitentiary institutions to which he should be handed over. Apart from the general justice of such procedure, it has the important advantage of easily rectifying the cruel consequences of judicial errors.

The proposal to deprive the law court of the right to pronounce predetermining sentences, to turn it into a kind of committee of learned jurists or a consultation of legal experts, would have seemed only a short time ago an unheard-of heresy, possible only for a miserable ignoramus, an utter stranger both to the practice and to the theory of law. Yet now this idea so wounding to professional pride is not only accepted in theory, but an important step has been taken in some countries to realize it in practice, by introducing *conditional sentences*. In certain cases a first offender, though sentenced to a definite punishment, is allowed to go free until he commits the same offence again, or some new crime; if he does, the new punishment is added on to his first sentence.

In other cases the sentence is conditional with regard to the term of imprisonment, which may be shortened according to the criminal's subsequent behaviour. Although these conditional sentences have as yet a limited application, as a matter of principle they are of enormous importance. They open a new era in penal justice and mean a new moral outlook concerned with a living man and not with the dead letter of the law. After the abolition of torture, this is the most significant success in the domain of legal procedure, and henceforth normal justice ceases to be a dream and begins to be a reality.

Deprivation of liberty for a longer or shorter term, determined not beforehand but in accordance with the real changes in the criminal's condition, plus compulsory work for his own benefit and for the compensation of losses he has caused to others — this is all that normal punishment should be. It consists in the conditional limitation of the criminal's personal rights and his rights of property as the natural consequence of his crime. This is what society must *take* from the criminal; but in exchange, it must *give* him active help in his reformation and moral regeneration. In view of this it is particularly necessary that prisons should be radically reformed and made into morally-psychiatric institutions.

There was a time when people suffering from mental disease were treated like wild beasts, chained, beaten and so on. Less than a hundred years ago it was considered quite normal; but now we remember it with horror. Since the rate of progress is continually increasing, I hope to live to a time when prisons and penal servitude of the present day will be looked upon in the same way as we now look upon the old-fashioned asylums with iron cages for patients. Although the penal system has undoubtedly progressed of late, it is still largely determined by the old idea of punishment as *torment* deliberately inflicted on the criminals.

In the true conception of punishment its positive end, so far as the criminal is concerned, is not to cause him physical pain, but to heal or reform him morally. This idea calls forth strong opposition on the part of jurists and of the 'criminal school' of anthropologists. From the legal side it is urged that to correct the criminal means to intrude upon his inner life, which the state and society have no right to do.

There are two misconceptions involved in this. In the first place, the task of reforming criminals is, in the aspect we are here considering, merely an instance of the positive influence which the society or the state ought to exert upon such members of it as are in some respects deficient, and therefore not fully possessed of rights. If such influence is rejected on principle as intrusion into the individual's inner life, it will be necessary to reject also public education of children, treatment of lunatics in public asylums and so on. And in what sense can it be said to be an intrusion into the inner world? In truth, by the fact of his crime the criminal has bared or exposed his inner world, and is in need of influence in the opposite direction to enable him once more to withdraw into the normal boundaries. It is particularly surprising that although the argument recognizes the right of society to put a man into *demoralizing* conditions (such as our present prisons and penal servitude, which the jurists do not reject), it denies the right and the duty of society to put him into conditions that might render him *moral*.

The second misunderstanding consists in imagining that reformation of the criminal means forcing upon him ready-made moral rules. But why regard incompetence as a principle? When a criminal is capable of reformation at all, it consists, of course, chiefly in *self-reformation*. External influences must simply put the man into conditions most favourable for it, help him and support him in this inner work.

But can criminals be reformed at all? Many representatives of criminal anthropology maintain that there is no escaping innate criminal tendencies which are incorrigible. That there exist born criminals and hereditary criminals there is no doubt; that some of them are incorrigible it is difficult to deny. But the statement that all criminals or even the majority of them are incorrigible is absolutely arbitrary and does not deserve to be discussed. If, however, all we may admit is that some criminals are incorrigible, no one can or has the right to be certain beforehand that this particular criminal belongs to their number; *all*, therefore, ought to be put into conditions most favourable for possible reformation.

. . . Public guardianship over the criminal, entrusted to competent persons with a view to his possible reformation — this is the final definition of 'punishment' or positive resistance to crime, compatible with the moral principle. Such punishment also best satisfies the society's unquestionable right of self-defence: a reformed criminal will no longer be dangerous to society and indeed will repay it a hundredfold for its care of him. Normal judicial procedure and a corresponding penitentiary system — real justice and mercy to the guilty without damage to the innocent — this is the fullest and clearest evidence of the true connection between legal justice and morality, or of the true idea of legal justice as the balance between two moral interests: social good and individual freedom. . . . If undue weight is given to the social good, criminals, like dangerous lunatics, ought to be simply destroyed. If undue weight is given to personal freedom, all compulsory action against both ought to be given up. Conscience and reason, and at the present time experience as well, point the right way which allows us neither inhumanly to destroy harmful people, nor inhumanly let them destroy others.

4

THE SECRET OF PROGRESS

Do you know this fairy tale?

A huntsman lost his way in a dense forest; tired out, he sat down on a stone beside a wide, raging stream. He sat there looking into the dark depths and listening to the woodpecker tapping and tapping against the bark of a tree. His heart grew heavy within him. 'I am as lonely in life as I am in the forest', he thought. 'I have long lost my way, wandering by different paths, and there is no way out for me. Solitude, misery and perdition! Why was I born, why did I come into this forest? What good to me are all those birds and beasts that I have killed?'

At that moment someone touched him on the shoulder. He saw a bent old woman, such as generally appear on such occasions — thin as thin can be, and her skin the colour of a locust pod or of an unpolished boot. Her eyes were sullen, two tufts of grey hair stuck out on her chin, and she was clothed in precious robes that had turned into tatters, through age.

'Listen, my good man, there is a place on the other side that is a regular paradise! Once you get there, you'll forget all your troubles. You'll never find your way to it yourself, but I'll take you straight to it — I come from those parts myself. Only, carry me across the stream, for I could not struggle against the current. As it is, I can hardly stand on my feet and am almost at my last gasp — and yet I don't at all want to die, not at all.'

The huntsman was a good-natured young man. He did not in the least believe the old woman's words about the place like paradise, it was not in the least tempting to wade across the stream, and not at all alluring to carry the old creature on his shoulders, but as he looked at her, she had a bout of coughing and shook all over. 'I can't let an ancient creature like her perish!' he thought. 'She must be over a hundred years old and have borne a lot in her day, so it's only fair to do something for her.'

'Very well, granny, climb on to my back, and mind you pull

your bones together, for if you fall to pieces there will be no picking them up in the water.'

The old woman climbed on to his shoulders and he felt a weight as heavy as if he had lifted a coffin with a corpse in it — he could scarcely move. 'Well,' he thought, 'it would be a shame to turn back now.' He stepped into the water, and suddenly the weight seemed less, and then it grew lighter and lighter with every step. And he felt that something miraculous was taking place. But he went straight on, looking in front of him. When he stepped ashore, he looked back : instead of the old woman an enchanting maiden, a real queen of beauty, was clinging to him! She brought him to her motherland, and never again has he complained of loneliness, or killed birds and beasts or lost his way in the forest.

Everyone knows some version of this fairy tale, and I too knew it as a child, but only today I felt its real meaning. The modern man hunting after the fleeting momentary goods and elusive fancies has lost his right path in life. The dark and turbulent stream of life is before him. Time like a woodpecker mercilessly registers the moments that have been lost. Misery and solitude, and afterwards — darkness and perdition. But behind him stands the sacred antiquity of tradition — oh, in what an unattractive form! Well, what of it? Let him only think of what he owes to her; let him with an inner heartfelt impulse *revere* her greyness, *pity* her infirmities, feel *ashamed* of rejecting her because of her appearance. Instead of idly looking out for phantom-like fairies beyond the clouds, let him undertake the labour of carrying this sacred burden across the real stream of history. This is the only way out of his wanderings — the only, because any other would be insufficient, unkind, impious : he could not let the ancient creature perish!

The modern man does not believe in the fairy tale, he does not believe that the decrepit old woman will be transformed into a queen of beauty. But if he does not believe it, so much the better! Why believe in the future reward when what is required is to deserve it by the present effort and self-denying heroism? Those who do not believe in the future of the old and the sacred, must at any rate remember its past. Why should he not carry her across out of reverence for her antiquity, out of pity for her decay, out of shame for being ungrateful? Blessed are the believers : while still standing on this shore they already see through the wrinkles of old age the brilliance of incorruptible beauty. But unbelievers in the future transformation have the advantage of *unexpected joy*.[1] Both the believers and the unbelievers have the same task: to go forward, taking upon their shoulders the whole weight of antiquity.

If you, the modern man, want to be a man of the future, forget not in the smoking ruins your father Anchises and the native gods. They needed a pious hero to transfer them to Italy, but they alone could give him and his descendants both Italy and power over the world. And that which we hold as holy is mightier than the Trojan gods, and we have to carry it further than Italy or the whole of the earthly world. *He who saves shall be saved.* That is the secret of progress — there is not and there can be no other!

[1] 'Unexpected joy' is the name of one of the miraculous ikons of Our Lady. Probably this is the reason for the italics.—*Ed.*

THE
EPILOGUE

A SHORT STORY OF
ANTICHRIST

THERE lived at that time a remarkable man — many called
... him a superman — who was as far from being a child in
intellect as in heart. He was young, but his genius made him
widely famous as a great thinker, writer and social worker by the
time he was thirty-three. Conscious of his own great spiritual
power, he had always been a convinced idealist, and his clear
intelligence always made clear to him the truth of that which
ought to be believed in: the good, God, the Messiah. He believed
in all this, but he loved only himself. He believed in God, but at
the bottom of his heart unconsciously and instinctively preferred
himself to Him.

... The inordinate pride of the great idealist seemed justified
both by his exceptional genius, beauty and nobility, and his lofty
asceticism, disinterestedness and active philanthropy. He was so
abundantly blessed with gifts from above that he was scarcely to
blame for regarding them as special signs of exceptional divine
favour; he considered himself as next to God, as the son of God
in a unique kind of way. In short he recognized himself for what
Christ really was. But this consciousness of his own higher dignity
expressed itself not as a sense of moral obligation to God and the
world, but as a conviction that he had rights and privileges over
others, especially over Christ. At the beginning he had no hostility against Jesus. He admitted His messianic dignity and significance, but he sincerely saw in Him merely the greatest of his
own predecessors; his mind, clouded by pride, could not understand Christ's moral achievement and His absolute uniqueness.
He reasoned thus: 'Christ came before me; I come second; but
that which in the order of time comes later is essentially prior. I
come last, at the end of history, just because I am the perfect and
final saviour. The first Christ was my forerunner. His mission
was to anticipate and prepare my coming.' With this idea in his
mind the great man of the twenty-first century applied to himself

all that is said in the Gospel about the second coming, understanding by it, not the return of the same Christ, but the replacement of the preliminary Christ by the final, that is, by himself.

... This man also justified his proud preference of himself to Christ by the following argument: 'Christ, in preaching the moral good and manifesting it in his life, was the *reformer* of mankind, but I am destined to be the *benefactor* of this partly reformed, and partly incorrigible mankind. I shall give all men what they need. Christ as a moralist divided men into the good and the bad, but I will unite them by blessings which are needed by the good and the bad alike. I shall be the true representative of the God who makes His sun to rise on the evil and on the good and sends rain on the just and the unjust. Christ brought a sword, I shall bring peace. He threatened the earth with the dreadful last judgment. But I shall be the last judge, and my judgment will be one of mercy as well as of justice. There will be justice too in my judgment, not retributive, but distributive justice. I will make distinctions between people and give everyone his due.'

In this beautiful frame of mind he waited for some clear call from God, for some manifest and striking testimony to his being the eldest son, God's beloved first-born. He waited, and meanwhile nurtured his selfhood on the contemplation of his superhuman gifts and virtues — as already said, he was a man of irreproachable morality and extraordinary genius.

The righteous and proud man waited and waited for a sanction from above to begin his work of saving humanity — and still the sanction did not come. He was thirty-three years old already; another three years passed. And suddenly there flashed through his mind a thought that sent a hot tremor into the very marrow of his bones: 'And what if...? What if not I, but that other ... the Galilean ... What if He is not my forerunner, but the real one, the first and the last? But then He must be *living*. ... Where is He?... What if He comes to me ... here, now. ... What shall I say to Him? Why, I shall have to bow before Him like the most stupid of Christians, shall have to mutter senselessly like a Russian peasant, "Lord Jesus Christ, have mercy on me a sinner", or grovel like a Polish countrywoman! I, the bright genius, the superman! No, never!' And instead of the former cold rational respect for God and Christ there was born and grew in his heart, first, a kind of terror, and then a burning, choking and corroding *envy* and furious, breath-taking hatred. 'I, I, and not

He! He is not living, He is not and shall not be. He is not risen, He is not risen from the dead! He rotted in the tomb, rotted like the lowest. . . .'

Foaming at the mouth, he rushed out of the house and garden and, leaping and bounding, ran in the black depth of the night along the rocky path. . . . The fury died down, and despair, hard and heavy as the rocks and dark as the night, took its place. He stopped at the sheer drop of the cliff and heard the vague noise of the stream rushing along the stones far below. Unendurable anguish weighed on his heart. Suddenly something stirred within him. 'Shall I call Him — ask Him what I am to do?' And the sad and gentle image seemed to rise before him in the darkness. 'He pities me. . . . No, never! He did not, He did not rise from the dead!'

And he threw himself down from the cliff. But something resilient like a water-spout supported him in the air, he felt a kind of electric shock, and some power flung him back. He lost consciousness for a moment and when he came to himself he was kneeling a few steps away from the edge of the cliff. He saw the outline of a figure glowing with a misty phosphorescent light and its eyes penetrated his soul with their intolerable sharp brilliance.

He saw those piercing eyes and heard — he did not know whether from within himself or from outside — a strange voice, toneless and, as it were, stifled, and yet clear, metallic and absolutely soulless as though coming from a phonograph. And the voice was saying to him: 'You are my beloved son in whom I am well pleased. Why have you not sought me? Why did you revere that other, the bad one, and His Father? I am your god and your father. And that other one, the beggar, the crucified, is a stranger both to me and to you. I have no other son but you. You are my only one, only begotten, co-equal with me. I love you and ask nothing of you. You are beautiful, powerful and great. Do your work in your own name, not in mine. I have no envy, I love you. I want nothing from you. He whom you regarded as God asked of His son boundless obedience, obedience unto death, even the death of the cross, and He did not help Him on the cross. I ask nothing of you, and I will help you. I will help you for your own sake, for the sake of your own dignity and excellence and of my pure disinterested love for you. Receive my spirit. Once upon a time my spirit gave birth to you in beauty, now it gives birth to you in power.'

At these words of the unknown being the superman's lips opened of themselves, two piercing eyes came quite close to his face, and he felt a sharp, frozen stream enter into him and fill his whole being. And at the same time he was conscious of wonderful strength, energy, lightness and rapture. At that instant the luminous outline and the eyes suddenly disappeared, something lifted him into the air and at once deposited him in the garden by the house door.

Next day not only the great man's visitors but even his servants were struck by his peculiar, as it were, inspired expression. They would have been still more impressed could they have seen with what supernatural ease and speed he wrote, locking himself in his study, his famous work entitled *The Open Way to Universal Peace and Welfare*.

. . . That book, written after the adventure on the cliff, showed in him an unprecedented power of genius. It was all-embracing and all-reconciling. It combined noble reverence for ancient traditions and symbols with broad and bold radicalism in social and political demands and precepts, boundless freedom of thought with the deepest understanding of all things mystical, absolute individualism with ardent devotion to the common good, the most lofty idealism of the guiding principles with thoroughly definite and concrete practical conclusions. And it was all put together with such consummate art that every one-sided thinker or reformer could easily see and accept the whole entirely from his own particular point of view, without sacrificing anything for *the truth itself*, or rising above his own self for the sake of it, or giving up his one-sidedness, or in any way correcting his mistaken views and aspirations, or trying to make up for their insufficiency.

. . . No one raised objections against this book, for it seemed to everyone a revelation of the all-embracing truth. It did such complete justice to the past, it passed such dispassionate judgment on every aspect of the present, it brought the better future so concretely and tangibly within reach, that everyone said: 'This is the very thing we want; here is an ideal that is not utopian, a plan which is not a chimera.' The wonderful writer carried all with him and was *acceptable* to everyone, so that Christ's words were fulfilled:

'I am come in my Father's name, and ye receive me not: if another shall come in his own name, him ye will receive.' For in order to be received, one must be acceptable.

True, some pious people, while warmly praising the book, wondered why Christ was not once mentioned in it; but other Christians replied: 'And a good thing too! In the past, everything holy was so bedraggled by all kinds of self-appointed zealots, that nowadays a deeply religious writer has to be very careful. And since the whole book is permeated by the truly Christian spirit of active love and all-embracing benevolence, what more do you want?' And all agreed with this.

Soon after the publication of the *Open Way*, which made its author the most popular man in the world, there was held in Berlin the international constituent assembly of the European States Union.

... The 'initiated' decided to concentrate executive power in the hands of one person, investing him with sufficient authority. ... The *man of the future* was elected almost unanimously life-long president of the United States of Europe. When he appeared on the rostrum in all the brilliance of his superhuman young strength and beauty and, with inspired eloquence, expounded his universal programme, the assembly, charmed and completely carried away, in a burst of enthusiasm decided without putting it to the vote to pay him the highest tribute by electing him Roman emperor. The assembly closed amidst general rejoicing, and the great elect published a manifesto beginning with the words, 'Peoples of the earth! My peace I give unto you', and ending as follows: 'Peoples of the earth! The promises have been fulfilled! Eternal universal peace is secured. Every attempt to disturb it shall be immediately met with overwhelming opposition. Henceforth there is in the world one central power which is stronger than all other powers, both separately and taken together. This invincible and all-conquering power belongs to me, the plenipotentiary chosen emperor of Europe and ruler of all its forces. International law is supported at last by sanctions that have hitherto been lacking to it. Henceforth no country will dare to say "war" when I say "peace". Nations of the world, peace be unto you!' The manifesto had the desired effect.

... Within a year a world-wide monarchy in the exact and proper sense of the term was founded. The seedlings of war were pulled out by the roots. The League of Universal Peace met for the last time and, having addressed an enthusiastic eulogy to the great peace-maker, dissolved itself as no longer necessary. In the second year of his reign the Roman and universal emperor issued another manifesto: 'Peoples of the earth! I promised you peace and I have given it you. But peace is only made sweet by prosperity. It is no joy to those who are threatened with destitution. Come unto me, all you that are cold and hungry and I will give you food and warmth.' Then he announced a simple and all-inclusive social reform that was already indicated in his book and had captivated at the time all noble and clear minds. Now that the world's finances and enormous landed properties were concentrated in his hands, he could carry out this reform and satisfy the desires of the poor without appreciable injustice to the rich. Everyone was paid according to his capacity, and every capacity was rewarded according to its merits and results.

... There was firmly established in all mankind the most important form of equality — *the equality of general satiety*. That was done in the second year of his reign. The social and economic problem was solved once for all. But though food is of first importance to the hungry, those who have sufficient food want something else.

Even animals when they have had enough to eat want not merely to sleep but to play as well. This is even more true of men who *post panem* have always demanded *circenses*.

The superman-emperor understood what the crowd needed. At that time a great magician surrounded with a halo of strange facts and wild fairy-tales came to him in Rome from the distant East.

This magician, Apollonius by name, unquestionably a man of genius, semi-Asiatic and semi-European, was a Catholic bishop *in partibus infidelium*. He combined in a marvellous way a mastery of the latest discoveries and technical application of Western science with a knowledge both theoretical and practical of all that is real and significant in the traditional mysticism of the East. The results of this combination were astounding. Apollonius mastered, for instance, the half-scientific and half-magical art of attracting and directing at his will atmospheric electricity, so that people said he *commanded fire to come down from heaven*. But while striking the imagination of the multitude by all kinds of unheard-of novelties he refrained for a time from abusing his power for any special purposes. And so this man came to the great emperor, worshipped him as the true son of God, and, declaring that in the secret books of the East he had found direct prophecies about him as the last saviour and judge of the earth, offered himself and his art in service to him. The emperor was charmed, accepted him as a gift from above, and bestowing splendid titles upon him, kept the magician permanently at his side. The peoples of the earth, having received from their master the blessings of universal peace and abundant food for all, were also given the chance of permanently enjoying the most diverse and unexpected signs and miracles. The third year of the superman's reign was coming to an end.

The political and social problems were happily solved; now there was the religious problem to deal with. The emperor himself raised it, and first of all with reference to Christianity. The position of Christianity at that time was as follows. It had considerably decreased in numbers — there were not more than forty-five million Christians on the whole of the globe — but it had pulled itself together morally and reached a higher level, so that it gained in quality what it had lost in quantity. Men who had no spiritual interests in common with Christianity were no longer numbered among Christians. The different denominations had lost about the same proportion of their members, so that the numerical relation between them was approximately the same as before; as to their mutual feelings, though there was as yet no complete reconciliation, the hostility between them had lessened considerably, and the differences had lost their former sharpness. Papacy had long been exiled from Rome and after many wanderings found shelter in St. Petersburg on condition that it was to refrain from propaganda, both there and within the country. In Russia it assumed a much simpler form. Without decreasing the necessary personnel of its colleges and offices, it had to spiritualize the nature of their activities, and also to bring down to the minimum its splendid ritual and ceremonial observances. Many strange customs that might be a stumbling block fell out of usage, though they were not formally abolished. In all other countries, especially in North America, the Roman Catholic hierarchy still had many representatives with an independent position, strong will and indefatigable energy; they made the unity of the Roman Church more closely knit than ever and preserved its international, cosmopolitan significance. As to Protestantism, which was still headed by Germany, especially after the reunion of a considerable part of the Anglican Church with Catholicism, it had freed itself from its extreme negative tendencies whose champions openly passed over to religious indifference and unbelief. Only sincere believers remained in the Evangelical Church; the men who stood at the head of it combined wide erudition with deep religious faith, and strove more and more to become the living image of the true ancient Christianity. Russian Orthodoxy had lost many millions of its nominal members when political events changed the official position of the Church, but it had the joy of being united to the best elements among the Old Believers and even among many sectarians of the positively religious type. The regenerated Church, while not increasing in numbers, grew in spiritual power, which showed itself very clearly in the struggle against extremist sects with a demonic and satanic tinge that had multiplied both among the masses and in society.

During the first two years of the new reign the Christians' attitude towards the emperor and his peaceful reforms was one of definite sympathy and even enthusiasm. But in the third year, when the great magician appeared, many of the Orthodox, Catholics and Evangelicals began to feel uneasy and to disapprove. The passages in the Gospels and the Epistles about the prince of this world and antichrist were read more attentively than before and excited lively comments. From certain signs the emperor guessed that a storm was gathering, and decided to make haste and clear up matters. Early in the fourth year of his reign he addressed a manifesto to all his faithful Christians of whatsoever denomination, inviting them to elect or appoint plenipotentiary representatives to an ecumenical council under his presidency. By that time he had transferred his residence from Rome to Jerusalem. Palestine was then an autonomous state, populated and ruled chiefly by Jews. Jerusalem had been a free city and was now made an imperial one. Christian holy places remained intact, but the whole of the broad terrace Haram-ash-Sharif, from Birket-Israin and the barracks on one side, and down to the El-Aksa mosque and 'Solomon's stables' on the other, was occupied by a huge new building. It included, in addition to two small old mosques a large 'Imperial' temple for the union of all cults, and two luxurious imperial palaces with libraries, museums and special accommodation for magical experiments and exercises. The ecumenical council was to open in this semi-temple and semi-palace on the fourteenth of September. Since the Evangelical denomination has no priesthood in the proper sense, the Orthodox and Catholic hierarchs in accordance with the emperor's wish decided, for the sake of uniformity among the delegates, to admit to the council some of their laymen known for their piety and devotion to the interests of the Church; and if laymen were admitted, the rank and file of the clergy and monks could not be excluded. Thus the general number of the council members exceeded three thousand, and about half a million Christian pilgrims flooded Jerusalem and Palestine.

There were three outstanding men among the council members. First, the Pope Peter the Second who, by right, headed the Catholic part of the council. His predecessor died on the way to the council, and a conclave convened at Damascus unanimously elected Cardinal Simone Barionini, who took the name of Peter. He was of humble origin, from the province of Naples, and became known as a Carmelite preacher; he had done much good work in combating a certain Satanic sect that had gained great influence in St. Petersburg and the neighbourhood and was leading astray both the Orthodox and the Catholics. He was made bishop of Mogilyov and afterwards a cardinal, and was singled out beforehand for the papal tiara. He was a man of about fifty, of medium height and strong build, with a red face, an aquiline nose and bushy eyebrows. Warm-hearted and impetuous, he spoke with fervour and sweeping gestures, and carried away rather than convinced his audience. The new Pope expressed distrust and disapproval of the world-lord, especially after the late Pope, setting out for the council, had at the emperor's insistence made the imperial chancellor and the great magician, the exotic bishop Apollonius, a cardinal. Peter considered Apollonius a dubious Catholic and an indubitable impostor.

The real, though unofficial, leader of the Orthodox was the Elder John, very well known among the Russian people. His official status was that of a bishop 'in retirement', yet he did not live in any monastery, but constantly travelled about. There were strange legends about him. Some people maintained that he was the risen Fyodor Kuzmich, that is, the Emperor Alexander I,[1] who had been born some three centuries before. Others went further and said that he was the real Elder John, i.e. the apostle John the Divine who had never died and of late appeared openly. He himself said nothing about his origin or his youth. He was very old but still vigorous, with yellowish and even greenish white

[1] There is a legend that Alexander I did not die in 1825 as recorded in history, but secretly left the palace disguised as a peasant and lived for many years a holy and ascetic life under the name of Fyodor Kuzmich.—*Ed.*

curly hair and beard, tall and thin, with full and slightly rosy
cheeks, lively bright eyes and a touchingly kind expression in his
face and voice; he always wore a white cassock and cloak.

The leader of the Evangelical members of the council was a
most learned German theologian, Professor Ernst Pauli. He was a
lean old man of medium height, with a huge forehead, sharp
nose and clean-shaven chin. His eyes had a peculiar ferociously
good-natured look. He constantly rubbed his hands, shook his
head, menacingly knitted his brows and thrust out his lips; as he
did so, his eyes glittered and he made gloomy and disjointed
sounds: *so! nun! ja! so also!* He was dressed for the occasion and
wore a white tie and a long clerical frock coat with some decora-
tions.

The opening ceremony was most impressive. Two-thirds of
the huge temple dedicated to the 'unity of all cults' were occupied
with benches and other seats for members of the council, and
one-third was taken up with a tall platform; there were two
thrones on it, one for the emperor, and a lower one for the great
magician (cardinal and imperial chancellor), and behind them
long rows of armchairs for the ministers, courtiers, and secretaries
of state, as well as longer rows at the sides for a purpose unknown.
The members had already celebrated their religious services in the
different churches, and the opening of the council was to be entirely secular. When the emperor came in with his suite and the
great magician, and the orchestra played 'the march of united
humanity', which was used as the imperial international hymn,
all those present rose to their feet and waving their hats called out
loudly three times: '*Vivat!* Hurrah! *Hoch!*' The emperor, standing
by his throne and with majestic benignity stretching out his hand,
said in a pleasant and sonorous voice:

'Christians of all denominations! My beloved subjects and
brothers! From the beginning of my reign which the Almighty
has blessed with such wonderful and glorious deeds, I have not
once had occasion to be displeased with you; you have always
done your duty in all faith and conscience. But this is not enough
for me. My sincere love for you, my beloved brothers, longs for
reciprocity. I want you, not out of a sense of duty but from heartfelt love, to recognize me as your true leader in every work under-
taken for the good of humanity. And so, in addition to what I do
for all, I should like to bestow special favours upon you. Christians, what can I do to make you happy? What can I give you,

not as to my subjects but as to my brethren and co-believers? Christians, tell me what is most precious to you in Christianity, that I might direct my efforts to it?'

He paused and waited. There was a low murmur in the temple. The members of the council were whispering among themselves. Pope Peter, warmly gesticulating, was explaining something to those around him. Professor Pauli was shaking his head and fiercely smacking his lips. The Elder John, bending down to an Eastern bishop and a grey friar, was quietly admonishing them in a low voice. After waiting for a few minutes the emperor addressed the council in the same kind voice, though now there was a hardly perceptible note of irony in it: 'Dear Christians', he said, 'I understand how difficult it is for you to make one straightforward answer. I want to help you in this too. Unfortunately you have been broken up into various sects and parties since time immemorial and perhaps you have no longer a common aim. But if you cannot agree between yourselves I hope to bring agreement between all your parties by showing them all equal love and equal readiness to satisfy the *true* desire of each. Dear Christians! I know that for many and by no means the least of you the most precious thing in Christianity is the *spiritual authority* which it gives to its lawful representatives — not for their own advantage, of course, but for the common good, since such authority is the basis of true spiritual order and of moral discipline which is necessary to all. Dear brother-Catholics! oh, how well I understand your view and how I should like to find support for my power in the authority of your spiritual head! That you may not regard this as mere empty talk and flattery, I solemnly declare: in accordance with my autocratic will the chief bishop of all Catholics, the Pope of Rome, is henceforth restored to his Roman see with all the rights and privileges that had ever been given it by my predecessors, beginning with the emperor Constantine the Great. And all I want of you, brother-Catholics, is an inner heartfelt recognition of me as your only defender and patron. Let those who regard me as such in their heart and conscience come to me here.' And he pointed to the empty seats on the platform.

With joyful cries '*Gratias agimus! Domine, salvum fac magnum imperatorem*' almost all the princes of the Catholic Church, cardinals and bishops, the majority of believing laymen and more than half of the monks went up on to the platform and, after low bows to the emperor, took their seats there. But down below, in the middle of the hall, straight and immovable as a marble statue, the Pope Peter the Second sat in his place. All who had surrounded him were on the platform. But the thinned ranks of monks and laymen closed around him, forming a narrow ring, and a restrained whisper came from there: '*Non praevalebunt, non praevalebunt portae inferni.*'

Glancing with surprise at the motionless Pope, the emperor raised his voice once more: 'Dear brothers! I know that there are among you some who value most in Christianity its *sacred tradition*, ancient symbols, ancient hymns and prayers, ikons and holy rites. And what indeed can be more precious to a religious mind? Know then, beloved, that today I have signed the statute and settled large sums of money on the world-museum of Christian archæology in our glorious imperial city of Constantinople for the object of collecting, studying and preserving all relics of church antiquity, especially the Eastern. I ask you to elect tomorrow from among yourselves a committee to discuss with me the measures that must be taken in order to make the present manners, customs and ways of living as conformable as possible to the tradition and ordinances of the holy Orthodox Church. Brother-Orthodox! Let those of you who appreciate my action and who can wholeheartedly call me their true lord and leader, come up to me here!'

A great number of hierarchs from the East and North, a half of the former Old Believers and more than half of the Orthodox priests, monks and laymen with joyful cries went up on to the platform, looking askance at the Catholics proudly seated there. But the Elder John sighed aloud and did not move. When the crowd around him had considerably thinned, he left his bench and moved nearer to the Pope Peter and his circle. He was followed by other Orthodox who had not gone up on to the platform.

The emperor spoke again: 'I know, dear Christians, that there are among you some who value most in Christianity personal conviction of truth and free inquiry into the Scriptures. There is no need for me to speak of my own attitude on the subject. You may know perhaps that in my early youth I wrote an extensive work on Biblical criticism which made quite a stir at the time and was the beginning of my fame. Probably in memory of this the University of Tübingen asked me the other day to accept from them an honorary diploma of doctor in theology. I gave instructions to reply that I accept with pleasure and gratitude.

And today, after instituting the museum of Christian archæology, I have signed the statute of the world-institute for free inquiry into the Scriptures from every possible point of view and in every possible direction, and for the study of all auxiliary subjects, with an annual budget of one and a half million marks. Will those of you who appreciate my attitude and can genuinely recognize me as their sovereign leader please come up here to the new doctor of theology.'

A strange smile twisted for a moment the great man's beautiful lips. More than half of the learned theologians moved towards the platform, though with some hesitation and delay. All looked back at Professor Pauli who seemed glued to his seat. He hunched his back, huddled himself together and hung his head. The learned theologians who had mounted the platform looked uncomfortable, and one of them, with a sudden wave of his hand, jumped straight down past the steps and ran, limping, to join Professor Pauli and the minority that had remained with him. Pauli raised his head and, getting up in an undecided sort of way, walked, followed by his staunch co-believers, past the empty benches and settled closer to the Elder John and the Pope Peter.

The emperor addressed them in a tone of sadness: 'What more can I do for you? Strange men! What do you want of me? I do not know. Tell me yourselves, you Christians forsaken by most of your brothers and leaders and condemned by popular feeling: what is most precious to you in Christianity?'

Then, straight and slender like a white church candle, the Elder John stood up and answered gently: 'Great emperor! Most precious to us in Christianity is Christ Himself — He Himself, and everything rests on Him, for we know that in Him all the fulness of Godhead dwells bodily. But from you too, sire, we are ready to receive every blessing if only we recognize in your bountiful hand the holy hand of Christ. And here is our straight answer to your question what you can do for us: confess now here before us Jesus Christ the Son of God, who came in the flesh, rose from the dead and is coming again — confess Him, and we will receive you with love as the true forerunner of His glorious second coming.'

He paused and looked steadily at the emperor. Something evil was happening to the great man. The same hellish storm raged within him as on that fateful night. He completely lost his inner balance, and all his thoughts were concentrated on not losing external self-control and not giving himself away too soon. He was making superhuman efforts not to throw himself with a wild yell at the speaker and tear at him with his teeth. Suddenly he heard the familiar unearthly voice: 'Be still and fear nothing.' He remained silent. Only his darkened and death-like face was contorted and his eyes flashed.

While the Elder John was speaking, the great magician, who sat wrapped up in a voluminous three-coloured cloak that completely hid his red robe of a cardinal, seemed to be doing some manipulations under it; there was a look of concentration in his glittering eyes, and his lips moved. Through the open windows of the temple a huge black cloud could be seen gathering, and soon everything turned dark. The Elder John was still gazing with fear and amazement at the silent emperor; suddenly he drew back in horror and, turning round, cried in a stifled voice: 'Children, it's antichrist!' At that moment there was a deafening crash of thunder, a huge ball of lightning flared up in the temple and enveloped the Elder. All were stock-still for a moment. When the Christians recovered from the shock, the Elder John lay dead.

The emperor, pale but calm, addressed the assembly: 'You have seen God's judgment. I did not wish for anyone's death, but my heavenly Father avenges his beloved son. The case is settled. Who would dare to oppose the Almighty? Secretaries! write: "The ecumenical council of all Christians, when the fire from heaven had struck the insane opponent of the divine majesty, unanimously recognized the mighty emperor of Rome and the world as their supreme leader and lord."'

Suddenly a word spoken loudly and clearly resounded through the temple: '*Contradicitur.*' Pope Peter the Second, purple in the face and shaking with anger, stood up and raised his staff in the emperor's direction. 'Our only Lord is Jesus Christ, the Son of the living God. And what you are — you have just heard. Begone from us, you Cain! Begone, you vessel of the devil! By the power of Christ, I, the servant of the servants of God, forever expel you, a vile dog, from God's fold and deliver you to your father, Satan! Anathema, anathema, anathema!'

While he was speaking the great magician restlessly moved under his cloak; there was a clap of thunder louder than the last anathema, and the last of the Popes fell down dead.

'This is how all my enemies shall perish at my father's hand!' said the emperor.

'*Pereant, pereant!*' cried the trembling princes of the Church.

He turned and, leaning on the shoulder of the great magician, slowly walked out of the door at the back of the platform, followed by all his crowd. There were left in the hall two corpses and a throng of Christians half-dead with fear. The only person who had kept his self-possession was Professor Pauli. The general terror seemed to have roused all the powers of his spirit. His very appearance changed — he looked inspired and majestic. With resolute steps he mounted the platform and sitting down in the empty seat of one of the secretaries of state took up a piece of paper and began writing. When he had finished, he stood up and read aloud: 'To the glory of our only Saviour, Jesus Christ. From the ecumenical council of God's churches, gathered in Jerusalem: After our most blessed brother John, the representative of Eastern Christianity, had denounced the great deceiver and enemy of God as antichrist, foretold in Holy Writ, and our most blessed father Peter, the representative of Western Christianity, rightly and lawfully excommunicated him for life, the council, in the presence of the bodies of these two witnesses of Christ killed for the truth, has decided: cease all intercourse with the excommunicated and his vile conclave, and, withdrawing to the wilderness, await the impending coming of our true Lord Jesus Christ.'

The crowd was filled with animation. There were loud cries of 'Adveniat! Adveniat cito! Komm, Herr Jesu, komm! Come, Lord Jesus!'

Professor Pauli made a postscript and read: 'Having unanimously adopted this first and last act of the last ecumenical council, we append our signatures thereto' — and he made a gesture of invitation to the assembly. All hastily mounted the platform and signed. The last to sign, in large Gothic script, was 'duorum defunctorum testium locum tenens Ernst Pauli.'

'Now let us go with our tabernacle of the last testament!' he said, pointing to the two dead men.

The bodies were put on stretchers. To the singing of Latin, German and Church-Slavonic hymns the Christians slowly walked to the exit from Haram-ash-Sharif. There the procession was stopped by a secretary of state, sent by the emperor and accompanied by an officer with a platoon of the guards. The soldiers stopped by the door, and the secretary read aloud: 'The order of his divine majesty: to instil reason into the Christian people and protect them from evil-minded men who cause trouble and sedition, we have thought fit to exhibit the bodies of the two mischief-makers, killed by fire from heaven, in the street of the Christians (Haret-en-Nasara) at the entrance to their chief temple, called the temple of the Sepulchre and also of the Resurrection, so that all may convince themselves of their actual death. As to their partisans who maliciously reject all our bene-factions and foolishly shut their eyes to obvious manifestations of the Deity, through our mercy and intercession with the heavenly Father they are spared death by heavenly fire which they deserve and are left entirely free except for the prohibition, for the sake of the common good, to dwell in cities and other populated places lest they disturb and offend innocent and simple-minded people by their evil inventions.' When he had finished reading, eight soldiers, at a sign from the officer, approached the stretchers on which the bodies were laid.

'Let it be done as written,' said Professor Pauli, and the Christians silently passed the stretchers to the soldiers, who carried them away through the north-western gates; the Christians went out by the north-eastern, and hastily left the town. They walked past the Mount of Olives along the road to Jericho, which the mounted police and two cavalry regiments had cleared of the crowds. It was decided to wait for a few days on the desert hills by Jericho. The following morning some Christian pilgrims of their acquaintance came from Jerusalem and told what had happened in Sion. After a state banquet all the members of the council were invited to the huge throne room (near the place where Solomon's throne is supposed to have stood), and the emperor, addressing the Catholic hierarchs, declared that the good of the Church obviously required of them immediately to elect a worthy successor of St. Peter; that under the present circumstances the election had to be held there and then; that the presence of the emperor as the leader and representative of the whole of Christendom would more than make up for omis-sions in the ritual, and that, in the name of all Christians, he suggested the sacred college should elect his beloved friend and brother Apollonius, so that the intimate bond between them would make the union between the Church and the state secure and indissoluble, to the benefit of both. The sacred college with-drew to a special room for the conclave and in an hour and a half returned with the new Pope Apollonius.

While the election was being held the emperor was gently,

wisely and eloquently persuading the Orthodox and Evangelical delegates to end their old dissensions in view of the new great era in the Christian history; he pledged his word that Apollonius would know how to do away forever with all the historical abuses of papacy. The Orthodox and Protestant delegates, convinced by his speech, drew up an act of union between the churches, and when, amidst joyful acclamations, Apollonius appeared on the platform with the cardinals, a Greek archbishop and an Evangelical minister presented their paper to him.

'*Accipio et approbo et laetificatur cor meum*', said Apollonius, signing the document. 'I am a true Orthodox and a true Protestant as much as I am a true Catholic', he added and exchanged friendly kisses with the Greek and the German. Then he walked up to the emperor, who put his arms round him and held him in his embrace for some minutes.

Meanwhile curious points of light flitted in all directions about the palace and temple; they grew and transformed themselves into luminous forms of strange beings; flowers never seen on earth before fell in showers from above, filling the air with a mysterious fragrance. Delightful heart-melting sounds of strange musical instruments floated from on high, and angelic voices of invisible singers glorified the new lords of heaven and earth. In the meantime a terrible subterranean roar was heard in the north-western corner of the central palace under *kubbet-el-aruah*, i.e. the cupola of souls, where according to the Moslem tradition lies the entrance into Hades. When, at the emperor's invitation, the assembly moved in that direction, all clearly heard innumerable high-pitched and piercing voices — children's or devils' — calling out: 'The time has come, release us, saviours, saviours!' But when Apollonius, pressing himself close to the wall, thrice shouted something to those under the earth in an unknown tongue, the voices were still and the subterranean roar subsided.

While all this was going on, an immense crowd of people surrounded Haram-ash-Sharif. When it grew dark, the emperor, together with the new Pope, came out on to the eastern balcony, raising 'a storm of enthusiasm'. He graciously bowed in all directions, while Apollonius continually took from large baskets, brought to him by cardinals-deacons, and threw into the air magnificent Roman candles, rockets and fiery sprays, pearly-phosphorescent or bright rainbow-coloured, that caught fire at the touch of his hand. On reaching the ground they all turned into innumerable different-coloured sheets of paper with complete and unconditional indulgences for all sins, past, present and future. Popular rejoicing surpassed all bounds. True, some people said that they had seen with their own eyes the indulgences turn into hideous toads and snakes; but an overwhelming majority were enthusiastic. Public festivities went on for a few more days, and the new miracle-working Pope performed things so wonderful and incredible that it would be quite useless to describe them.

During this time the Christians on the desert heights of Jericho devoted themselves to fasting and prayer. On the evening of the fourth day, after dark, Professor Pauli with nine companions made their way to Jerusalem with asses and a cart, and went by side-streets to Haret-en-Nasara, approaching the entrance to the temple of the Resurrection, where the bodies of Pope Peter and the Elder John lay on the pavement. The streets were deserted at that hour, for the whole town had gone to Haram-ash-Sharif. The sentries on duty were fast asleep. The rescue party found that the bodies were untouched by corruption and had not even grown stiff or heavy. Putting them on the stretchers and covering them with cloaks brought for the purpose, the party returned by the same circuitous way to their people. As soon as they put the stretchers on the ground, the spirit of life returned to the dead. They stirred, trying to throw off the cloaks that covered them. With joyful cries all rushed to help them, and soon both the risen men were on their feet, safe and sound. And having come to life, the Elder John said: 'Well, my dear children, so we are not parted after all. And this is what I tell you now: it is time we fulfilled Christ's last prayer about His disciples that they should be one, as He and the Father are one. For the sake of this unity in Christ, my children, let us honour our beloved brother Peter. Let him pasture Christ's sheep at the last. There, brother!' — and he embraced Peter.

Professor Pauli came up to them. '*Tu es Petrus!*' said he to the Pope. '*Jetzt ist es ja gründlich erwiesen und ausser jedem Zweifel gesetzt.*'[1] And he warmly pressed Peter's hand with his right hand and gave his left to John, saying: '*So also, Väterchen, nun sind wir ja Eins in Christo.*'[2]

That was how the union of the churches took place on a dark night, in a high and solitary place. But the night's darkness was

---

[1] 'Now this is thoroughly proved and established beyond all doubt.'
[2] 'So now, Father, we are really one in Christ.'

suddenly lit up with a bright light, and a great sign appeared in the sky: a woman clothed with the sun, and the moon under her feet, and upon her head a crown of twelve stars. The sign remained in the same spot for some time, and then slowly moved southwards. Pope Peter raised his staff and cried: 'This is our banner! Let us follow it!' And he walked in the direction of the vision, followed by both the elders and the whole crowd of Christians — towards God's Mount, Sinai. . . .

At this point the MS. breaks off, and Mr. Z. tells the end of the story as he heard it from 'Father Pansophius' before Pansophius's death.

When the spiritual leaders and representatives of Christianity retired to the Arabian desert, where crowds of the faithful devotees of truth flocked to them from all countries of the world, the new Pope was able without hindrance to demoralize with his miracles all the other, superficial Christians, not disillusioned about antichrist. He declared that by the power of his keys he had opened the doors between the earthly world and the world beyond the grave, and indeed intercourse between the dead and the living, and also between men and demons, become a thing of everyday occurrence, and there developed new and unheard-of kinds of mystical fornication and idolatry. The emperor began to consider himself firmly established on the religious ground, and at the insistent suggestion of the secret 'father's' voice declared himself to be the only true incarnation of the supreme Deity; but at this point he was faced with new trouble from an utterly unexpected quarter: the Jews rose up against him. This nation, numbering at the time some thirty millions, had a share in preparing and consolidating the superman's world-wide success. And when he moved to Jerusalem, secretly encouraging the Jewish rumours that his main purpose was to establish Israel's world domination, the Jews acknowledged him as the Messiah, and their enthusiastic devotion to him knew no bounds. But suddenly they rebelled, breathing anger and vengeance. This sudden change, no doubt predicted both by the Scriptures and the tradition, was explained by Father Pansophius perhaps rather too simply and realistically. The fact was that the Jews, who regarded the emperor as a full-blooded and perfect Israelite, accidentally discovered that he had not even been *circumcised*. On that very day the whole of Jerusalem and on the next day the whole of Palestine were in revolt. Boundless and ardent devotion to the saviour of Israel, the promised Messiah, was replaced by hatred, as boundless and as ardent, for the perfidious deceiver, the impudent impostor. The whole of Jewry rose up like one man, and its enemies saw with surprise that in its real depths the soul of Israel lived not by calculations and greed for gain, but by the power of heartfelt emotion — by the hope and wrath of its centuries-old messianic faith.

The emperor, who had not expected such a sudden outburst, lost his self-control and issued an edict sentencing to death all rebellious Jews and Christians. Many thousands and tens of thousands who had not had time to arm were slaughtered without mercy. But soon a million-strong army of Jews gained possession of Jerusalem and surrounded antichrist in Haram-ash-Sharif. He had at his disposal only a part of the guards and could not cope with the massed enemy. With the help of his Pope's magical arts the emperor succeeded in making his way through the besiegers' ranks, and soon again appeared in Syria with an innumerable army of different heathen tribes. The Jews set out to meet him with small hope of success. But just as the advanced guards of both armies were about to meet, there was an earthquake of unheard-of violence: under the Dead Sea, in the vicinity of which the emperor's troops encamped, a huge volcano burst open and rivers of fire, merging into one flaming lake, swallowed up the emperor with all his numberless regiments and his inseparable companion Pope Apollonius, whose magic proved of no avail. The Jews ran towards Jerusalem in fear and trembling, calling on the God of Israel to save them. As they came in sight of the holy city, the sky was rent in two by a great lightning reaching from east to west, and they saw Christ coming down from heaven in royal array with wounds from the nails in His outstretched hands. At the same time a crowd of Christians led by Peter, John and Paul was approaching Sion from Sinai, and from all sides other enthusiastic crowds were running: those were the Jews and Christians executed by antichrist. They came to life again and reigned with Christ for a thousand years.

WAS SOLOVYOV A CONVERT TO ROMAN CATHOLICISM?

TEN YEARS after Solovyov's death the paper *Russkoe Slovo* (April 21, 1910) published a statement by Fr. N. Tolstoy, a priest of the Uniate Church in Moscow, that on February 3, 1896, in the presence of witnesses, Solovyov received communion from him, having first read aloud the Creed in 'the form adopted by the Roman see for Christians joining the Catholic Church', and handed in a written profession of faith, identical with the one published in *La Russie et l'Église universelle* (see Introduction, p. 20). This statement was later confirmed by two witnesses. Soon after, on November 2, 1910, the paper *Moskovskiya Vedomosti* published the account of the Orthodox priest S. Belyaev who received Solovyov's death-bed confession and gave him communion. According to Belyaev, Solovyov said to him that he had not been to confession for some three years, since at his last confession he had an argument with the priest on a question of dogma (he did not say which) and was not admitted by him to holy communion. 'The priest was right', he added, 'and I argued with him solely out of pride and a wish to carry my point; afterwards we exchanged some letters on the subject, but I would not give in, though I knew very well that I was wrong. Now I am quite aware of my error and sincerely repent of it' (quoted in *L.*, III, 215–17).

It follows from these two statements that after communicating in a Uniate (Græco-Catholic) church, Solovyov did not break off relations with the Orthodox Church. It might be said that his last communion proves nothing, for even a regular Catholic on his death-bed might call in an Orthodox priest in the absence of a Catholic one. But it would certainly be out of order for him under normal circumstances, soon after communicating in a Catholic Church, to go to confession and seek communion from an Orthodox priest, as Solovyov did in 1897.

The canonical rules laid down by the Catholic Church for converts may or may not have been strictly observed on February 3, 1896 (d'Herbigny says that one exception was made for Solovyov: 'there was no formal abjuration, for it was considered unnecessary'), but in any case the very fact of his having been given communion shows that the Catholic Church regarded Solovyov as a convert. Solovyov's subsequent behaviour, however, equally shows that he took a different view of the matter. The statement he made on his death-bed to Fr. S. Belyaev (and also the absence of evidence to the contrary) implies that his ecclesiastical contact with the Catholic Church was confined to that one particular occasion. His sister, Madame M. Bezobrazov, and his intimate friend, the philosopher Lopatin, both testify that to the end of his life he denied being a Catholic.[1] But then what could have induced him to communicate in a Catholic church and what did he mean by doing so?

Fr. N. Tolstoy says that Solovyov did not receive communion in the Orthodox Church after 1892 because since that year Orthodox priests refused it to him, evidently under pressure from the Synod. This explanation is utterly untenable. To say nothing of there being no occasion for such 'pressure' — since after 1889 Solovyov did not write about church matters — it was from the nature of the case impossible. Solovyov led a wanderer's life, so that every priest in Russia would have had to be warned against him, and even this would have been to no purpose, since the custom of the Russian Church is to admit people to communion (after confession and absolution) whether personally known to the priest or no. Besides, the absence of any such action on the part of the Synod is clearly proved by the fact that no difficulty whatever was raised about Solovyov receiving communion before he died.[2] If he really had not communicated after 1892, that was simply due to his withdrawing from church life at that period (see Introduction, p. 23).

At first sight the case is further complicated by the circumstance that in his private letters and public answers to accusations of 'popery' Solovyov had frequently asserted that he was Orthodox and had no intention of leaving his church; the last statement to that effect was in 1891 (L., III, 199). He was definitely opposed to individual conversions to Catholicism as 'harmful to the universal cause' (the union of the churches), though he added that he could not 'throw a stone at converts' who do so from sincere 'even if mistaken conviction' (L., III, 193 and 172, 1886). But curiously enough this is, perhaps, just where the explanation of the riddle is to be found. So long as Solovyov remained on purely ecclesiastical ground and worked for the reunion of the churches in strictly canonical order, it naturally seemed to him

[1] Fr. N. Tolstoy confirms this, but his explanation is that Solovyov joined the Catholic Church *of the Eastern rite*.

[2] D'Herbigny turns Fr. N. Tolstoy's surmise about the 'pressure' brought to bear upon the priests into a definite assertion that 'secret instructions were given to the clergy to refuse communion to him'! This would have been tantamount to a secret excommunication — an unheard-of case, I think, in the history of the Church, and for many reasons impossible in this particular instance.

wrong and harmful for separate individuals to act on their own initiative. But in the 'nineties Solovyov's views underwent a definite change (see Introduction, especially the letter to Tavernier): he no longer ascribed decisive significance to ecclesiastical authority; he believed henceforth only in the universal Church, consisting of the minority of Christians true to the spirit of Christ and having no visible boundaries; his 'religion of the Holy Spirit' was from the conventional point of view the faith of a religious free-thinker. His communion in a Catholic church was not the action of a man who had found in Catholicism the only true Church, but the action of a religious free-thinker who in virtue of his faith in the one universal Church considered himself entitled to ignore the actual division of the churches. He had always believed that every Christian as having 'the unction from the Holy One' had the sovereign right to judge of church matters, and now it included for him also the right to *act* 'in accordance with the spirit of Christ'. And since he retained his conviction of the necessity for all faithful Christians to unite round 'the traditional centre of unity — the see of Rome' (see Introduction, p. 20), he wished to testify to this faith by communicating in a Catholic church. The Catholic creed repeated by him accorded with his convictions, though he interpreted it freely, according to his religion of the Holy Spirit. While remaining a member of the Orthodox Church (this is emphasized in his personal confession which, evidently at his own initiative, he included in the rite of communion) he considered himself entitled to ignore its requirements.

This is indirectly confirmed by another fact which also explains the meaning of the statement he made at his last confession. An intimate friend of the Solovyov family, Madame K. Yeltsov (Professor Lopatin's sister), was at their house on the day when in 1897 Solovyov confessed to an Orthodox priest (owing to illness, Solovyov was staying at his mother's), and she has revealed the name of that priest.[1] It was Fr. Ivantsov-Platonov, Solovyov's teacher at the Theological Academy, who had known for years both him and his 'Catholic' convictions (in the 'eighties they had a controversy in print — see Vol. 4, 634–39). Obviously it was not on the ground of those convictions that Ivantsov-Platonov refused to give Solovyov communion, otherwise he would not have come ready to administer it at all. In the paper he submitted to Strossmayer about the union of the churches Solovyov testifies *from personal experience* that the Russian Orthodox Church admits to holy communion persons who profess Catholic dogmas questionable for it (*L.*, I, 187, note). The only new thing about Solovyov's ecclesiastical attitude that Ivantsov-Platonov could have learned from his

[1] K. Yeltsov, *Sovremenniya Zapiski* (Reminiscences about Solovyov), V. 28, p. 257.

confession was the fact that a year before he had communicated in a Roman church. From the canonical point of view Ivantsov-Platonov was bound to say that by this act Solovyov had cut himself off from the Orthodox Church and to refuse him communion unless he repented. But Solovyov, believing as he did in the right of every Christian to act in church matters in accordance with his religious conscience, defended his action and would not repent of it. This was the subject of their dispute. Before dying, Solovyov admitted that he had been in the wrong: not renouncing any of his general religious convictions, he repented of his unauthorized communion in a Catholic church.

From the age of thirty to the end of his life Solovyov was conscious of himself as a member of the one indivisible universal 'Orthodox-Catholic' Church, though his interpretation of it underwent a change. But formally and canonically he always regarded himself as belonging to the Russian Orthodox Church, and, if his last confession be taken into account, such he remained to the end, even from the purely ecclesiastical point of view.

SOURCE OF CONTENTS

I. GOD AND MAN

1 God, the divine basis of creation and man. From *Chteniya o Bogochelovechestve* (*Lectures on God-Manhood*), 1878, Lectures 7 and 8.

2 The essence of Christianity. From the article *On Counterfeits*, 1891.

3 The idea of humanity. From *The Idea of Humanity in Auguste Comte*, a paper read by Solovyov in 1898 at the St. Petersburg University Philosophical Society, on the centenary of Comte's birth. In the first philosophical work of his early youth, *The Crisis of Western Philosophy*, Solovyov criticized positivism, but here he gives an appreciative account of Comte's idea of humanity, and, in connection with it, expounds one of the main conceptions of his own philosophy.

4 The collapse of the mediæval world-conception. A paper read at the meeting of the Moscow Psychological Society in 1891.

II. THE CHURCH OF CHRIST

1 The union of the churches

a The great dispute and Christian politics. Written in 1883, this is Solovyov's first and most important work on the subject of church union. I give here Chapters IV, VI and VII in abridged form. In the original the subject is discussed in connection with the relations between Russia and Poland and the destinies of the Russian Church.

b The Church as the universal organization of the true life. The concluding pages of the introduction to *The History and the Future of Theocracy*, Vol. I; Solovyov sums up in them the fundamental idea of this work. It was planned in three volumes, but only Vol. I, *The Philosophy of Biblical History*, was published. Parts of it appeared in the Russian theological journal *Pravoslavnoe Obozrenie* (*Orthodox Review*) in 1885, and the whole was printed in 1887 at Zagreb in Croatia. Ideas which Vols. II and III were to express form part of Solovyov's French book, *La Russie et l'Église universelle*.

2 The Jews and the Christian problem. 1884. Considerably abridged. Solovyov regarded as providential the fact that the greater part of the Jewish people live in Poland and Russia, and accordingly he discussed the Jewish problem in connection with the problem of relations between Poland and Russia. He thought that it was at bottom the problem of relations between Orthodoxy and Roman Catholicism. This aspect of the subject is omitted as historically out of date.

III. BEAUTY AND LOVE

1 Beauty in nature. 1889. Considerably abridged.

2 The meaning of art. 1890. Considerably abridged.

3 The meaning of love. Five articles under this title were published in the periodical *Problems of Philosophy and Psychology* in 1892–94. Considerably abridged.

IV. MORALITY, LEGAL JUSTICE, POLITICS

1 The idea of the Christian state. A fragment from the essay on *The Philosophy of History*, 1891.

2 Morality, politics and the meaning of nationality. 1883. Abridged from the introductory article to two volumes of essays under the general title *The National Question in Russia* (Publ. Vol. I in 1888, Vol. II in 1891).

3 Morality and legal justice. Selections from the book *Morality and Legal Justice, Essays on Practical Ethics*. 1897. This book is an addition to Solovyov's general system of ethics *The Justification of the Good* (1895–96).

4 The secret of progress. 1897. First published after Solovyov's death in his collected works (Vol. IX in the second edition).

THE EPILOGUE

A short story of antichrist. The concluding portion of Solovyov's last work *Three Conversations* (1899–1900). It is concerned with the truly Christian attitude to evil, and in particular with justifying active opposition to evil by force, as against Tolstoy's doctrine of non-resistance. It is written in the form of dialogue, after the pattern of Plato's dialogues. The chief characters are 'the general', representing the morality of the military class, 'the prince', representing Tolstoy's theory, 'the politician', representing the standpoint of *Realpolitik*, and Mr. Z., who expounds Solovyov's own ideas. At the end of the third conversation Mr. Z. reads the MS. of a Russian monk Pansophius (the name suggests 'Sophia' and the doctrine of 'pan-unity'). Mr. Z. (Solovyov) adds: 'In my opinion this work gives in the form of fiction or of an imaginary historical narrative all that seems most likely to be true about this subject according to the Scriptures and church tradition.' The story begins with the description of the Mongolian invasion of Europe and the fifty years of Mongolian domination; finally the Mongols are expelled, and democratic order and liberal enlightenment triumph in Europe. The story is given here with a few abbreviations.

SOLOVYOV'S WORKS AVAILABLE IN ENGLISH TRANSLATIONS

War and Christianity from the Russian Point of View: Three Conversations. With an Introduction by Stephen Graham. 1915. (Constable's Russian Library.)

Another translation of the same work:

War, Progress and the End of History: Including a Short Story of the Antichrist. Translated from the Russian by Alexander Bakshy. With a biographical notice by Dr. Hagberg Wright. (University Press, London, 1915.)

The Justification of the Good: An Essay in Moral Philosophy. Translated by Natalie A. Duddington, 1918. (Constable's Russian Library.)

Plato. Translated by Richard Gill. With a note on Solovyov by Janko Lavrin. (Stanley Nott, London, 1935.)

God, Man and the Church: The Spiritual Foundations of Life. Translated by Donald Attwater. (J. Clarke & Co., London, 1938.)

The Meaning of Love. Translated by Jane Marshall. (Geoffrey Bles, London, 1946.)

Lectures on God-Manhood. With an Introduction by P. P. Zouboff. (Dennis Dobson, London, Dublin, 1948.) (Contains a bibliography of literature on Solovyov.)

Russia and the Universal Church. (Geoffrey Bles, London, 1948.)